ACTING IN CLASSROOM DRAMA
A CRITICAL ANALYSIS

ACTING IN CLASSROOM DRAMA
A CRITICAL ANALYSIS

GAVIN BOLTON
Visiting Professor
University of Central England

with a Foreword by

DAVID DAVIS
Head of International Centre for
Studies in Drama in Education
University of Central England

Trentham Books
in association with the
University of Central England

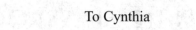

To Cynthia

ACKNOWLEDGEMENTS

My thanks are due to Jack Gilliland and Mike Fleming who have given me encouragement and supportive criticism. I am also grateful to Peter Slade and Dorothy Heathcote, who were kind enough to read the relevant parts of the text and to give advice, and to David Davis for writing the Foreword to this book and to the University of Central England, Faculty of Education, for their generous support. This volume is part of an ongoing series on Drama Education being published in partnership by Trentham Books and the University of Central England.

Thanks are also due to Marie Langley for supplying the photograph used on the back cover, from her drama lesson on 'fear', with a pre-school class of children.

First published in 1998 by Trentham Books Limited

Trentham Books Limited
Westview House
734 London Road
Oakhill
Stoke on Trent
Staffordshire
England ST4 5NP

British Cataloguing in Publication Data
A catalogue record for this book is available from the British Library
ISBN 1 85856 109 4 p.b
ISBN 1 85856 120 5 h.b

Designed and typeset by Trentham Print Design Ltd., Chester and
printed in Great Britain by Henry Ling Limited, Dorset.

CONTENTS

AN APPRECIATION OF GAVIN BOLTON'S 'ACTING IN CLASSROOM DRAMA' – BY WAY OF A FOREWORD[1]

In his essay 'Identity and the Modern Novel' Jerome Bruner writes of the crisis that comes when the person who has been highly creative has to face the doubt that this may not continue and that repetition and stagnation may set in. There is no fear of this happening to Gavin Bolton. In this book of entirely original research he not only offers a new definition of the acting behaviours that can be found in school drama but redefines his own position once again.[2]

He starts and finishes the book with a quotation from David Hornbrook which is claiming that there is no conceptual difference between a child acting in the classroom and the actor performing in the theatre. In the pages in between Gavin Bolton submits this to rigorous scrutiny and searches the end of the nineteenth and the whole of the twentieth century to find what has been written about acting in school drama.

Far from seeking to lock horns with Hornbrook, Bolton is at pains to find an approach that is inclusive. He is quite content for Hornbrook's claim to be true for the type of drama that Hornbrook himself is advocating (theatre/performance focused work) but is challenging the notion that it could cover what has come to be known as 'living through' drama. Bolton's massive scholarly research does enable him to arrive at a definition that is inclusive and wider than Hornbrook's approach. He offers a definition of acting behaviour that finds a generic unity in all forms of school acting but allows for different species to exist. Bolton quietly suggests by his detailed survey that Hornbrook's assertion is incorrect and damagingly narrow.

What emerges early on in this book is a fundamental difference in how acting behaviours are seen by Finlay-Johnson and Caldwell Cook (early examples of teachers using drama for education). This difference develops into two categories of acting behaviour and the seeds of a third category are found in the work of the child psychologist Isaacs. Her work on make-believe play is a revelation. Already in 1930 she is challenging Piaget's notion that children generally follow an age related pattern of mental development by finding from her own research, different levels of ability at different ages including higher than expected levels of mental ability in play. Here is a contemporary of Vygotsky (about whom she possibly knew nothing) reaching similar conclusions to the ones he was reaching. She appears to follow a tradition in psychology exemplified by Sully, who affirmed that children do not 'act' or 'perform' in make-believe play which seems to suggest that this is a generically different activity to theatre acting. What Bolton brings out is that Isaacs saw the power of make-believe play as an activity to release the child from the here and now and this formulation, at the same time as allowing difference in the activity, could have provided the generic link between play and theatre. It is this possibility which is developed as the book proceeds and is the means whereby Bolton is able to search for a generic unity between what has been central to his teaching, the value of dramatic playing as he formerly called it, and other forms of acting behaviour. Bolton muses on the missed opportunity in the history of drama teaching when Isaacs' colleague Langdon published a book on drama teaching which while acknowledging the importance of make-believe play saw it as but an activity to be left behind as soon as possible for drama proper.

One of the invaluable and stimulating things this publication does is to draw attention to a whole range of writers and publications which may otherwise have been neglected. One such writer is Hourd who wrote 'The Education of the Poetic Spirit', a book on the uses of drama to teach literature. Her use of Eliot's phrase 'the paw under the door' to indicate the power of indirectness and also her emphasis on 'inner understanding' (or innerstanding as Heathcote would call it later) are indicative of post-war interest in the psychological potential of drama in classrooms.

Another significant area this book visits is the influence of Movement and Dance on drama particularly through the eurythmics of Jacques-Dalcroze and the movement of Laban, (who taught and influenced Heathcote when she was a student at Bradford). Jacques-Dalcroze saw rhythm and movement as the basic aesthetic sense of the whole person fundamental to being and to the arts. Thus a climate was developed which enabled Slade to develop his unique practice.

Drawing on influences such as these Slade burst on the scene at the Bonnington Conference in 1948 with the claim that child drama is different to theatre. I had not realised before the influence on and importance of Slade for Bolton. What Slade was arguing was that child drama was not about performing and more than just play. It was an art and linked to the spontaneous expression of the child's whole being in movement and dance. In Way's hand this became a more explicit polarisation between drama and theatre. This became played out in arguments between those who saw something special happening in this spontaneous involvement and those who saw in it the death of theatre form. Bolton could be seen in the 1960s as someone who argued against Slade's 'playing' at drama. However it is now possible to see that a more accurate description of a central part of Bolton's journey has been to provide both a deeper and more significant form of make-believe playing to develop rather than totally replace Slades's spontaneous play forms. Bolton's concern has been to build on this make-believe play form and to imbue it with theatre form so that it holds the inherent power of 'being' in the event that play has. Most importantly he has been concerned to argue that this new dimension to dramatic art is also in a generic unity with drama/theatre as an art form. His search has revolved around exploring the quality of involvement in the immediate 'moment' of the drama. (This is not meant to imply that there is no inside /outside reflective dialectic operating for Bolton here: in fact the search for the opposite has also characterised his work.). The search for this 'moment' has been an elusive one. Holub, that delightful combination of scientist and artist writes in an essay called *The Dimension of the Present Moment*:

> *The fact that I cannot imagine the present moment has always worried me. By the present moment I mean a conscious individual state or process, an experience; the larger-scale present is rather*

easier to grasp. What is a moment, what is this moment in which I evidently exist, unlike nature, which according to Whitehead's famous quotation does not exist in a moment? (p.1)

Much that has characterised Drama in Education over the last forty years or so has been the search for productive involvement in this present moment: Heathcote's 'now time', Bolton's 'It is happening to me now', O'Neill's 'I am watching it happen to me now'. It has involved the search for ways to involve young people in this elusive present moment in a way where something significant is happening to them, where they are contributing to what is happening and where they are to some extent conscious of the significance of the experience in a way that takes them into and beyond that present moment.

Holub is referring to the difficulty of capturing the present in daily living. 'Living through' drama can slow down time and create a fictitious moment through which to live and which can be given detailed attention. Brook (quoted towards the end of this book) refers to this 'moment' in theatre terms;

> *It is the truth of the present moment that counts, the absolute sense of conviction that can only appear when a unity binds performer and audience. This appears when the temporary forms have served their purpose and have brought us into this single, unrepeatable instant when a door opens and our vision is transformed.*

This seems to encapsulate the search for the 'same' sort of experience and yet how to arrive at the 'same' place in child drama has been a contentious issue in the history of drama in education. Is it a theatre moment? Is it a moment of spontaneous play rising to the level of art? Is it a moment brought into being by a teacher manipulating the art form for and with the pupils? There used to be the search for a 'moment of awe'. In this volume Bolton quotes Slade writing rhapsodically of such a moment. 'I felt the light dying. If not of a real sun, it was the light of 'real theatre' when a great scene comes to a close.'

It was from Heathcote that Bolton drew most inspiration in his search for a productive form for drama in schools and with her invention of teacher in role it was possible to have a form of 'living through' where the dimensions of the art form could be introduced 'partly cooked' (as

Bolton describes it in this publication), rather than working from the raw materials as in theatre work. 'Living through' drama for Heathcote involved being there in the present and presence and also being outside, as Bolton explains. The chapter on Dorothy Heathcote in this publication is in my view the definitive account of the essential features of her work to date. It is clear from this account that she left behind the notion of drama being a 'man in a mess' which is how she characterised it in the film 'Three Looms Waiting', and he is able to show how and why that no longer served her from the early to the mid 1970s onwards. It is revealing that this line of descent (drama being seen as essentially 'man in a mess') was really continued by Bolton himself and O'Neill who was a student of his and was strongly influenced by him. This influence she has now made her own in what she has called 'Process Drama'. It is typical of Bolton that he does not count himself as one of the pioneers of Drama in Education. However it is the pursuit of the connection between classroom drama and make-believe play that has marked the quite unique quality of Bolton's contribution to Drama in Education. I suspect this has not been fully appreciated or understood yet. (A genealogy of Drama in Education would be interesting but does not belong here!)

This book provides a rich survey of drama teaching and influences on drama teaching over the last century in the search for the different sorts of acting behaviours that have existed. That only three are offered and in a generic unity is tempting, provocative and extremely worthwhile. I am convinced that this book will become a seminal publication in the field of drama in education.

References

Bruner, J.S. (1962) *On Knowing – essays for the left hand* London: Belknap Press, Harvard University

Holub, M (1990) *The Dimension of the Present Moment and other essays* London; Faber and Faber

Notes

1   This is the first time I have been in the position of writing a foreword to a book. I have found the task curiously difficult. Before I knew what was happening it was becoming a book review and then a replacement introduction to the one already provided by the author. When I realised this I found myself offering a precis of the book! Then the tempation grew to write about some of the things that had been

thought-provoking and stimulating for me as I had read the thesis and then the book of the thesis. Before I could look round this had then become an examination of some of the key issues around which the book is built which would have had its proper place in a separate paper. Finally I have settled for referring to enough of the main areas of the book to focus some of the key issues without giving away too much of the detail of the theory that unfolds. I have also given few references as these are all to be found in the main body of the text. I am left in awe of foreword writers everwhere.

2   In 'Drama as Education' he writes that his claim was mistaken in 'Towards a Theory of Drama in Education' where he argued that there is a continuum of contrasted activities in drama; exercise, dramatic playing and theatre which when combined form Type D drama or artistic dramatic involvement. It should rather rest on the disposition of the child towards the activity not on the activity itself, that is on a disposition to *be* in the event or to *communicate* the event. In this present volume he redefines his position again and being in the event is no longer on a continuum with communicating but is in a dichotomous relationship to it and furthermore is redefined to distinguish it from Heathcote's 'living through' drama and from make believe play.

3   An example of the quality and extent of the research behind this book is the way in which everything in the admirable chapter on Slade was checked out with Slade himself. The taped interviews and letters now form part of the history of drama in education archive which Bolton has established at Durham University.

David Davis
International Centre for Studies
in Drama in Education,
University of Central England,
Birmingham

CLASSROOM ACTING – A HISTORY AND CONCEPTUAL FRAMEWORK

INTRODUCTION

Background to the selection of the topic

When John Allen HMI[1], in 1979, argued that drama in schools is 'basically and essentially no different from drama anywhere else', he was drawing attention to the Aristotelian view of drama as 'Mimesis' which Allen translates as 'an act of recreation'. What is interesting about his argument is not that he had uncovered something profound, but rather that as an Inspector with special responsibility for Drama he should feel obliged to remind educationists of what might be thought of as self-evident. The development of drama education in this country has been such that, whereas early pioneers would have taken Allen's assertion as axiomatic, by the second half of this century leading drama educationists appeared to be more interested in persuading teachers that differences between one kind of practice and another were critically more important than any common ground. I know this to be the case, for my early teaching career seemed to coincide with increasing rivalry among fashionable trends[2]. By the time I read John Allen's book I saw his statement as a timely reminder to people who were in danger of forgetting what was 'basic and essential' to the subject we taught. In the same year, 1979, I had published my first attempt at a theoretical model which purported to embrace the idea of a generic base for all dramatic activities while acknowledging different orientations. I introduced the notion of a continuum of intentions, at the extremes of which theatre and make-believe play pursued their contrasted ends while sharing common ground in the middle. Much of that 'middle ground', I claimed, represented dramatic activities typically found in our classrooms.

However, I was not so ready to accept David Hornbook's assertion which came ten years later. He wrote[3]:

> It is my contention that conceptually there is nothing which differentiates the child acting in the classroom from the actor on the stage of the theatre.

This appeared to challenge the very basis of progressive drama education, for deeply embedded in my own professional theory and practice was the assumption that what actors do on stage is fundamentally different from what children do in the classroom: the artifice required of the professional actor in projecting to the back of the auditorium for a long run of a play seemed so far removed from my expectations of pupils' classroom Role-Play that, in a review of his book[4], I dismissed his position as untenable.

It nevertheless remained as an issue at the back of my mind, causing me to consider, in particular, whether the kind of language employed by various leaders in the field, to describe acting in their classrooms, revealed the extent to which their conceptual understanding of acting behaviour matched Hornbook's. In a brief scan of major publications spanning this century, I discovered that exponents of drama education had little to say on the subject. Various pioneers in classroom drama appear to have been urged to communicate their innovatory philosophy, methodology or teacher-techniques and consequent educational or aesthetic outcomes, but that concern did not spread to acting itself. The same could be said for research papers[5]. For the most part, acting behaviour has been taken for granted, not seen as something of interest *per se*[6].

And yet its presence as a phenomenon has featured *implicitly* in almost every publication on drama education, for any innovation in philosophy or methodology inevitably had bearing on the writer's expectations of and perceptions of acting behaviour. Apart from dropping in an adjective such as 'natural' or 'sincere' or 'accurate' or 'imaginative' to describe the expected quality of such behaviour, acting was rarely discussed in more detail. Indeed many writers in the second half of the century, because of the association of 'acting' with theatricality, avoided using the word 'acting', alternatively favouring 'acting out', 'living through' or 'improvisation'.

There are signs, towards the end of the century, however, that the term 'acting' may once more become part of a teacher's vocabulary. Andy Kempe, for instance, in his 'scrapbooks' for use by senior pupils[7], whilst avoiding inviting the pupils to 'act', does refer to them as 'actors'. Michael Fleming[8], conscious of the danger of its carrying inappropriate overtones, nevertheless appears to be recommending that a return to its usage in an educational context be given serious consideration.

What this book is about

The purpose of this book is indeed to give the term 'acting' serious consideration – in two ways. It is my intention both to provide an historical perspective and to recommend a reformulation of classroom acting behaviour. I shall investigate, using publications written during the century, how the concept of acting appears to have changed during that period and, further, I shall use drama exponents' implicit or explicit perceptions of acting behaviour as a basis for a revised conceptual framework. This reformulation attempts to make a case for embracing, in the classroom, many different kinds of acting behaviours that go beyond the limits and responsibilities expected of a stage actor, while nevertheless including both 'stage' acting and that kind of acting behaviour associated with 'teacher-in-role' led drama – which latter strategy I believe to be in serious danger of neglect in the present day dependence on too narrow a view of drama practice.

Each chapter of this book, therefore, will present an account of a pioneer or a trend in drama education with a view to eliciting the underlying assumptions about acting behaviour the relevant publications betray. A tension will sometimes arise between my twofold determination to be faithful both to an historical account and to the argument I wish to pursue. I have tried to make each of the first nine chapters stand, in their own right, as a fair summary of the publications of the time, but because the bias is towards *acting*, this has necessarily skewed my choice of contributors to the field. Some notable drama teachers, such as Maisie Cobby, Alan Garrard, Tom Stabler, Brian Watkins, John Fines, Ray Verriour, David Davis and Jonothan

Neelands, who would normally claim a place in an historical account may appear to be neglected.

An historical account of classroom drama in England through (1) pioneers and (2) trends

By selecting from a combination of pioneers and trends, the major publications of the century will be analysed from four perspectives:

(1) It will be necessary, briefly, to place both the pioneer and the identified trend in a historical context, so that innovations may be understood against an educational or theatrical background.

(2) A sufficient account of the methodology of each pioneer or trend will be given for the reader to visualise the prescribed dramatic activity.

(3) Inferences will be drawn from the publications about the various authors' assumptions about classroom acting behaviour.

(4) Where appropriate, a discourse will be opened up on some aspect of acting behaviour, which, while deriving from the publication(s) under review, will embrace both the relevant writings of subsequent authors and my own theoretical position, thus anticipating the conceptual framework of the concluding chapter.

The British Pioneers in Drama Education

Each of the chosen pioneers has in some fundamental way changed our conception of classroom practice. This factor alone might be sufficient to qualify an exponent of drama education as a pioneer, but other aspects reinforced the selection of the five names. 'Pioneers' are so defined because they fulfil the criteria that they:

a. brought about a radical change in conception of classroom practice;

b. introduced innovatory praxis, backing up new methods in their own skilled practice with a theoretical exposition;

c. provided a published account from which a reader might base his/her understanding of the innovatory praxis;

d. became a figure of sufficient interest, either contemporaneously or retrospectively, for others in the field to publish their own account of that figure's contribution to drama education;

e. devoted a career to promoting classroom drama.

On the basis of the above criteria, the 'pioneers' in this country number but five: Harriet Finlay-Johnson (1871-1956); Henry Caldwell Cook (1886-1937); Peter Slade (1910-); Brian Way (1923-); and Dorothy Heathcote (1926-). That is not to suggest that there were or are no other major figures in the field of Drama Education. For example, an outstanding innovator earlier this century was Marjorie Hourd, but she fails to meet criteria (d) and (e), in that her contribution to drama teaching has not been sufficiently acknowledged, and her interest in classroom drama was but part of a greater concern with creative writing. Contributors to the field such as E. M. Langdon advanced a new theory without revolutionising practice; while E.J. Burton and Maisie Cobby inspired progressive practice, but added little theoretically. Figures such as Ken Robinson and Robert Witkin were better known for their extensive theoretical input than for innovatory practice. There are, of course, many contemporary leaders in the field to whom it will be necessary to refer, and there are, of course, leaders in the field from abroad whose publications and practice have made their unique mark, but this book is confined, in the main, to the British scene, although it is hoped that its conclusions will have much wider application.

The main source of information about the pioneers' work will be their own publications, and published comments from others. Where appropriate, connections will be made with the educational, theatrical or political climate of the times. A broad outline will be given of changes in classroom drama practice throughout the 20th century, with a view to determining where each pioneer stood in relation to its overall development.

Trends between the World-Wars in Drama Education
Following publications by the first two pioneers, in 1911 and 1917 respectively, there is a gap of 37 years before the first book by the third pioneer is published. Those 37 years saw considerable changes in drama practice which cannot be attached to one particular innovator. To do justice to that period which, while lacking any one hugely in-

fluential figure, nevertheless saw an increase in the popularity of drama, I have elected to follow developments in *ideas* as reflected by both ideology and methodology. Although the publications I shall examine in this connection are interesting in their own right, they have been chosen as illustrative of a trend in attitude to acting behaviour rather than as illuminative of an author's work.

During that inter-War period drama in the classroom came to mean many different things to different people. It was against this background of conflicting claims for the subject that the three remaining pioneers took up their work in the second half of the century. Understanding these later pioneers in part depends on identifying the extent to which each embraced, modified, rejected or demolished the pre-World-War Two trends.

This book is a condensed and revised version of a doctoral thesis[9]. In the process of rewriting, I have removed hundreds of footnotes which I saw as essential for a research document, but as amounting to unreadable pedantry if retained in a book. Detailed referencing has therefore been cut down as far as possible, although the reader, seeing how many have been retained, could be forgiven for doubting my determination with the scissors!

Notes

1   Allen, John (1979) *Drama in Schools: Its Theory and Practice* Heinemann Educational Books London, p.119.

2   In 1971 I read a paper to the 'Clifton Conference' entitled 'Drama and Theatre in Education: a Survey', in which I lightheartedly recalled my early drama teaching days during which I tried to cope with conflicting philosophies by becoming a compulsive 'course attender'. [in *Drama and Theatre in Education* by Dodd, Nigel and Hickson, Winifred {Eds} (1971) Heinemann London

3   Hornbrook, David (1989) *Education and Dramatic* Art Blackwell Oxford, p.104

4   Bolton, Gavin (1990) 'Opinion – Education and Dramatic Art – A Review' in *Drama Broadsheet* Spring 7 (1) pp 2-5

5   The most recent research publications in the field [See Taylor, Philip (Ed 1996) *Researching Drama and Arts Education* Falmer London and Somers, John (Ed 1996/7) *Research in Drama Education* Vol 1 Nos 1and2 Vol. 2 No 1, on the whole confine their attention to research methodology, the content of particular examples of drama or an analysis of teacher behaviour.

6   The exception among publications is the School's Council Secondary Project *Learning Through Drama* (1977) by Lynn McGregor, Maggie Tate and Ken Robinson Heinemann London which sees acting as the central activity.

7   See, for example, *A South African Scrapbook* by Andy Kempe and Rick Holroyd (1994) Hodder and Stoughton London

8   Fleming, Michael (1994) *Starting Drama Teaching* David Fulton London

9   Bolton, Gavin (1997) *A Conceptual Framework for Classroom Acting Behaviour* Ph.D thesis, University of Durham

SECTION ONE
FINLAY-JOHNSON AND
CALDWELL COOK

CHAPTER ONE

HARRIET FINLAY-JOHNSON
(1871-1956)

This chapter will begin with a brief comparison of the first two pioneers, its broad brush strokes indicating their contrasted school situations, their not dissimilar aspirations and the political climate they shared. An account will follow giving some evidence of the occasional appearance of other classroom dramatic activity in both the private and public sector in the early days of Finlay-Johnson's and Caldwell Cook's teaching. The educationist, J.J. Findlay, will be cited as an example of a progressive thinker recognising an educational potential in drama.

A biographical comparison between Harriet Finlay-Johnson and Henry Caldwell Cook
They taught the same age group, but in conspicuously contrasted circumstances. Whereas Harriet Finlay-Johnson was Head-teacher of a village elementary school in East Sussex, class-teaching with the 8-13 age group, Henry Caldwell Cook entered the private sector and was appointed as English Master to teach the 'junior' forms (ages 11-14) at the Perse School, a prestigious, residential, boys-only, independent school in Cambridge.

Both pioneers wrote their books retrospectively, Finlay-Johnson[1] early in her retirement after thirteen years at Sompting School, Caldwell Cook early in his recruitment to the trenches ('somewhat uncongenial employment', as he describes it) after a mere three years as a teacher. Whereas the former publication is described by its author as

3

methodological, which, for the most part, it is, Caldwell Cook's book, on the other hand, is an educational treatise in which he writes broadly about principles of 'progressive' teaching of which his particular practice is seen by many as illustrative. They both wrote passionately about drama in their classrooms and, within the differing demands of the whole curriculum of the Elementary School compared with the specialised requirements of the English teacher's classroom, they gave it equal prominence.

Their dreams
There is no record of whether they read each other's writings. Each would no doubt have responded sympathetically to the somewhat romantic tone of the other's style. It is a romantic tone adopted under the darkening clouds of war. Finlay-Johnson prophetically asks:'Am I quite wrong when I say that childhood should be a time for absorbing big stores of sunshine for possible future dark times?', not realising that within four to five years many of the boys in her class would be killed in the Great War. Caldwell Cook, in the spring of 1914[2], wrote with poignant foreboding:

> None but a visitation of wrath seems possible today. Let us build a fane, and therein, over the consecrated altar, shall the unknown god be declared. The sun shines all over the earth, but no flowers grow on the cinder-heap which is kept arid by the daily piling up of ashes.

The Progressive movement in Education, of which our two pioneers were among the early representatives, was born under a shadow and out of a dream of better things. From France, Caldwell Cook writes in 1915 in the Conference of New Ideals in Education[3]:

> Whenever I have spoken seriously with a man or woman I have told them of my dream. Even the invigoration of a frosty morning, or the enchantment of the moon at night, have always made me think: Here is gone by another morning or another evening which might have made some occasion of good hap in the Play School. The one thing upon which my heart is fixed is to make this dream come true in this our England.

As the earliest pioneers in England of classroom dramatisation, it is not surprising that their writing about the value of drama in schools is passionate, optimistic, romantic and often sentimental[4], as though entry into the wonderland that drama permitted gave credence or expression to their deepest aspirations.

On the surface, at least, this faith in the 'Romance' is in keeping with the visions of other 'Progressive' reformers. Selleck suggests that the whole Progressive movement in education is characterised by a search for something even deeper than its appeal to 'freedom' and 'individuality', that it represented a search for an alternative to ugliness, moral corruption and industrialism, a search for the means to escape from the reality of war.

Perhaps the practice of drama has never entirely lost its escapist sense of other-worldliness, of 'such stuff as dreams are made on'. Its mystery and amorality beckons and repels[5]. To introduce drama into one's classroom, it might be thought, is a daring thing to do, opening up the wickedness of theatre or the forbidden territory of the subconscious. Educationists may offer a rationale for justifying or denying the inclusion of Drama in the curriculum, but (who knows?) the true explanation may lie in their more gut-level response to its mysteries.

Dramatic activity in the classroom at the beginning of the century
Harriet Finlay-Johnson, perhaps more than any other pioneer in classroom drama, can claim the right to that title, on the grounds that she appeared to have no model to follow or surpass, no tradition to keep or break. She was the first in the field, or at least the first whose classroom drama practice was to be recorded.

A small number of publications at the beginning of the century make passing reference to classroom dramatic activity. It seems that such activity was to be found in either the kindergarten or the public school. Brief references to the latter seem to be generally favourable in tone, whereas dramatic activity in the kindergarten occasionally comes in for criticism.

The independent sector
The reading aloud of Shakespeare had found a sufficiently firm place in the independent sector for James Welton in 1906 to offer teachers a

procedural model: that the play should be read three times, focusing respectively on (1) the story, (2) the characters and (3) the language, and then the scenes 'may be acted or at least recited[6]'

Another form of dramatisation to be found in public schools was the practice, introduced by classics masters such as W.H.D. Rouse of the Perse School who encouraged the direct speaking of Greek and Latin dialogue. According to Coggin and others[7], the long-held suspicion of public performances of plays was suspended by some schools when it came to performing classical texts.

In a private preparatory school in Weymouth, its headmistress, Miss E.M. Gilpin, headmistress from 1898 to 1934 had no reservations about the performance of plays, claiming, in 1920, that 'everyone has something of an actor in him'. In addressing the Drama League sponsored conference she boldly prophesies[8]:

> The Day of the emancipation of the teaching of Drawing has come, that of the teaching of Music has dawned, and I hope that of the teaching of Drama in schools is at hand.

The Kindergarten
Margaret MacMillan (1901), the distinguished Scottish educator, is perhaps the first British advocate of play opportunities in the infant classroom. She is not visualising a mimetic context as much as, in the spirit of Dr Montessori's innovative work in Italy, a freely experimental one, providing an opportunity for 'brain and limb' to learn control 'as a whole[9]'. She makes no reference to any kind of dramatic actions.

H.L. Withers, on the other hand, in a lecture to the Froebel Society in 1901[10], in which Withers' address is recorded under the title: 'The Distinction between Work and Play', refers disparagingly to 'action-plays' to be found in kindergartens. While seeing the value of 'bio-logical play', as Karl Groos[11] called make-believe play, for the pre-school child, Withers goes on (p.258):

> But I never saw a child yet, left to itself, act the part of a daisy, or a tree with the leaves rustling, or any other vegetable or inanimate objects which it is supposed to represent in many 'action-plays.' These are not instinctive, self-expressive games; they are not play, they are not work. The words in which they are written are often

inexcusably feeble and drivelling, and the music with which they are accompanied is sometimes not even tenth-rate. A good many of them want 'reforming altogether.'

Withers' (1904) complaint is against the kind of drilled actions to rhyming scripts (written by the teacher or other adults) modelled on Froebelian practice. N.J.R. Crompton[12] designates these action rhymes as the first British instance of classroom dramatic activity and traces the source of some of the material referred to in a publication by an infant teacher, Mabel Bloomer[13], headmistress of Hyndburn Park Council School, Accrington, directly to Froebel, whose action songs, *Mutter und Kose Lieder*, were produced in Germany in 1843 and translated into English by Frances and Emily Lord in 1886. Crompton (1978) sees Froebel 'as the spiritual father of drama-in-education' and he confesses that 'it is tempting to see *Mutter-und Kose Lieder* as the ultimate source...'. For Crompton, Harriet Finlay-Johnson's unique achievement was in extending the principles of Froebelian practice from the infant to the junior school, but, as we shall see, teacher-directed 'action songs' were not to Finlay-Johnson's taste. She writes[14]

> Why not continue the principle of the Kindergarten game in the school for older scholars? I did so, but with this difference: instead of letting the teacher originate or conduct the play, I demanded that ... the play must be the child's own.

We shall see that her progressive view of pupil autonomy created a 'game' for the older children that made immeasurably greater demands than the Froebelian 'action-songs' and broadened the scope of the playing opportunities advocated by Margaret Macmillan.

J.J. Findlay, in 1902, early in his long career, when he was headmaster of The Cardiff Intermediate School for Boys[15], regretted, somewhat wistfully, that 'the drama plays a very small part in modern life,' but confirms that it 'survives in the Greek and Latin plays performed in a few schools.' He then adds: 'and it has been revived in the imitative Games of the Kindergarten', referring to the kind of 'action-game' disparaged by Withers (above).

It seems likely that Professor Findlay was the first British educationalist to refer to Drama as a classroom activity. Interestingly, he is not sure in which chapter of his book he should discuss it. Having placed it under 'The Art of Language', he has second thoughts: 'We have classified the drama with Language, because it is so largely a matter of speech: but, as acting, it may more properly be transferred to the next group, [which Findlay calls 'The Arts of Representation'] because it aims at natural representation'. This uncertainty expressed by Findlay in 1902 of where to place Drama in a curricular hierarchy marks the beginning of a century-long dispute.

His introduction to the notion of some kind of dramatic activity leading to Drama as part of the curriculum could be said to be more visionary than realistic, although he had actually seen some experimentation in an American school[16]. Based at the University of Chicago, John Dewey was at that time beginning to take interest in the idea of appointing specialists in each art to the Experimental School, specialists 'who are making the same combination of artistic skill with insight into Education.' Findlay writes: '...much may be expected in time from Professor Dewey's School in Chicago...'.

It seems that the first authoritative publication[17] to recognise the possibility of dramatising as a legitimate part of classroom activities was a Board of Education document, published in 1905, three years after Findlay's seminal text. It should be pointed out, however, that there is one reference only to dramatic activity in some 100 densely printed pages, not enough to warrant its inclusion in its detailed index. It occurs in the section of 'Teaching English' dealing with 'Practice in Speaking English[18]'. Part of this practice was to include[19]:

> Simple rhymes and games of a dramatic cast, which are at first a form of (verse or prose) repetition, but might possibly (in connection with the paragraph below) be developed into something more spontaneous if classroom conditions allow.

Stories told first to the class by the teacher, afterwards retold by individual children. These should proceed from the simple nursery tale of the recurrent type to freer forms of fairy story, in all of which, however, there is a certain reiteration which seems essential to this form of literature and is a great aid to reproduction. With the older infants an attempt might be made to dramatise these.

A hint, here, of 'something more spontaneous' in the kindergarten. There is no reference to the use of dramatisation in the upper end of the elementary school, and yet that is the age-group with which the first pioneer of this study evolved her dramatic methods. Indeed Miss Finlay-Johnson had started her experimentation eight years earlier.

Introduction to Harriet Finlay-Johnson – adulation and notoriety

Miss Finlay-Johnson was appointed Head Teacher of Little Sompting School, near Worthing, Sussex, in 1897 and stayed until she married in 1910. The attention her work received is so bound up with its publicisation by the Chief Inspector for Schools, Edmond Holmes, that it is not possible to give an account of its methods without constant reference to his interpretation of them. She wrote her book, *The Dramatic Method of Teaching*, at his persuasion, in 1911, a year after her retirement. He became a regular visitor to her school a few years after her appointment. His books[20], published after his enforced resignation[21] in the same year as her retirement, attempted to give a theoretical frame to her approach. He used Finlay-Johnson's methods as a model in the 'What Might Be' half of his book, labelling her his 'Egeria'. The result was that a school that had attracted a pilgrimage of admiring visitors during Miss Finlay-Johnson's period of headship became a centre for destructively motivated investigation (for instance, the charge that Miss Johnson had 'faked' exercise books was part of the vicious rumours spread about her work) after she left.

One can only muse on whether the practice of dramatisation as a method of teaching would have become popularised much earlier in this country if Miss Johnson's teaching had not accidentally come within the firing-line of a minor educational scandal. On the other hand, Sompting School and its headteacher's innovatory methods may never have reached public notice if Holmes had not drawn attention to them, for Holmes was a key figure in the 'New Education', and is identified with what became known as 'The Progressive Movement'.

Harriet Finlay-Johnson's Dramatic Method: as justified by her own and Edmond Holmes' publications
Finlay-Johnson's justification for the method: 'arousing a keen desire to know'

Miss Johnson believed that young 'scholars', as she called them, would learn if and when they want to learn. She discovered that such a desire for knowledge can be aroused by dramatisation[22]:

It has always been an axiom in matters of school method that one of the first essentials in teaching any subject should be 'first arouse the desire to know'. When our scholars began to dramatise their lessons, they at once developed a keen desire to know many things which hitherto had been matters of pure indifference to them. For instance, after their initial performance of scenes from 'Ivanhoe', they soon began to study the book closely to supply deficiencies in dialogue, and when the dialogue was rendered according to the book it had to be memorised (voluntarily), and this led to searching questions after meanings and allusions – some of which the elder scholars soon learned to find in the dictionary.

Her book records many examples of teaching literature, but also History, Geography, Shakespeare, Grammar and Spelling, Arithmetic and Nature Study (a subject she at first saw as the centre of all education until, in the latter years of her thirteen at Little Sompting, it was superseded by dramatisation as the core activity). Dramatisation, Finlay-Johnson claims, provides the means of 'arousing a keen desire to know'; it was to be an incentive (my choice of word) to learning[23]. Even the most unpalatable subject-matters laid down by the school authorities could be taught through dramatisation, concealing, as Miss Johnson puts it 'the powder in the jam.' Such a functional use of an art form was contrary to the generally accepted Kantian position of 'disinterestedness' as a necessary feature of artistic response.

Harriet Finlay-Johnson's approach, however, involved much more than sweetening medicine, for it embraces some of the features that later characterised the Progressive movement: 'integrated knowledge'; 'activity-method'; 'pupil-autonomy' – and 'dramatisation' gradually and uniquely became Finlay-Johnson's means of achieving such goals:

(1) when she writes: 'Children...have a wonderful faculty for teaching other children and learning from them', she is seeing this mutual learning in the context of 'preparing a play';

(2) when she writes of making children 'self-reliant, mainly self-taught, and self-developing', she is seeing these maturing attributes in the context of 'preparing the play';

(3) when she speaks of developing in her pupils a 'habit of mind' in approaching 'thoroughly' any acquisition of knowledge or skill, she is seeing this seeking after high standards in learning in the context of researching for 'the play'.

(4) Likewise the incentive of 'getting our play ready' allows her to revolutionise the traditional 'teacher-pupil' relationship. The teacher is to be regarded as 'fellow-worker' and 'friend':

There could be plenty of liberty without licence, because the teacher, being a companion to and fellow-worker with the scholars, had a strong moral hold on them, and shared the citizen's right of holding an opinion – being heard, therefore, not as 'absolute monarch' but on the same grounds as the children themselves.'

The educational goals to be reached through dramatisation according to Finlay-Johnson can be summarised from the above paragraphs as follows:

Children will be 'keen to know'.

Children teach and learn from each other.

Children will become self-reliant and mainly self-taught

Children will acquire an habitual 'thoroughness' in approaching knowledge or skills.

Children are to see the teacher as 'companion' and 'fellow-worker'.

The first four of these goals are related directly to the acquisition of knowledge. According to Finlay-Johnson, dramatisation creates a motivation to learn and a responsibility towards learning, a shared responsibility. The notion of children teaching each other, however, is not a characteristic that the Progressive Movement in Education entirely supported, for many saw the New Education in terms of an individual's independence rather than his/her dependence on a group[24].

It may seem remarkable that with no model to follow, this village school-teacher, so early in the century, should have discovered the effectiveness of dramatisation for learning and be able to describe that effectiveness in terms of motivation, responsibility and co-operation. What she does not do is explicitly suggest that the knowledge acquired through drama is necessarily qualitatively different, although this may be implied, for Finlay-Johnson is anxious for her pupils to understand 'the fitness of things'[25], making connections they perhaps could not have made without the concrete experience of the dramatic location. The following extract is illustrates this point vividly[26]:

> That the children were set thinking for themselves by means of playing their own version of Shakespear's 'Henry V.' is proved by the fact that on the next 'Unseen Reader' morning, following the first performance of 'Henry V.', there was a great rush for historical works of all kinds, and very shortly we heard remarks as 'Why, it was my son, Henry VI., who caused Joan of Arc's death! (from the boy who had impersonated Henry V.). 'Yes, and when Jack died ('Jack' was Henry V. for the nonce!) 'Katherine married Owen Tudor, and that's where the Tudor line came from,' said another. 'How do you know that?' said I. 'I traced it on this table,' was the reply. I looked at the book shown me. It was opened at a genealogical table! Fancy that studied voluntarily by an ordinary boy!

Edmond Holmes' justification of Miss Finlay-Johnson's method: 'self-realisation'

Holmes devoted his book, What is and What Might Be to a study of Finlay Johnson's methods without referring to her by name. He frames his account of the work of Sompting School in rather quaint terms: the school becomes 'Utopia' and its headteacher, 'Egeria'. Thus he writes: 'In Utopia 'acting' is a vital part of the school life of every class, and every subject that admits of dramatic treatment is systematically dramatised.' His book is a diatribe against traditional state education and in moving from the first half, entitled 'What Is or The Path of Mechanical Obedience' to the second half 'What Might Be or The Path of Self-Realisation', he offers a picture of the 'ideal'.

Holmes' book inspired many young progressives, but also created controversy. As Selleck explains: '...successful attempts were made to discover who Egeria was and where her school was situated; whispers went around that it was not the utopia Holmes had claimed and Holmes indignantly answered them.' He sought to defend his first book by writing a second.

In In Defence of What Might Be (1914), Holmes gives a succinct explanation of what led him to describe Miss Finlay-Johnson's work, which for him epitomises the 'growth' theory of education[27]:

> Neither Rousseau's nor Froebel's exposition of it (the growth theory of education) had quite satisfied me. Rousseau, as it seemed to me, left too much to Nature and too little to the teacher. Froebel, as it seemed to me, left too little to Nature and too much to the teacher. As my visits to 'Utopia' had convinced me that 'Egeria' had managed to adjust, almost to a nicety, the respective claims of nature and the teacher, I thought it might be well if I were to describe her school and her work, and try to interpret her philosophy of education.

He sees the work at Sompting School as harnessing six parallel instinctive desires in a child[28]

(1) to talk and listen

(2) to act (in the dramatic sense of the word):

(3) to draw, paint and model:

(4) to dance and sing:

(5) to know the why of things:

(6) to construct things.

He describes these as the 'communicative', 'dramatic', 'artistic', 'musical', 'inquisitive', and 'constructive' instincts. He goes on to explain that 'Two of these are sympathetic; two are aesthetic; two are scientific. The realisation of these instincts leads to the development of corresponding 'faculties', the 'sympathetic' claiming sovereignty over the others: '....training their imaginative sympathy – a sovereign faculty which of all faculties is perhaps the most emancipative and expansive...'

Implicit in Holmes' theoretical gloss is the notion of dramatisation (along with other communicative activities) as 'sympathetic', which implies that a participant's attention is directed outwards. Holmes puts it: '...teaching them to identify themselves, if only for a moment, with other human beings... leading them into the path of tolerance, of compassion, of charity, of sympathy.' For Holmes acting fulfils the emancipative requirement of growth, an 'escape from self'. This, as we shall see, is in marked contrast to some later play theorists and drama educators who see the purpose of dramatisation as 'finding oneself'[29].

Holmes gives apparently unqualified support to dramatisation. He writes, 'However rude and simple the histrionic efforts of the children may be, they are doing two things for the actors. They are giving them a living interest in the various subjects that are dramatised, and, by teaching them to identify themselves, if only for a moment, with other human beings, they are leading them into the path of tolerance, of compassion, of charity, of sympathy...' There can be no doubt about the genuineness of this support; but one is left feeling that his use of 'Egeria's' achievements in dramatisation as illustrative of his own 'growth' philosophy overrides any interest in promoting dramatisation per se, rather than as evidence of a methodology worthy in itself of close attention. That in the latter years of her thirteen at Sompting, Miss Finlay-Johnson turned more and more to drama, eclipsing her earlier interest in Nature Study as a base-line, seemed not to be significant to Holmes. It can only be concluded that his advocacy was not, at heart, a promotion of drama as a method. That this is the case is perhaps also partly borne out by his 1914 defence which barely mentions Drama, an omission which further suggests that critics of his 1911 publication did not see Drama as significantly part of their complaint against either his book or the educational system it advocated. This was not because they approved of Drama but because the critics of the School tended to have paid their visits after its notorious headteacher had left it and thus did not actually see any drama. Perhaps for this reason Holmes did not feel driven to defend its usage. A further example of Holmes's ambivalence is revealed in a Foreword, for he manages to write a three-page eulogy of Finlay-Johnson's methods, prefacing a book bearing the term 'Dramatic Methodology' in its title, without once referring to Drama.

One can only conclude that his support for 'acting' in the classroom was more apparent than real, that he failed to recognise the critical role played by dramatisation in 'making knowledge work'. Had he done so, one feels that he would have made drama itself a less peripheral feature of his argument[30].

Characteristics of acting behaviour in Harriet Finlay-Johnson's classroom

Harriet Finlay-Johnson's style of practice was that of an enthusiastic team-manager, coaching from the sidelines, as it were, as pupils engaged in their endeavours. Unlike her successors, she does not feel impelled in her publication to give an account of what she did, but only what the children achieved.

Miss Finlay-Johnson gives us relatively few clues about the acting itself. Her chief concern seems to be that her readers should understand that whatever was created dramatically was the children's own invention[31]:

> ...instead of letting the teacher originate or conduct the play, I demanded that, just as the individual himself must study Nature and not have it studied for him, the play must be the child's own. However crude the action or dialogue from the adult's point of view, it would fitly express the stage of development arrived at by the child's mind and would, therefore, be valuable to him as a vehicle of expression and assimilation (which is, after all, what we need), rather than a finished product pleasing to the more cultivated mind of an adult, and, perhaps, boring to a child.

The phrase 'however crude the action' recalls Holmes' 'however rude and simple', suggesting that 'from the adult's point of view' there were indeed some deficiencies. What they were is not spelled out, but the view expounded by Finlay-Johnson, that in an educational context adult perception becomes irrelevant, is to anticipate the work of Franz Cizek in Vienna[32], who, in the 1920s, revolutionised the educational approach to the visual arts.

One of the dangers of attempting to trace a history of ideas is that one's present perspective causes one to misinterpret what an earlier writer means. Here is an example of such a trap. By referring (in the quotation

above) to dramatisation as 'a vehicle of expression and assimilation...
rather than a finished product', it seems that Finlay-Johnson may be
entering the process/product debate still raging today[33] – and, ahead of
her time, siding with the 'process' voices. However, it could be that she
is adopting the sporting notion that it is the act of participating in the
drama that is more important than the final outcome, and, of course,
such a position does not necessarily imply that there should not be a
final outcome. Or she may even intend her phrase '...rather than a
finished product' to be read as 'rather than a finished product'. She
may simply be saying that the consequence of her pupils' having the
chance to express their own version in their own way will inevitably be
a product of less finesse than if a teacher had ordered the material and
directed the activity. The notion of 'process' as an alternative to
'product' may have been outside her frame of reference.

What Harriet Finlay-Johnson is conscious of in this connection, is the
need to do away with 'acting for display', a point she makes twice in
her book. She overcomes this impediment as far as she can by 'doing
away with an audience', turning the non-actors into stage-managers or,
as we shall see from examples below, into active commentators or
spectators.

'Dramatisation', in the sense of reformulating knowledge from
curriculum subjects into a dramatic sequence or story was occasionally
to be extended to include acting Shakespeare[34]. She does not, however,
comment on any ill-effect wrought by the presence of an adult audience
of parents and other local villagers. However, she cannot resist
referring to the occasion when 'a great Shakespearean actor and actress
who saw them' ['Rosalind' and 'Celia'] ' waxed quite enthusiastic over
their natural way of deporting themselves..'. She herself saw their
acting as 'so exceedingly good, dramatic and convincing in their parts
that their performance really approached pure Art.' She is not explicit
about what she means by 'pure art', but her recall of The Merchant of
Venice is vividly expressed in conventional 'performance' terms[35].

> Their impersonation of the various parts, far from being calculated
> to draw a smile (which might be expected when young children
> attempted to act complex characters), were earnest and interesting.
> Shylock and Portia, ...realised their parts wonderfully, and yet they
> were played in an original manner, because the action and gesture

were their own, and neither taught by an instructor nor copied from players seen previously. They had merely the text of Shakespeare to depend upon. That they read this aright was proved by the fact that in such speeches as Shylock's, commencing 'How like a fawning publican he looks!' the boy impersonator used a venomous kind of undertone; and when Bassanio enters next and Shylock has to say, 'I am debating of my present store, ' andc., the boy changed his tone at once to a conciliatory, cringing tone, although no such directions are given in the play.

Clearly, from the above description, drama was at times conceived of and appreciated as classical scripts to be carefully rehearsed for showing to an audience. There is evidence in the book that plays were performed many times and no doubt the constant stream of visitors, created a strong sense of 'getting our play ready', but she does not record the school's attempts at more formal, public performances.

The making of scenery, properties and costumes were to be taken seriously for both dramatisation and the performance of a play and involved non-acting members of the class. It is clear that both pupils and teacher gained satisfaction (in keeping with a Naturalistic tradition of Western Theatre) from this theatrical notion of representational realism. Indeed she sometimes went to great lengths to ensure a 'realistic' environment[36].

Likewise the convention of appropriate 'casting' was unquestioningly followed. That the great stories from History or from Shakespeare were predominantly male oriented seemed not to be a matter for regret, and certainly not something that could be overcome by having girls play male roles. Indeed, not only was casting controlled by gender; physical attributes influenced choice: 'It took but a few seconds for the boys to settle on a rosy, rotund boy for a jovial Friar Tuck...' One wonders if it is the same overweight boy she refers to later in commenting on what happy memories past students must have of their Christmas Carol performance:

> The name Fezziwig will bring back to them the fat, rosy boy (stuffed in the region of the waistcoat with dusters to complete the illusion!) who sat up at the spindle-legged desk, once the hermit's cell for Friar Tuck, and beamed over spectacles, which sat with difficulty on his snub little nose...

Getting the appearance of a role right was but part of theatre orthodoxy, and like any traditional theatre-goer, Finlay-Johnson slips into such phrases, especially in relation to performing Shakespeare, as 'living in the part'. What was educationally innovative within this orthodoxy was that their teacher allowed the pupils to do the casting and rehearsing themselves, and that acting was seen as a legitimate part of school time.

Clearly some of the dramatisations were carried out with the intention, not of further rehearsal or presentation, but of further study, the dramatic 'game' being a catalyst for alternative classroom activities, such as research, writing or just 'learning on their feet'. It appears that the pupils in their 'shopping' games', for instance, spontaneously played at handling money, measuring and weighing etc. while in role as shop-keepers and customers.

That there was to be an audience to their fictional 'shopping' no doubt increased the self-consciousness of the participants, some of whom at least may well have been out to impress their classmates with their 'shopping' skills. Indeed, if this were the case, then it would be impossible for them to see themselves purely as 'shoppers', as they had an audience to entertain, an essentially different context from the kind of absorbed 'playing at shopping' envisioned perhaps by Margaret Macmillan (1901) in the kindergarten's play corner. Nor is this the formal audience to a Shakespeare performance, but rather an audience 'looking on'. It may be more appropriate to think of the rest of the class as critical 'spectators', as interested supporters of the game, rather than as an 'audience'.

The only recorded occasions when the dramatic fiction was played out independently of the presence of even a 'looking in' audience were at 'playtimes', 'dinner times' and 'after school'. 'Once', writes Miss Johnson, 'I found the boys playing at 'Princes in the Tower', and the game was so good I immediately commandeered it for school use.' Even the most spontaneous 'playing', if it occurred in school time, would not escape the 'scrutinising' by peers. There were times in school hours when some of the boisterous out-of-doors drama playing verged on 'pure' adventure play. For example, following the reading of Bevis, the pupils set up for themselves an imitation 'raft' (packing-case) on a 'river' (the school brook) – and they sailed, removing boots and stockings before doing so. Miss Johnson's account goes on, however, with: 'The raft went on voyage to all parts of places and (my italics) *the chorus sat along the banks to explain matters*'. Thus what must have had the appearance of a lively, juvenile pastime on a hot summer's day, was elevated into an excursion worthy of interpretative commentary, the 'chorus' directing the muddy-legged wallowers into thinking they are discovering diamonds in South Africa. Another function of the spectators is to take copious notes, so that even the dialogue emerging from this kind of 'fun' is recorded for re-use. The very instant of experiencing (in this case an adventure) is to be fed back to them as dialogue worthy of inspection. We have here, therefore, the introduction of a further dimension to the 'game': an active audience, functioning as commentators or recorders, as if they are part of what is being created. This is slightly but significantly different from the 'Shopping' game, for in that instance the onlookers had no responsibility for the fiction itself.

Thus, in this kind of example of spontaneous play, the acting behaviour is for the most part likely to have been modified by a conception of 'audience' that is far from traditional. A dramatisation occurs that is inwardly interactive, that is, the participants have to concentrate on and with each other in order to make sense of what they are doing. Their acting behaviour, however, is also, in part, directed outwards towards the watchers, who have a vested interest in what is going on as part-creators, and who are consciously treating what is going on as a 'product' to be talked about, written about or, more significantly, concurrently manipulated by choral interjection. Thus we have a special mode of acting behaviour, which to an extent anticipates the freer kind of playing associated with experimental progressivism of the kindergarten of the 1920s and yet is, in Finlay-Johnson's classroom, critically modified by others who are to treat the activity as a 'product-in-the-making'; the 'meaning-making' of the event is partly controlled by the audience to it

Generalisations about acting behaviour drawn from Harriet Finlay-Johnson's classroom dramatisation

The pupils as dramatists and stage-managers

'Dramatisation', for Finlay-Johnson, appears to have a precise meaning, the enactment of curriculum subject-matter. At its weakest it could simply be regarded as a kind of mnemonic for memorising information, rather like a rhyme for recalling the order of the British monarchs. No doubt some of the 'singing-rhymes' of the kindergarten were for this kind of purpose. Dialogue put into the mouths of different characters is a more elaborate form of representation than a singing rhyme with greater potential for inventive expression and for managagement hazards. Harriet Finlay-Johnson required her pupils to do the inventing *and* the managing, and before they could do the inventing they often had to search for the relevant information or knowledge.

Finding, selecting, re-ordering and dramatically interpreting first through scripting and then through enactment became a sequential pattern for her upper elementary age group. Each one of these steps had its own internal refinement process, for instance, if we take the first two lines of their 'Sweetpea' play:

Scholar;   Oh, here is a pretty Sweetpea hanging over the fence!

Sweetpea: He is wrong. I am not hanging over it at all! I climbed up here on purpose to look over at the sun. If he tries to pull me down, he will find I am holding on quite firmly. (pp 238-9)

This scripting by the pupils involved empirical research, selection of which items to include in their presentation, what characters to have and how to arrange their interaction with some humour and (towards the end of their play) a philosophical parallel drawn between the deviousness of Sweetpeas and children![37] Only a dramatist's sense could have the 'scholar' lay himself open to contradiction in his very first line (see above).

Acting characterised as knowledge-bearing

The final phase of the sequential pattern is presentation in which, as Finlay-Johnson describes, they enact 'scholars out on a ramble'. Rather like an ice-berg, the actual presentation is but the 'tip' of the work. However, to suggest that the presentation, in this kind of process, is less important than what has gone before, is to miss the point, for the presentation is critically part of the sequence. Nevertheless a reasonable and perhaps useful way of describing the acting is as a channel for newly acquired knowledge. This is its principal function in the Sompting School curriculum. One can understand how Holmes (1911) came to place Drama, not with the other arts, but as one of the two 'sympathetic' faculties, with an 'outward' orientation towards things and people outside oneself. By 'self-expression' Finlay-Johnson did not mean, as Freudian influenced exponents of drama were later to do, expression of inner experience, but a creative and collaborative act of selecting from a body of knowledge and finding their own dramatic form for its presentation. The notion of drama as being expressive of a personal inner experience is going to dominate much of its history in the the later pages of this book. The conceptual framework I shall be putting forward in the final chapter requires a fundamental reformulation of this long held assumption.

Ownership of knowledge

And it is *their* knowledge. Although not a term used by Finlay-Johnson, [or, indeed, by any of the chosen pioneers] the expression 'ownership' seems appropriate and in keeping with the spirit of her methodology. Traditionally, at that time, knowledge was perceived as a 'given' for pupils to absorb; Finlay-Johnson spurred her pupils on to find it and remould it, making it their own – for the sake of the play. This 'for the sake of' is the key to the method. Making a play provided an impetus for learning, offering the pupils an incentive outside the perceived purpose of schooling.

An overarching cultural context – a 'game'

I want to suggest that dramatising knowledge amounted to something rather more than an 'incentive'. I believe it provided a different order of school experience. Conventional schooling may be regarded as being at one remove from living, a special context with its own laws, set aside for certain periods in a child's life. Now to engage in the making of fiction as a major task *within* the school context is to enter an alternative culture with alternative laws, so that not only is knowledge reframed but matters such as school discipline and teacher-pupil relationship are open to readjustment.

To understand the apparent confusion that Harriet Finlay-Johnson showed in her sometimes random substition of the labels of 'game' and 'drama', we may need to appreciate that her use of 'game' may not have applied in her mind to a particular kind of activity as much as to a new order of doing things, a 'game' of temporarily creating an alternative culture within a school culture. On the other hand, it could be that she wanted drama to be seen as a 'serious game'.[38]

Looked at this way, we see the play-making and play-performing as part of a totality of a 'game'. It is the concept of 'game' that gives over-arching significance to the dramatic work. It colours everything that occurs in the dramatic endeavours, including a tolerance for 'crude action or dialogue from the adult's point of view referred to above. The classroom acting is conditioned by the 'game'. It is as if this alternative culture 'permits' the acting.

This may, in part, explain why Holmes (1911) is not able to enthuse about dramatisation *per se* while writing that 'In Utopia 'acting' is a vital part of the school life of every class...'. It may be that he sensed something inappropriate and unrealistic in even suggesting to elementary school teachers of that time that they invite their pupils to 'act' the material of their lessons. Without the underlying cultural infusion provided by the 'game', acting in a classroom could appear to be as unbecoming as running in church.

That such an alternative culture could be introduced was no doubt due to the special circumstances surrounding an enterprising teacher, a head-teacher, no less, along with her sister as the only other member of staff, in a two-class village school. The way in which Finlay-Johnson set up her dramatic method was undoubtedly peculiar to her and that school, but from it I suggest we may learn that dramatic activity in an educational setting may benefit from, if not depend upon, some kind of overarching cultural influence that gives plausibility to the acting.

How to 'do away' with an audience
This aspect of classroom acting behaviour will be pursued throughout the century as a central issue. Harriet Finlay-Johnson draws attention to it early in her book, suggesting that 'display to an audience', and even the 'idea (my underlining) of an audience' should be 'done away with'. She had three strategies: (1) turn them into stage-managers or

'crowds' (2) turn them into critical, note-taking onlookers (3) turn them into co-creators and directors[39]. In the final chapter of this book, however, it will be necessary to offer an alternative interpretation of what Finlay-Johnson might have meant by her expression 'display to an audience'

Notes

1   Miss Finlay-Johnson became Mrs. Weller, on marrying a member of her adult Shakespeare Group.

2   Cook, Henry Caldwell (1917) *The Play Way: An Essay in Educational Method* Heinemann London p.21

3   *Report of the Conference of New Ideals* (1915) p.193

4   Beacock D.A.[*The Playway English for Today: The Methods and influence of Caldwell Cook* Thomas Nelson London p.80] complains about the danger of over-sentimentality in Cook's writing.

5   Philip Coggin writes: 'From the days of Plato it has been a constant criticism of the stage that the portrayal of wickedness and evil must inevitably lead to their encouragement. And though the dramatist has always argued that he showed virtue and vice in their true colours, it has always been a difficult argument to answer.' p.249 [Coggin, Philip A. (1956) *Drama and Education: An Historical survey from Ancient Greece to the present day* Thames and Hudson London]

6   Welton, James. (1906) *Principles and Methods of Teaching* University Tutorial Press London *ibid* p.162. Interestingly, on the previous page he casts doubt on the value of boys actually seeing performances of Shakespearean plays because '...doubtless it tends to limit the imagination of the pupils to the actors' ideas of the characters.' (p.161)

7   The story of the 19th/early 20th centuries' resistance to the putting on plays in Schools and Universities is recorded by Vail Motter [1929] *The School Drama in England*, Longmans, London, by Philip Coggin [1956] *ibid*, and by K.M. Lobb [1955] in *The Drama in School and Church* George G. Harrap., London.]. Whereas during the early part of the 19th century public performance in schools was banned on moral grounds, the resistance from Universities took the form of academic prejudice.

8   Gilpin, E. M. (1920) ['The Dramatic Sense as a Factor in Education', a paper read before the Conference of Educational Associations, Drama League Session, at University College, January 1920, in Drama July 1920 p.177].

9   Macmillan, Margaret (1901) *Early Childhood* Swan Sonnenschein London p.32

10   See *The Teaching of History and other Papers* edited by J.H. Fowler (1904) University Press Manchester

11   Groos, Karl (1899) *The Play of Man* Appleton Press

12   Crompton, N.J.R. (1978 unpublished) *A Critical Evaluation of the aims and purposes of Drama in Education* Thesis M.Phil University of Nottingham

13   Bloomer, Mabel (1911) *A Year in the Infant School* Blackie London

14   Finlay-Johnson H. (1911) *The Dramatic Method of Teaching* Nisbet, London p.19

15   Findlay, J.J. (1902) *Principles of Class Teaching* Macmillan and Co Ltd London p.79

16   Frances W. Parker School, Chicago, founded in 1901 and named after America's pioneer in 'child-centred' education

17   Board of Education (1905) *Suggestions for the consideration of Teachers and Others* concerned in the Work of Public Elementary Schools HMSO

18   It is interesting to note that Oral English was, according to this 1905 Board of Education publication, to have priority in the kindergarten and infant school over Learning to Read

19   Board of Education (1905) *ibid* p.30 included in *The Companion to the Red Code* (1908) National Union of Teachers, London

20   Holmes, Edmond, (1911) *What is and What Might Be* Constable London and (1914) *In Defence of What Might Be* Constable London

21   He had managed to enrage the National Union of Teachers with his undiluted attack in his first book on Elementary Education. He claimed afterwards that he had intended attacking the system, not the teachers who were part of it. For an account of this 'turbulent inspector' see: 'Utopia Reconsidered: Edmond Holmes, Harriet Johnson and the School at Sompting' by M.T. Hyndman in *Sussex Archaelogical Collection* 118 (1980) pp 351-357.

22   Finlay-Johnson, H. (1911) *ibid* pp.36-7 It seems likely that Finlay-Johnson was the first teacher to apply the term 'dramatisation' (or dramatization, as OED prefers) to education; its dictionary definition is 'conversion into dramatic form'.

23   Later writers, notably, Dorothy Heathcote and Cecily O'Neill, were to use the word 'lure' and 'pretext' respectively to describe the means of arresting pupils' attention in the dramatic theme.

24   Indeed, a feature of the progressive movement was an avoidance of inter-pupil activity (See Selleck, R.J.W. [1972] *English Primary Education and the Progressives* 1914-1939 p.51). A typical conference speech at the time came from Lillian De Lissa, Principal of Adelaide Kindergarten Training College, Australia. Delivered at the first Montessori Conference held at East Renton in 1914, it argued: 'The psychology of a group is quite different from the psychology of an individual, and the teachers should be concerned with individuals, for it is they who make the strength of the nation'. (From Report of the Montessori Conference, 1914 p.51.

25   Finlay-Johnson, H. (1911) *ibid* p.70 This phrase 'the fitness of things' is echoed years later by Mary Midgely [Midgely, M. (1980) *Beast and Man: The Roots of Human Nature* Methuen London] who says: 'Understanding is relating; it is fitting things into a context.' p.18 Mike Fleming (1982) A Philosophical Investigation into Drama in Education Ph.D thesis, University of Durham (unpublished), p.157 [footnote] quotes D.W. Hamlyn: '...all learning is in one way or another connecting things...'.

26 Finlay-Johnson, H. (1911) *ibid* p.110

27 Holmes, E. (1914) *ibid* p.2

28 Holmes, E. (1911) *op cit* p.165

29 Burton, Bruce (1991) in his *Act of Learning* Longman Cheshire, Sydney, divides the drama education pioneers into those who 'perceive the drama process as a valuable learning experience about oneself' and those who ' choose to use it as an educational tool to stimulate learning about specific fields of human experience.' p.52

30 Differences among progressive practitioners, according to Selleck (1972 *op cit* p.23) were sometimes overlooked in favour of perceiving unity in opposition to 'the old ways'. Edmond Holmes, for instance, seemed not to see any fundamental difference between the classroom practice of Harriet Finlay-Johnson and that recommended by Maria Montessori, for whose book, *The Montessori Method*, translated into English in 1912, he wrote an equally enthusiastic preface. In Montessori's approach the child in the classroom is certainly invited to discover through play, but the form of the play (she used the telling term 'auto-play') is a solitary investigation of the 'Montessori' apparatus, with the teacher as a benign, perceptive observer of each child. According to her critics, Montessori, like Rousseau, was opposed to make-believe activities. W.H. Kilpatrick writes of her work [Kilpatrick, in *Montessori Examined* (1915) Constable London p.43]: 'There is very little of dramatisation. On the whole, the imagination, whether of constructive play or of the more aesthetic sort, is but little utilised' One cannot be surprised by this absence of make-believe in a method whose creator regarded fantasy as something education should help the child to overcome. Such a view is expounded by Montessori in *The Advanced Montessori Method* Vol 1. Ch. 9. Perhaps the most striking denial of differences comes from Norman MacNunn, who, at the East Runton conference in 1915 on 'Montessorism in Secondary Schools' [p.86 of the report] averred that: '...difference in the ideals...of Madame Montessori and of Miss Finlay-Johnson are infinitely less essential than the community of aim.'

31 Finlay-Johnson, H. (1911) *op cit* p.19

32 See: Viola, Whilhelm (1936) *Child Art* Franz Cizek Vienna

33 Such is the concern of today's leaders that two publications this decade emphasise 'Process' in book titles: O'Toole, John (1992) *The Process of Drama: Negotiating Art and Meaning* Routledge London and O'Neill, Cecily (1995) *Drama Worlds: a framework for process drama* Heinemann New Jersey

34 Harriet Finlay-Johnson's interest in Shakespeare led her to start an amateur Shakespeare group in the village. Ironically, this out-of-school activity led to her meeting the man she was to marry and, consequently, to retirement from teaching.

35 Finlay-Johnson, H. (1911) *ibid* pp 138-9

36 On page 70 she describes plays that gained in verisimilitude when they were performed in a near-by disused chalk-pit, 'where they could scale heights most realistically' or 'under the shade of the greenwood tree'.

37 Sweetpea: White Sweetpea....has cruelly twined her tendrils even around the Cornflower's blossoms, forcing them to support her.

Schoolmaster: I have known some children like that. They will let others do the work...

38 To borrow a term used a decade later by Artaud, Antonin (c. 1920s) in *Selected Writings* (1976) edited by Susan Sontag, Farrar Strauss and Giroux, New York, pp 156-7

39 'Doing away with the audience' must have seemed a strange conception to those contemporaries encouraging Drama, such as Miss Gilpin referred to above (p.15). We shall see that Caldwell Cook sought a degree of active cooperation from the audience, while retaining a Western theatre stance, but that subsequent exponents adopted other methods. For instance, Peter Slade and Brian Way, more than a generation later, evolved a system whereby there was no audience at all and in their professional Children's Theatre work they wove a degree of participation by the audience into the actor's presentation, although the 'spectator' function of the audience was retained. It is interesting that, by the 1960s Jerzy Grotowski, in adult professional theatre was experimenting with similar methods. According to Shomit Mitter [Mitter, S. (1992) *Systems of Rehearsal* Routledge London, p.100] 'In *The Ancestors...* they treated the audience as fellow actors by including them in the action. In subsequent productions, situations were created in which the audience had definite roles imposed upon them.' Interestingly, as Grotowski became dissatisfied with these experiments, he 'did away' with the audience by harnessing their spectator function: 'In *Dr. Faustus*, the central character had begun by asking the spectators to be his witnesses. A role was still 'imposed' upon the audience but it had been made congruent with their 'natural' role as observers.' (p.101) Perhaps when Grotowski [in an interview included in *Towards a Poor Theatre* and entitled 'The Theatre's New Testament' (1968, translated 1965) Simon and Shuster, pp 41-2] declares: 'It is therefore necessary to abolish the distance between actor and audience by eliminating the stage, removing all frontiers. Let the most drastic scenes happen face to face with the spectator so that he is within arm's reach of the actor, can feel his breathing and smell his perspiration.', he could have added, 'as in the classrooms of Harriet Finlay-Johnson and Henry Caldwell Cook'!

CHAPTER TWO

HENRY CALDWELL COOK
(1886-1937)

An introduction – an independent school setting: the English Master

Caldwell Cook[1] was employed[2] as a member of staff at the Perse School in 1911 by a headmaster, Dr. W.H.D. Rouse, who was warmly receptive to this young teacher's ideas. Rouse had already established in the school the 'Direct Method' of teaching Modern and Classical Languages[3]. Beacock writes[4]:

> Thus it was to the right man that Caldwell Cook came, and to an atmosphere suitable for the fulfilment of his hopes. An enthusiastic advocate of dramatic work, he found to his joy that Dr. Rouse believed acting to be one of the most potent methods of learning...

As with Finlay-Johnson, Caldwell Cook's use of dramatisation can only be understood in the fuller context of the deeply-held, revolutionary views of schooling he maintained throughout his career. His romantic image of himself as a 'Playmaster', along with the quaint choice of title for his book, The Play Way, a title which caused some embarrassment to those who wanted to support his views and methods[5], are but outer trappings of a serious challenge to the traditional image of a school-master and to the educational system in general:

> The educational system has in fact not been evolving at all, it has been congealing. And now it has become clogged, stuck fast. The educational system has ceased to be educational.

27

This 'Playmaster's' career deteriorated towards the end. C.W.E. Peckett, an ex-pupil of Cook's and subsequently headmaster of The Priory School for Boys, Shrewsbury, describes how the new head-master replacing Rouse, who retired in 1928, closed the Mummery and told Caldwell Cook 'to stop all this nonsense'. Peckett adds: 'Of course he resigned; he couldn't teach conscientiously any other way. He died of an excess of alcohol – who can blame him? – and a broken heart.'[6] He suffered a debilitating, nervous illness caused by shell-shock in the Great War, leading to a breakdown in 1933. He was not able to return to teaching again. John Allen, in an unpublished essay, dated approximately 1965, writes: 'Henry Caldwell Cook died suddenly in 1937, almost unnoticed'.

The Play Way: An Essay in Educational Method

A close investigation will reveal that Caldwell Cook's expression, 'Play Way' covers a complexity of meanings, which together make his contribution to education unique. It is not possible to understand the status of his dramatic work and the kind of acting that took place in his classroom without a grasp of his broader conception of what education is about and how he played a part in the Progressive movement of his day. It will be necessary, therefore, to examine the philosophy of his practice in some detail. For the sake of clarity, the discussion will be conducted under separate headings, isolating those characteristics of his Play Way concept which coincide with the 'Progressive' Education Movement of the period: 'action', 'freedom', 'individuality', and 'self-government'.

Four 'Progressive' Concepts in Caldwell Cook's ideology

The 'Play Way' as Present Action

Caldwell Cook made a number of attempts at explaining what he meant by 'Play Way'. Following Froebel, he proposes that 'boys and girls of the upper school should have as much play as the infants in the kindergarten'. Early in his book he appears to support the commonly held view that child play is a form of practice, a preparation for adult life: 'It would not be wise', Caldwell Cook writes, 'to send a child innocent into the big world...But it is possible to hold rehearsals, to try our strength in a make-believe big world. And that is Play.'

His 'rehearsal' metaphor lies uneasily with his later definition, for Caldwell Cook goes on to express faith in personal engagement as a factor in learning: '...by Play I mean the *doing* anything one knows with one's heart in it. The final appreciation in life and in study is to put oneself into the thing studied and to live there active. And that is Playing.' The italics are Caldwell Cook's; such emphasis on 'doing' and 'active' and 'following one's heart' suggests a full engagement with the present rather than practice for the future. Indeed, much as he concurred with the message of Holmes' *What is and What Might Be* with its appeal for a swing in education from the 'Path of Mechanical Obedience' to the 'Path of Self Realisation', his instinct as a practising teacher led him to see the pathway, not merely as the means of reaching a goal, but as the goal itself. As Caldwell Cook put it, 'The claim here put forward is not for the destination, but chiefly for the journey' and that we should give our attention 'to what is usually called the means, and make that our end' He reasserts the point: 'The world goes on, and the life of each individual with it, not in telling what has to be done, nor in saying what remains to do, but in the present doing of present deeds.' Such a philosophy, borne out by his practice, appears to deny a view of education as 'rehearsing'.

The Play Way as Freedom

Having argued that education is in the 'doing', Caldwell Cook feels impelled to affirm that pupil 'Play' activity must be seen as something more than an amusing way of learning. According to Caldwell Cook, it is a way of freeing the imagination, so that the deepest levels of a person can be 'brought into play'. 'Freeing' children to learn is a key part of the conceptual luggage of the 'Progressives'. Typically, Montessori claimed that 'The fundamental principle of scientific pedagogy must be, indeed, *the liberty of the pupil*; – such liberty as shall permit a development of individual, spontaneous manifestations of the child's nature.'[7]

Caldwell Cook's view of himself as a 'Playmaster' seems to fit another view of 'freedom' popular with his fellow reformists: a freedom from restraint, in such matters as discipline, arranging classroom furniture and choice of curriculum. Caldwell Cook's approach could be described as non-traditional in all these matters, although he was not as radical a 'Progressive' as his contemporary Homer Lane[8], for example, who was prepared to tolerate confusion and chaos as necessary channels to self-discipline.

Some confusion appears to show itself when Caldwell Cook describes the need for a teacher to be a 'necessary part of the scheme', and at the 'very centre', and then, appearing to correct himself, he adds: '...or, better still, he is at the circumference'. This apparent contradiction is perhaps explained by the subtle nature of this teacher's relationship with his classes. It is not, for Caldwell Cook, a choice of either imposing or letting go, but rather, a conception, both sophisticated and paradoxical, of always being present by appearing to be absent, or as he elegantly phrases it: '...an influence continuously operative, though not constantly assertive.'

Although Caldwell Cook saw the necessity at times of giving instructions, for the most part, he allowed the pupils to choose how they wanted to work, and how they wanted to evaluate each others' work, while taking it upon himself to decide what material to introduce to them. Any hint of compromise with the excesses of Progressivism should not, however, diminish his image as a passionate believer in his own methods. The teacher, according to Caldwell Cook, must have 'a genuine interest in the play', joining in with the pupils' interests[9] '...honestly and heartily, not with any idea of amusing the boys, but because he is of like passions with them.'

The Play Way and Individuality

'Individuality' may well have been the 'supreme educational end'[10] of the Progressive movement, and yet it is in relation to this particular concept that it is possible to detect a departure from Progressivism in Caldwell Cook's approach. This apparent defection, it should be said, is not something of which he or his contemporaries appeared to be aware. Although Caldwell Cook at times appears to be taking a typically 'progressive' stance in respecting 'the individual': 'A master must of course understand boys. But it is not enough for him to understand boys in a general way. He must know the particular boys now under his guidance...', it is noticeable that he fails to talk about getting to know each individual. Rather, it appears to be the teacher's responsibility to get to know 'particular boys' (in the plural), as though it is a particular group, rather than its individual members, that is to be understood. An examination of Caldwell Cook's writing reveals that although occasionally he refers to 'the child', he is more comfortable with the 'group' references: 'the class'; the 'form'; the 'Littlemen'; 'boys'; 'the players; 'the playboys'. Such a usage of collective nouns in the mouths of traditional teachers often denies a recognition of pupils as separate persons, but for Caldwell Cook the terms imply 'co-operative' rather than 'collective'[11]:

> Although the members of a class are seldom enough treated as individuals, it is even more rare to find a class treated as a conscious group. The boys are either addressed collectively, or they are set to do each version of the same task separately. It is an excellent plan to treat the class, whenever possible, *as a body of workers* [my italics] collaborating.

Historians of twentieth century education have had little difficulty in identifying the principal ideals and associated concepts that have qualified pioneers for the designation 'progressive', and to varying degrees such historians have given some prominence to the part played by Henry Caldwell Cook in the 'Progressive Movement'[12], but it is worth reiterating the point, already made in connection with Harriet Finlay-Johnson, that the key notion of 'collaboration within a group', of a class as 'a body of workers' and of inter-dependence in learning has not, it seems, been given much practical attention[13]. Selleck while listing the concepts commonly associated with the progressive movement, such as 'individuality', 'freedom' and 'growth' etc., makes no mention of group collaboration.

The Play Way and Self-Government

Caldwell Cook was interested in the few experiments of self-government in schooling already begun when he started teaching. He refers in his book both to the 'Junior Republics' in North America and to the school, 'The Little Commonwealth', for delinquent boys recently opened in Dorset by Homer Lane[14], an American, who became its first headmaster in 1913.

The American model of 'self-government' gained support from and indeed may have derived from the writings of the great American philosopher and educationist, John Dewey. It is not difficult to identify in Caldwell Cook's approach to teaching three of the basic tenets of

Dewey's educational philosophy, described, for example, in Democracy and Education published in 1916, a year before Caldwell Cook's own publication. Dewey advocates a method of teaching which sets up 'a genuine situation of experience' in which there is 'continuous activity'. The three educational ideals: active, experiential learning; democratic responsibility; and the conception of teaching and learning as a partnership between pupil and teacher characterise Caldwell Cook's practice – as they did Harriet Finlay-Johnson's. What is missing from Dewey, however, is any consistent support for dramatisation.

More important then to Caldwell Cook than his cherished concepts of 'freedom', 'activity' and 'self-expression' is the notion that schooling should be conducted as a microcosm of society: '...a school must be as far as possible a *little State in itself...* [Caldwell Cook's. italics]..'. Any classroom dramatisation had to submit to rules of procedure, election of officials, a system of rewards and punishments, and the right of free-speech. Hence Caldwell Cook's 'The Junior Republic of Form 111b' or, less politically, 'Littlemen' and 'Ilonds'. Typically, Caldwell Cook writes[15]:

> In 11b (average age under twelve) it chanced appropriately in connexion with our reading of 'Le Morte D'Arthur' that certain boys should be knighted for single deeds of prowess or for general renown. Thus it happened that a certain six came to be known as The Knightly Guard. There was the Knight Captain, who held supreme sway, while the rest divided among them the control of the homework and the desks, and those other cares with which a Knight could be charged. In this form the officers have a fuller responsibility. A Knight of the Guard holds a daily wapenshaw to assure himself that all have fit and ready their equipment of pens, ink and paper; and the Knight Captain marshals his men orderly from one room to another.

This quotation may appear merely to be reiterating the point about self-government, but it seems that Caldwell Cook was offering his boys, as we have seen Finlay-Johnson offered her pupils, an 'alternative culture'. Whereas Finlay-Johnson's approach provided no more than a fictitious 'game' that granted a licence to their dramatisation, Caldwell Cook's 'alternative culture' was more deeply concerned with identity.

The Play Way approach endows the pupils with a long-term, collective identity. This, above all, is its distinctive feature.

Caldwell Cook the English Master – a summary of his classroom practice

The kind of titles Caldwell Cook has chosen for the chapters of his major publication, *The Play Way* are indicators of where his priorities lay as a teacher of English. After introductory chapters discussing his 'Play Way' philosophy and principles, he gives the following headings to his chapters: 'Littleman Lectures' in which he describes the eleven year old boys' endeavours with oral composition, attention being given to content, style, wit, grammar, figures of speech and quality of speech; 'Ilonds and Chap-Books' in which the drawing by the pupils of their own imaginary islands (Caldwell Cook was impressed by Stevenson's use of this stimulus for Treasure Island and from which sprang stories, poems and further drawings, all being recorded in the boy's personal note-book ('chap'-book); 'Playtown', an account of an out-of-school (most of the boys lived-in) activity for a chosen few boys involving the building in the back-yard to Caldwell Cook's own house in the school grounds of a large-scale model countryside with river, railway, bridge, farm, hostel, market-place etc. and then its citizens, designated characters about whom stories could be built; 'Acting Shakespeare in the Classroom'[16] is about how to introduce dramatisation to boys through the use of stories and ballads – 'dramatising almost everything we read', as Cook put it, before advancing to acting Shakespeare; 'Miming and the Ballads', a chapter giving instruction in conventional signing and in the telling of anecdotes or the representation of a ballad through gestures; and 'Play-making' in which the boys create their own drama, either by representing 'real-life' (often too 'cheap and sensational' according to Caldwell Cook), or by using literary sources.

The above chapter headings alone must have mystified and even shocked traditional teachers of English. Indeed Caldwell Cook seems to be determined to offend his fellow professionals. He pokes fun at a fellow English master at Rugby School whose enthusiasm for teaching a Shakespearean text is unmistakable in spite of Caldwell Cook's cynicism. The author of 'Notes on the Teaching of English in the Lower Middles', notes written with enthusiasm and wit, is ridiculed by Caldwell Cook to a point of caricature. The Rugby English master's besetting sin was, apparently, to recommend that before the 'parts' are assigned for the reading round the class of a play, the text should be minutely examined by the boys. Using the metaphor of 'the huntsman' the Rugby teacher suggests that after a lively reading of some twenty or thirty lines by the 'huntsman'[17]:

> The meaning is examined: dug out of the words, torn out of the idioms, enticed out of the allusions. Every bush is beaten, and hares started up, whether historical, mythological, moral, geographical, political, etymological, architectural, or ecclesiastical, are pursued, and, if possible, caught.

Such intellectual dissection, even seen as a 'fun-of-the-hunt' pursuit, is anathema to Caldwell Cook to whom the meaning of a play-text lies in action. That the Rugby master intends, after this close analysis by his boys, the play should be 'read dramatically with any amount of coaching in emphasis and inflexion by the master...' , fails to impress Caldwell Cook, for it is too late: 'As well hand over your dog to be hanged, drawn and quartered, tarred and feathered, and then whistle him out to run!' Not only too late, but inappropriate, for Caldwell Cook knew that 'dramatic reading' for most teachers of English, including the Rugby master, implies 'boys reading in turn while seated in their desks.' He goes on: 'I insist that to ignore action is to ignore the play. A book in hand is not a very serious impediment to a boy who has the chance to stab someone or to storm a city wall.'

This was not, for Caldwell Cook, merely a matter of methodological preference, but a fundamental belief in the possibility of pupils' finding the true meaning of a text (Shakespeare, in particular, but he treated ballads, myths and legends in the same way) from inside the action.

An analysis of Caldwell Cook's use of dramatisation in the teaching of Literature

Early in his book he sums up his method with the word 'make': doing drama is *making* a play and the way to go about it is to get on and do it. 'You must fall straight away upon the actual work, and you will find out what you are doing as you go along.' The pupils' 'making' was most often linked with their reading: 'We early formed a habit of dramatizing almost everything we read', but it becomes evident as

Caldwell Cook goes into his methods in more detail that 'falling in' to the drama was not entirely haphazard. His warning: 'The thing must be acted extempore in the classroom. But unless you happen to have a special knack of casting stories into dramatic form you may find yourself in difficulties at the very start.', reveals his strength as a teacher-artist: his interest essentially lies in dramatic form and it is this aspect of art that he set out to teach from the very beginning with his young pupils. 'But at first I used to give the boys suggestions of a scheme of action. This was a very simple aid, but without it the boys never would have found the acting successful.'

He goes on to give an instance of how he unhesitatingly interferes: 'But the master intervenes. This is not the way to tell a story dramatically. They are in too much a hurry to reach the climax.' He explains to the boys about to 'make' their Beowolf play how to lead up to the arrival of Beowolf by having earlier scenes building the Hall Heriot and, with some irony, celebrating this achievement, ignorant of Grendel's imminent attack. Typically, Caldwell Cook notes: '...when your playboys become expert in acting and play-making they will, at such a juncture as this, interpolate a comic scene in which the builders rag one another and make comments upon life in general. This interpolated comic scene is of course borrowed from Shakespeare as instanced in the porter in 'Macbeth' and the grave-digger in 'Hamlet'. Caldwell Cook continually draws on Shakespeare as a principal source for learning about dramatic structure: 'One is not born with a working knowledge of playmaking and dramatic conventions. We have learnt all we know in this kind from Shakespeare. The best way to make a start in classroom acting is to take a play of Shakespeare and act it. The boys will there find everything is set down for them in the book.'

Clearly this 'Play Way' approach to 'playmaking' is not a free-for-all romp but a serious harnessing of dramatic structure. Furthermore, Caldwell Cook demands not just a literary understanding of dramatic form, but a grasp of the physical structure of the Elizabethan stage. Thus the pupils are to experience a 'double refraction' of the material they are handling: they are to adapt the material of the Beowolf story in a way that satisfies (1) dramatic form as opposed to narrative form and (2) architectural constrictions as opposed to a 'real life' presentation. Even in, or rather, as we shall see, especially in the enactment of

Shakespeare, Caldwell Cook requires this conscious 'distancing' from the performers. The pupils are to respond to Shakespeare's juxtaposition of scenes and, further, they are to adapt their acting to fit an imaginary Elizabethan stage: 'All the while the boys are playing Shakespeare in the classroom they consider themselves subject to most of the conditions of an Elizabethan playhouse stage.' Thus, in acting Macbeth, their goal is not to recreate the atmosphere of Glamis Castle, but to achieve an authentic representation of the original staging of Glamis. His argument is that to get to the heart of a play it is necessary that '...you get some knowledge of the conditions in relation to which this particular play was wrought actable.'

Whereas most of the material dramatised was drawn from legends, epic poems or plays, Caldwell Cook occasionally (and, one feels, against his better judgement) permits his pupils to make up their own plays from '...the incidents of everyday life.' Even here the material is to be subjected to literary and architectural constraints. The most casual adventure is to match Shakespeare's example in the selection of scenes; scenes are to be plotted to fit a supposed Elizabethan stage; and the language to be poetic in spirit although not necessarily in verse. It is a pity Caldwell Cook does not supply the reader with sample texts, illustrating a style that is 'poetic in spirit'.

Caldwell Cook's reasons are as instructive as they are clear. He argues that 'a conscious pursuit of realism is inadvisable for boys', because it is 'beyond their powers' to represent 'things as they are', because it fails to teach the boys about theatre conventions and because it neglects boys' 'ready comprehension of a romantic theme' and their 'fitly imaginative treatment of it.' Thus it seems that not only is the dramatic action to be conventionalised, the content is to be romanticised. It has already been pointed out in the introduction to Harriet Finlay-Johnson and Henry Caldwell Cook that an aspect of Progressivism was its search for the Romantic. Caldwell Cook's avoidance of realism may also derive from his intuitive understanding as an artist educator.

Characteristics of the acting behaviour in Caldwell Cook's classroom

Caldwell Cook taught some lessons in the Mummery and others in the regular school classroom. [A visitor to the School gives a description of a typical lesson he observed in the Mummery with the 'First Year's']. Between lessons boys were required to learn their lines, ready to be plunged further into the theatrical environment of spotlights, drawn-curtains, swords, arrasses and thrones. The focus of their attention is on 'making a play', with all that implies of pleasing an audience. Mostly that audience was just the rest of the class, usually busy with sound-effects and other forms of stage-managing, and the master. Together, Caldwell Cook claimed, the boys can '...revel in din and clash and horrors, and learn to appreciate literature in its highest form...'.

Leaving aside the effect of this invitation to bring 'din and clash and horrors' into the classroom on the average schoolmaster of the day, it is worth questioning Caldwell Cook's assumption that such raucous activity leads to an appreciation of 'literature in its highest form'. This point has already been touched on in relation to Harriet Finlay-Johnson's own observation that 'however crude the action' it has value to the child. Visitors, including those from the Inspectorate[18], to both schools were impressed with the pupils' achievements in literary appreciation. From the evidence, it cannot be doubted that the method worked, and yet there are arguments that do indeed cast doubt on a faith in juvenile recitation of text accompanied by crude action as an entry into the meaning of a play. Such an argument is put forward forcefully by W.S. Tomkinson[19], a contemporary of Caldwell Cook and also a distinguished teacher of English.

Mr. Tomkinson is not convinced by the enthusiasts for what he calls 'the Dramatic Method'. He is particularly suspicious of the presentation of Shakespeare: 'A dramatic presentation of Shakespeare focuses attention primarily on the action, and not on the poetry.'[20] One cannot help but feel that this bald remark is intended as a personal attack on Caldwell Cook as much as for the general reader, and yet Tomkinson appears to share with Caldwell Cook a vision of the teacher as an artist embarking on the reform of oral expression; but for Tomkinson oral expression should not include dramatisation. 'There is no danger of the

Dramatic Method being over-looked in present-day practice', he comments somewhat ruefully. He goes on: 'The real danger, as it appears to me, lies in the teacher's forgetfulness of its pitfalls and limitations.'

This may be the first appearance in any publication of an attempt seriously to challenge the efficacy of the 'dramatic method'[21]. Tomkinson's reference above to the reductionist effect of a dramatic presentation of Shakespeare should not be taken merely as his disapproval of a particular method with a difficult text but rather as part of a fundamental belief he holds relating to drama as an inadequate vehicle for the presentation of truth and reality. Tomkinson justifies his position by citing the use of the Dramatic Method to teach History. He concedes the point that the only way the true meaning of a past event can be brought into the classroom is indeed through Art, but the Art of Narrative or Poetry, not Drama. For Tomkinson, Drama is an inappropriate art form and he offers a convincing anecdote to support his case[22]:

> Let the teacher make an experiment. Let him take such a piece of writing as Stanley's Murder of Becket, or Napier's Death... and read it to his class... The effect, if the reading is good and emotional, will be impressive... Now present the scene dramatically. Becket's murder (I take the subject of my own experiment) will be received by actors and audience alike with undisguised amusement. The atmosphere – and good history teaching is largely the presentment of correct atmosphere – will be falsified and debased. Imagination, by which alone we possess the past, will be overpowered by the crude realism of history in action. In grasping at the substance you have even lost the shadow.

Tomkinson is drawing a conclusion here from his own practice that the amateurish dramatising of an event, whether it be from History or from Literature actually diminishes the 'substance', by concentrating on the least important dimension of its meaning: crude action.[23]

As if anticipating his critics, Caldwell Cook reasserts his belief with emphasis: '...it is not generally recognised that by letting them act the plays from the beginning you make it possible for boys under fifteen to appreciate some of the most difficult and moving passages of tragedy. To know this as a fact surely gives great support to my belief that *a true feeling for art values may be expected to arise out of the trial practice of the arts.'* (Caldwell Cook's italics). He goes on to give two instances of supreme achievement. A 14 year old boy's reading/acting of 'Hamlet' Caldwell Cook describes as follows:

> Hamlet began the scene with an air of assumed madness, snapping out the words in a high-pitched voice. But with 'Come, come, and sit you down,' his whole bearing changed to suit his altered purpose. He became outwardly calm, but spoke in a tense voice full of restrained excitement. Just that voice, in fact, which so frightened the queen that she cried out on murder... The boys all watching in breathless interest. No one moved in his seat... A change from pathos in 'This was your husband,' to contempt in 'This is your husband' – no easy thing for a boy to express – was very effective, and the tone in 'Ha! have you eyes?' rose to a kind of shriek, which seemed to make clear once and for all that the madness of Hamlet was neither real madness nor assumed, but hysteria...

> The other boys (at the end of the scene) remained sitting and no one spoke a word. The atmosphere showed that no comment was needed, so I praised it as the finest piece of work I had ever seen in the school; and the class dispersed.

It is not Caldwell Cook's way to isolate, as he has done here, a particular boy's performance; usually he sees the work as a collaborative effort. However, he was obviously keen to give the reader a picture of the best that could be achieved. Caldwell Cook is seeing some kind of perfection here. His readers are left to ask whether for him it lies in the technique of the performance, in a young actor struggling to convey the meaning of the text, or in a pupil's personal discovery of a truth in the text – or a combination of these. Quality of acting is not something an author can convey for the reader: he can only attempt to share his response to it. Such an attempt, as has been seen with Harriet Finlay-Johnson in her description of 'Rosalind' and 'Celia', is barely in keeping with either author's overall principles. Nevertheless it is a form of evidence that Caldwell Cook's own emphasis on finding the action of the plays did not deny the pupils access to deeper meanings within the text.

One wonders why Tomkinson, also a gifted teacher, could not cite similar examples from his own classroom. Many teachers will respond to Tomkinson's and others' reservations about the superficiality wrought by the 'din and clash and horrors' of mere activity. It may be, therefore, that there is a dimension of Caldwell Cook's teaching that is missing for other proficient members of the profession. Some might suggest that it is his genius[24]; it seems to be commonly accepted that he was an exceptional teacher. That he stood alone led HMI Phillips to conclude his 1922 report with '...it would be very dangerous for teachers to be encouraged to visit the School with the idea that they will find there something that they might and should imitate. That being so, it seems clear that if an application is ever made for an Art 39 grant for this experimental work, it would be well for the Board not to entertain it.'

Having one's work dismissed as distinguished but too idiosyncratic to be useful to others may be a slight that most pioneer teachers suffer. If Caldwell Cook's success lies in his methodology rather than, or as well as, in his genius, then there is a chance that we can learn how, for example, a boy of 14 can reach a stage of being able to give a moving and intelligent performance of the scene between 'Hamlet' and his 'Mother' after the pupil concerned had merely 'read over the scene beforehand' and had seen 'Mr. Poel's production at the Little Theatre'. If this represented a final stage in Caldwell Cook's hands (it took place during the pupil's 'final year' with Caldwell Cook), one might wonder what earlier elements in training the youth led to that kind of success. It is not enough to say, for instance, that Caldwell Cook's enthusiasm and love for Shakespeare won over a group of young boys who wanted to please their English master.

A return to the argument put forward earlier, related to the filtering of the text through the architectural frame of an Elizabethan stage may, in part, account for the apparent accessibility for his pupils of a difficult text. Caldwell Cook writes: '...the most remarkable fact about Shakespeare's skill in stage-craft is the way he tells his actors at every important moment exactly what he wants them to do. Could anything be at once more interesting for the boy-players to notice and so helpful to them in their acting of plays? The mister[25] in charge has only to read the book with care to find all the directions literally waiting for him.'

He continues later: 'He who has not tried putting himself and his players entirely into Shakespeare's hands, and playing all his games exactly as he directs they should be played, has missed half the fun so generously given by this amazing craftsman.'

Engaging with Shakespeare, then, is to be a 'game', a 'treasure hunt' for the hidden clues. It is conceivable that Caldwell Cook had found, perhaps intuitively, a method of teaching that involves a deliberate use of *refocusing*, so that the immediate, explicit problem for the learner is transformed from an intellectual one into a practical one: the meaning of the text becomes in the eyes of the pupils 'merely' a matter of 'theatrical staging'; its other complexities remain unacknowledged, unspecified, unspoken and yet open to being engaged with subconsciously.

In the above discussion of his philosophy, I reached the conclusion that the most distinctive and critical feature of 'Playway' was that the notion of schooling as a 'little state' gave pupils a collective identity. Thus everything the pupils did was to be done or seen in the light of their respective roles in the 'Junior Republic of Form IIIb'. This sense of identity filtered through to how they saw themselves in his English lessons. They were prestigious 'Littlemen' or 'Ilonds' or 'Junior Republic of IIIb. They tackled their plays as a 'company' or 'band' of players: *thus each member of the group was already 'in role' before taking on another role.* This belonging to a company, it seems reasonable to assume, gave each player a sense of savoir faire before he even started to play his 'second' role. This 'banner of prestige' may have spread in many directions[26]: it created an atmosphere of collaboration; it reduced the weight of responsibility for performing the play from individual shoulders; it encouraged the idea that no problem is unsolvable; it reduced 'showing off', because it was felt to be a group effort; it continually fed on public recognition gained from streams of visitors, Press and School Magazine reports, Headmaster's praise, in-school and public performances and, above all, from the 'total belief in the game'[27] espoused by their own teacher, Caldwell Cook who is seen by them as part of the game, continually re-affirming their identity.

Generalisations about acting behaviour in Cook's classroom

There seem to be five aspects that add to our understanding of class-room acting: (1) drama as collaboration (2) pupils' identity as 'players' (3) indirect approach to a text (4) a 'platform' mental set (5) avoidance of 'realism'.

Drama as collaboration

Drama, more than any other classroom subject requires group co-operation. This occurs in its preparatory stages and in performance. It appears to have a reciprocal effect on relationships in the classroom:

(1) its practice appears to develop in the teacher a particular way of looking at 'the-child-in-the-group', that is, as an individual member within a cast of 'play-makers' (using the term in both its broadest and narrowest senses), and

(2) its practice appears to develop in the pupils a propensity for learning from each other through group responsibility.

Pupils' 'identity' as players

In the previous chapter on Harriet Finlay-Johnson, it was argued that the invitation to 'dramatise everything' implicitly established an 'alternative culture'. Caldwell Cook took this overarching dimension a stage further by explicitly devising such an alternative culture, in which organisational rules were established and a code of behaviour laid down. Thus pupil identity was modelled on the standards set by the sub-culture. We shall not come across another example of such dual identity until we examine the 'enterprise identity' of Dorothy Heathcote's 'Mantle of the Expert' approach.

Adams is perhaps the only educationist who recognised this critical dimension of Cook's 'Play Way'. Adams appreciated that 'make-believe' is certainly essential to the concept of 'Play Way', but it is not the 'make-believe' associated with dramatisation. It is the 'make-believe' of a game, in this case a large-scale game in which the players 'play at' being members of a fictional society. Adams puts it: 'Scouting is carried out entirely on the lines of the Play Way. It is essentially a game, full of make-believe...'

Indirect approach to a text

It is possible to identify in Caldwell Cook's method a structure for engagement that appears to be dependent on the teacher refocusing the task away from the main goal of study[28] to a connected but subsidiary goal, which becomes the focal task for the pupil. Caldwell Cook's own way of expressing it seems not incompatible with this notion:

> It will occur time and again that what was at first undertaken only as a method of dealing with certain subject-matter will become itself the main concern.

He proceeds to give an example, showing how, in the kindergarten, what was ostensibly the study of 'The Daffodil', became much more: 'Here then are many of the finest experiences of life centred round the alleged study of one flower. *The value has come, not from the subject, the 'alleged study' but from the method of treating it.*' (my italics)

Here we have an early example of a teacher grappling with the notion of 'unintentional' learning. Later learning theories identify an element in learning as 'unintentional', 'passive'[29] or 'tacit'[30] learning. It is Michael Polanyi's notion of 'subsidiary' awareness that becomes of central importance here[31]. Mike Fleming of Durham University in his doctoral thesis (1982) goes as far as to say: '...the teaching of the subject (drama) is to a large degree undertaken with an implicit conception of unintentional learning.'[32] The teacher may deliberately direct the pupils' attention away from a primary target. 'Refocusing' in this way allows for a flexibility in teaching which, possibly, neither Caldwell Cook's critics nor his admirers fully grasped. By inviting his pupils to concentrate on Shakespeare's text as a stage-management problem of how to deliver that text authentically within the prescribed Elizabethan staging, the usual business of trying to do justice to the poetry is put on hold. This has a number of consequences, not the least useful being that the teacher can interrupt the work without upsetting it. As Caldwell Cook puts it: '... the play-method allows the master or the boys to hold up the dramatic narration of the story from time to time.' Such interruptions, normally destructive to a 'text-centred goal', are natural to a 'stage-management centred' goal.

A 'platform' mentality

I have purposefully selected this slightly pejorative term to describe an aspect of acting behaviour that is conventionally associated with formal presentation in a theatre. In the concluding chapter on Harriet Finlay-Johnson I referred to a prescribed space – front of the classroom – from which the actors unidirectionally faced their audience – in their desks. This spatial feature of acting behaviour, derived from proscenium arch theatre, was to become deeply embedded in a teacher's expectations of classroom drama.[33]

Caldwell Cook's ambition was to emulate theatre tradition, first by devising a makeshift platform with curtains in his regular English classroom and then, on acquiring the 'Mummery', designing an Elizabethan stage with curtain tracks and lighting paraphernalia. Using this particular design he was, of course, breaking with modern, proscenium arch with footlights tradition while retaining a basic actor-audience division. Thus classroom acting became, ideally, something done in a well-lit defined space and from an appropriate height to give the audience a good view, with curtains signalling the start and finish and division of scenes. This 'platform' concept was to govern school hall architecture for two generations, but with the proscenium arch, not the Elizabethan stage, as the dominant style.

Teachers whose facilities fell far short of this ideal, could at least reinforce the tacitly accepted notion that acting was prepositionally governed. Both in the professional theatre and in the classroom acting it was understood that something that came *from* an actor in his space and directed *to* an audience in their space. However, this was not a matter of straightforward communication, as, say, in a public address (and to that extent the 'platform' metaphor breaks down), for the division between the respective spaces created a *virtual* barrier, which was seen by theorists of the time as a necessary distancing element of theatrical art.[34] Such a barrier emphasised the artificiality of acting and the artifice needed by the actor to overcome it. The actor's skill in projecting both voice and gesture to 'the gods' was to be matched in miniature in the classroom or school hall. For some commentators at the end of this century such as David Hornbrook, this image of the classroom as a stage in miniature is sufficient as a defining feature of drama education.

There is an another assumption tacitly built into this notion of acting as performance: the actor is inviting the audience to stare at him or her; indeed performing is dependent on such staring, a reversal of most social codes. It was Dorothy Heathcote (1995) who first drew attention to the way, say, English or History teachers, keen to use Drama, may not always appreciate that their pupils have not 'given permission to stare'. Again, whether or not permission from the pupils is implicitly given is dependent on the 'overarching image' built into the classroom context. If, for example, the participants are members of a School Drama Club or have 'opted' to do drama, then tacit 'permission to stare' has been built in. In the final chapter of this book I shall probe further this notion of attention from an audience as a defining factor in characterising what is going on.

Avoidance of realism
It is in keeping with Caldwell Cook's determination to break away from the proscenium arch that he steered his pupils away from realism, but his motive went beyond an architectural predilection. The current thrust of progressive theatre at the time of Caldwell Cook's 1917 publication was towards social realism, in content dealing with political and social issues, in style attempting a detailed and faithful reproduction of 'real life' with a life-like setting, life-like costumes and life-like (everyday) dialogue. The actor's 'naturalistic' art lay in appearing to be living within the picture frame of the proscenium.

Caldwell Cook lists three major objections to a 'conscious pursuit of realism'[35]:

> 2 (i) Because it is frankly beyond their powers, since realism implies a representation of things as they are, and boys have not experience enough to go beyond impressions and appearances;

> (ii) because it would be outside the scope of our educational purpose, since true realism implies a certain sacrifice of conventions and the avoidance of types of character and situation, while our purpose as teachers is to ensure that by the exercise of play-making the boys shall become familiar with these very artistic conventions, and with the dramatic situations and characters which have become typical from their frequent occurrences in literature we are taking as our model; and

(iii) the pursuit of realism by boys is inadvisable because it implies the abandonment of that tower of their artistic strength, the ready comprehension of a romantic theme, and fitly imaginative treatment of it.

There are a number of observations to be made here which can usefully be summarised as follows: (i) the elusiveness for immature pupils of significance in 'everyday life' material; (ii) a diet of 'romantic' material (Shakespeare; legends; Bible Stories; epics) deals in broad 'types' of characters and situations, most suitable for pre-adolescent boys; and (iii) training in dramatic action in a school setting should centre on the theatrical conventions appropriate to this kind of 'Romantic' material.

In recommending an earlier theatrical style for his pupils, Caldwell Cook is making a pedagogical, not an artistic point. He argues that boys of the 11 to 14 age group are not ready for naturalism, in spite of their obvious taste for replicating 'school life' or some 'adventure in modern times'. He favours the 'Romantic' theatre of fantasy, myth and legend in which characters, broadly drawn, are heroic, villainous or innocent victims. He wants the many stage conventions that 'Realistic Theatre' sort to dispense with to be accessible to his pupils. Above all, he wants their drama to be 'poetic'. Caldwell Cook may be the first drama educationist to use the term 'poetic' in relation to a theatrical style, even for prose drama. He no doubt saw a danger in the literalness of some realistic theatre. The dramatic art he wanted his pupils to learn was to be freed from representational accuracy in favour of abstract expression. I want to suggest that once again a central strand of Caldwell Cook's dramatic work was either not understood or ignored by his successors and that consequently some school drama suffered from the cult of realism in the theatre.

Notes

1   For a detailed list of writers who have recorded Caldwell Cook's history, see Bolton, G. (1997), University of Durham Phd. thesis.

2   'Employed' is not quite the right word for, according to his biographer, D.A. Beacock, he declined to accept a salary for the first year.

3   W.H.D. Rouse in *Journal of Education*, December 1901

4   Beacock, D.A. (1943) *The Playway English for Today: The methods and Influence of H. Caldwell Cook Thomas* Nelson and Sons London p.10-11

5　See, for example, Sir John Adams [*Modern Developments in Educational Practice* (1922) ULP] who is concerned (pp 205-6) that the title of Cook's publication misleads likely readers in respect both of staging school plays and avoidance of hard work.

6　From a letter written to John Allen and subsequently published in: Allen, John (1979) *Drama in Schools: its Theory and Practice*, Heinemann London, p.12

7　Montessori, Maria (1912 – translated 1919) *The Montessori Method* William Heinemann, London p.28

8　See Bazely, E.T. (1928) *Homer Lane and the Little Commonwealth* Allen and Unwin or Neill, A.S. (1962) *A Radical Approach to Education* Gollanz

9　It should be noted that the Perse school was a 'boarding school' with most of the boys and teachers resident

10　Ballard, P. B. (1925) *The Changing School* University of London Press p.201

11　Cook, Caldwell H. (1917) *ibid* p.37

12　For instance, Sir John Adams, the Professor of Education, University of London, R.J.W. Selleck, School of Education, University of Melbourne and W.A.C. Stewart, Professor of Education, Institute of Education, Keele University refer in their publications to Cook's contribution to the progressive Idealism.

13　The image of a class of children as 'a body of workers' had already entered some educational literature, albeit as part of an expression of idealistic hope rather than an account of known practice. For instance, J.J. Findlay, Professor of Education at Manchester University is drawing on the model presented by the Scout Movement when, in 1911, he fancifully writes: 'Thus the class of a primary school re-shapes itself to our imagination not so much as a group of individuals sitting at separate desks, each imbibing instruction for himself from a teacher or a book, but rather as a hive of busy workers ...' (Findlay, J.J. (1911) *The School: An introduction to the study of Education* Williams and Norgate London, p.243). It should perhaps be noted that whereas Findlay's 'busy workers' metaphor is drawn from bees Finlay-Johnson's and Caldwell Cook's usage could be drawn from field or factory.

14　Lane, Homer (1928) *Talks to Parents and Teachers* Allen and Unwin London

15　Cook, Caldwell H. (1917) *ibid* p.65

16　A footnote on Page 183 runs as follows: 'This chapter should have been on 'Acting in the Classroom,' but in writing it I found that apart from matters in connexion with Shakespeare, there was very little of importance to say, which is not dealt with in the Chapters on 'Miming' and on 'Playmaking.' After all, if you can act Shakespeare you can act anything, and if you cannot act even Shakespeare you might as well sit down again.'

17　This excerpt from the Rugby Master's Notes is quoted by Cook [1917] on p.195 of *The Play Way*

18　The extent of the support of the Chief Inspector for Schools, Edmond Holmes, of Finlay-Johnson's approach has already been discussed but an examination of the unpublished report (Ref: S.B. 5081/13 F.I. 1922) by HMI T.W. Phillips on Mr.

Cook's work, reveals a heavily qualified respect for Caldwell Cook's achievements. For example, in one paragraph he writes: 'It is clear that the character of the work is such as to appeal particularly to boys in the years preceding adolescence, and it is therefore important that a special care be taken not to carry it to too late a stage. A boy may suddenly become sceptical about it all, in which case it does him more harm than good. There seemed to be some indication that this actually happens at the present time.'

19 Tomkinson, W.S. (1921) *The Teaching of English* Oxford University Press

20 Tomkinson, W.S. (1921) *ibid* p.48.Tomkinson has on an earlier page begun his chapter on Practice in Speech with this curious put-down of Cook {Tomkinson, W.S. (1921) *ibid* p.19 [1928 ed]}: 'There were brave men before Agamemnon; and brave speech reformers before Mr. Caldwell Cook.'

21 By contrast *The Committee Report on The Teaching of English in England* published in the same year (1921) gives strong support to what it calls 'Drama in Education', but it is also aware of difficulties in introducing Shakespeare to young pupils pp 309-328.

22 Tomkinson, W.S. (1921) *ibid* p.46

23 Such a view echoes that of Harley Granville-Barker, the distinguished British theatre director and entrepreneur, [Granville-Barker, Harley (1946) *The Uses of Drama* T. and A. Constable, Edinburgh]. He too had reservations about school children's and amateur participation in what he saw as professional territory. Granville-Barker, however, was discussing public performances; Cook and Wilkinson are disagreeing about classroom practice.

24 D.W. Hughes, an ex-student of Caldwell Cook, writes in Beacock's book '...that Caldwell Cook was a genius, in the true sense of that overworked word, I have not the slightest doubt.' Beacock D.A. (1943) *op cit* p.114. Dr. W.D. Rouse, the headmaster who employed him, in writing the Foreword of Beacock's book wrote: 'He was a true genius, and simply bubbled over with new ideas, all brilliant. Visitors thronged to see his work, and he welcomed all. I miss him profoundly, and he will never fade from my memory'.

25 'Mister' is one of Caldwell Cook's designations for the boy whose turn it is to be in charge of lesson procedures: 'The word 'official' did not please us long, and none of the words in common use, such as 'monitor,' 'prefect,' 'captain,' 'director,' 'manager,' seemed to us fitly to describe the boy-official-in-charge-of-the-lesson, so I introduced the word Mister' Cook, Caldwell (1917) *ibid* p.206.

26 Caldwell Cook does not discuss the matter in these kind of analytical terms, although the spirit of the élitist enterprise is well-illustrated in his article for the School Magazine, giving advance notice of the creation of the 'Perse Players': 'Their constitution will be quaint, their shows conducted with formal ceremony, and the whole tenor of their doings above the common. Their art, though simple and near to the interests of ordinary people, will be so far removed from the aimless vulgarity of present-day diversions as to seem in keeping with another lovely age...' [Quoted by B.A. Beacock in *The Play Way English for Today op cit*

p.68]. A glance at Page X1 of the 1913 publication of *The Perse Players No. 3* reveals an impressive line-up of honorary members, including Frank Benson, William Poel, Harley Granville-Barker and Cecil Sharp, well-known theatre figures whose printed names are then followed by 'Master of the Players'; 'Officers'; and 'Players and Members', some forty in all made up of adults and scholars, one of whom, it is interesting to note, includes a certain 'F. R. Leavis'.

27   For Dorothy Heathcote, two generations later, this characteristic of 'total belief in the game from a teacher who is part of the game' became a central feature of her work.

28   Shomit Mitter (1992), in his *Systems of Rehearsals* [Routledge, London, p.36], observes a similar deliberate use of indirectness in Peter Brook's work with actors: 'Paradoxically, the movement away from meaning, creates conditions in which meaning may be discovered the more prodigiously.'

29   See, for example, Dunlop, F.N. (1977) 'Human Nature, Learning and Ideology' in *British Journal of Education Studies* Vol XXV No 3, October, pp 239-257)

30   For example, Polanyi, Michael (1958) *Personal Knowledge: Towards a Post-Critical Philosophy* Routledge and Kegan Paul

31   It is of interest to this study that one of the examples Polanyi cites of focal and subsidiary awareness is from the context of an actor's 'stage-fright' – caused, according to Polanyi, by a reversal of awareness levels in the actor, who is concentrating on how he should act instead of on the fictional context. (Polanyi, p.55)

32   Fleming, Michael (1982) *A Philosophical Investigation into Drama in Education* Unpublished Doctoral thesis, University of Durham, p.129

33   'Where space is available a standard-size stage should be marked out on the classroom floor with tapes' writes Howard Hayden [Hayden, Howard (1938) 'Drama in the Classroom' in *School Drama: It's Practice and Theory* by Guy Boas and Howard Hayden (Eds) Methuen London pp 32-37]

34   The seminal article of the time was 'Psychical Distancing as a Factor in Art and an Aesthetic Principle' in *British Journal of Psychology* 5, June 1912 pp 85-118 in which Edward Bullough argued that theatre, because of its obvious physical divisions between performer and audience, more than any other art supports the maintenance of distance between the art object and the spectator (See p.104 of Bullough's text)

35   Cook, H. Caldwell (1917) *ibid* p.271

SECTION TWO
TRENDS BETWEEN WORLD WARS

CHAPTER THREE
ACTING AS PLAY

TWO EDUCATIONISTS' VIEWS OF PLAY AND EDUCATION: 'Play as a metaphor for progressive classroom practice' and 'Play as part of classroom practice'

This is the first of the four 'trends' making up the second section of this book. Labelled 'play', it seems to provide the strongest link with the two pioneers of Section One, especially with Caldwell Cook whose authorship of *The Play Way* gave credence to 'play' as a progressive educational shibboleth.

This chapter discusses the influence of two professors of education, Sir Percy Nunn (1920) and Susan Isaacs (1930). It will be argued that the former's well-intended enthusiasm for linking play and education amounted to a *discouragement* of acting as a classroom activity and that the latter's experience of teaching young children led, potentially at least, to significant theoretical support for the notion of classroom acting. As they added little, in the long run, to teachers' understanding of the place of drama in the classroom, it might be thought that the attention given to them in this study is misplaced. Although this book is not a straightforward history of events relating to the development of classroom drama, it is concerned with how ideas about acting behaviour evolved through the innovative methods of the selected exponents. In order to understand the full extent of our next chosen pioneer's (Peter Slade's) impact on drama education thinking, it will be necessary to indicate what ideas and practices preceded him. Some of those ideas, for instance, those of Frances Mackenzie and Irene Mawer,

53

as we shall see, popularised forms of amateur acting behaviour that were anathema to Slade; others, for example, those of Marjorie Hourd and R.L Stone, initiated methodologies which Slade to some extent emulated. But these and others we shall be mentioning were all 'fellow travellers' in drama education and to that extent shared an interest and a language with Peter Slade. It is the ideas of progressive educational experts of this period not associated directly with drama but having a view of its place, whose concept of acting as a potential in education has relevance to this study. Sir Percy Nunn and Susan Isaacs, both hugely influential figures in the twenty years before World War Two, have been selected because each articulates a progressive doctrine based on Play that appears to go so far in support of classroom acting and then holds back. We shall see that Nunn manages to extol the value of make-believe without recommending its practice and that Isaacs goes as far as developing a rationale for linking make-believe with learning, but fails to implement it. Between them, it could be said, they created a kind of vacuum of missed opportunities. This gap in leading educationists' support for drama perhaps created the most serious deterrent to progress in classroom acting – and gave Peter Slade his greatest challenge.

A final section of the chapter will turn to the first major publication purporting to base dramatic classroom practice on a developmental theory of Play. Published in 1948 *Dramatic Work with Children*, written by E.M. Langdon, a London University Institute of Education colleague of Dr. Isaacs, outlines the kind of dramatic activity in which each age group might be expected to be engaged. We shall see that this theoretical input from the 1940s added a developmental dimension to the place of drama in schools. For instance, the first attempts to draw attention to the difference between 'pretending' and 'acting', and between 'playing' and 'a play' appear.

Play as a metaphor for progressive classroom practice
What the 'progressives' shared was a desire to link education and 'play'. Such a term caught the new educational spirit of the times: it captured the Rousseauesque image of the innocent child; it related to the Darwinian explanations of development drawn from the studies of playful behaviour in the young of animals; it carried experiential overtones of an Existential philosophy; it implied 'activity' and

'exploration'; it appeared to open a door to paedocentric education; it offered a conception of aesthetic education and physical education; and, in the practice of Finlay-Johnson and Caldwell Cook, it made connections with theatre.

Sir Percy Nunn represents those leaders in the field of education who relied on the concept of 'play' to promote their own version of 'Progressivism'. Richard Courtney, in his seminal 1968 publication, *Play, Drama and Thought*[1] selects Nunn as the between-Wars inspiration to later Drama teachers such as Peter Slade and E.J. Burton and sees Nunn's aphorism 'the richer the scope for imitation the richer the developed individuality' as a trigger for legitimising classroom drama. I will argue, however, that Nunn's interest in Play was metaphorical rather than practical and that such usage took the activity of Drama down a cul-de-sac.

The major published work of this most distinguished Professor of Education, London University, was *Education: Its Data and First Principles*[2] which became a basic text for student teachers for the next thirty years. He devoted two chapters to 'Play' and 'The 'Play-Way' of Education' and made continual references to 'play' throughout his text. Nunn's earlist reference in the book to 'play' activities arises from a discussion of the importance of 'Routine and Ritual'. He points out how young children love the routine and repetition of nursery rhymes such as 'Ring-a-ring-of-Roses'. It is rhythm of movement and song that is fundamental in its appeal, man being governed by his rhythmic sense, physiologically, cosmically and artistically. Nunn gives approval to the teachers of 'Eurhythmics', a practice I shall be examining in Chapter Six, devoted to combining dance, movement and musical appreciation. Nunn alludes to the kinship between ritual and great dramas and adds 'We may, therefore, with greater confidence give it (ritual, that is) a larger place in the education of the young, using it as a means of intensifying and purifying social emotion'.

Nunn's section on 'Play', begins: 'The spirit of play is an intangible and elusive sprite, whose influence is to be found in corners of life where it might least be expected.' He goes on to define this 'sprite': '...she manifests her presence there in activities whose special mark is their spontaneity – that is, their relative independence of external needs and stimuli.' In his attempt to find a biological explanation of the phenomenon of 'play', Nunn sees the 'surplus-energy' theory as having a minor, but not unimportant, place. However, he is more interested in 'play' as a creator of energy rather than as a channel for unwanted energy; and he is keen to balance the 'anticipation theory' of Groos[3] with the 'recapitulation theory' of Hall[4]. In his view they complement each other, Groos seeing 'play' as engaging the intellect, Hall perceiving it as 'motor heredity'. The latter view leads Nunn to make the passing comment that '...dancing, eurhythmics and *acting* (my italics)...' might be substituted in schools for some of the more formal physical exercises, a more stimulating way of 'securing...mastery over the body...' Notice this introduction of 'acting' as one of a number of possible activities belonging to *physical* education.

In Nunn's view the critical feature of 'play' is that it revives in the child the capacity for 'self-assertion'. While recognising that 'games' and 'sports' can to some degree promote this capacity, their purpose is more in tune with the notion of 'relaxation', and as such are attractive forms of 'escape', lacking the potential of inventive and imaginative play.

Nunn moves on to discuss the connection between play and work recognised by thinkers such as the 18th century German philosopher, dramatist and poet, Friedrich Schiller.[5] The common ground between the two is whatever is morally and aesthetically beautiful. He goes on: 'It is not an accident that the noblest achievements of antique art were won by the race that cherished the humane and healthy Olympic games, not by the race that loved the horrible sports of the gladiatorial arena.'[6] Nunn then extends the 'surplus energy' theory by arguing that it is 'the play phenomenon' that changes a craft from being merely functional to having beauty: 'The flint weapon, the pot, became more than a mere weapon, a mere pot; they became beautiful.' He concludes that what is required in schools is for the pupils to '*play* (Nunn's italics) with their materials – and beauty will inevitably appear.'

Nunn now moves to discuss an aspect of play that is of central interest to a book on acting behaviour: 'make-believe', which he refers to as an 'element' in play. He immediately pours a cold shower on any fanciful interpretations his readers might have on the meaning of make-believe. He warns: '...much that is attributed to the child's faculty of making-believe may be due not to the transforming power of imagination but to ignorance and a sheer inability to see the world around him as it really is.'[7] This reminder, placing Nunn firmly within the Anglo-Saxon empirical tradition, of a distinction to be drawn between 'the cold world of fact and the subjective world of purpose, thought and fancy' is followed by his drawing of analogies between make-believe and insanity and the child's tendency to 'fibbing', while conceding that such analogies should 'not be pressed too far.' Having issued these warnings against any extreme stance, Nunn proceeds to establish a position somewhere between the orthodox Froebelians who, according to Nunn, invite gratuitous make-believe and the Montessorians who 'regard make-believe as frivolous and a form of untruth'

Nunn does not seem to rate the function of make-believe beyond seeing it as the child's temporary means of compensating for environmental inadequacies. Making-believe is 'merely a biological device to secure that his self-assertion during the formative years of life shall not be frustrated by his inability to control the real conditions of his activities'[8], those real conditions applying to 'inconvenient facts' as much as absent objects. He argues that make-believe play is developmental in the negative sense that the child's ideas are 'forced into ever-increasing congruence with the external world,' as he matures. It appears, then, that make-believe play, when 'untruths' are no longer needed to bolster the activity, is to disappear from the child's behavioural spectrum. Nevertheless, Nunn argues, 'the *power* [my italics] of make-believe remains, and may still perform an essential function in securing the development of spontaneity.'

Nunn seems to be accepting that make-believe play is functionally necessary for a young child's exploratory learning and that its 'power' is what remains beyond the infant stage. Any hopes advocates of dramatisation in the junior or secondary classroom might have had of support for that activity from Sir Percy Nunn must have been dashed by that word 'power', for he spends the next few pages making it quite clear that make-believe as such is to be left behind. (One may speculate that Caldwell Cook, teaching in Cambridge and Mrs. Harriet Waller [née Finlay-Johnson] must also have been disappointed by lack of support for their chosen practice from this major 1920 publication.) It is its 'power', not the activity itself, that is to be harnessed. For Nunn, as for Professor Adams, Nunn's colleague and previous incumbent of the London University Chair of Education , the supreme example lies in the Scout Movement, which Nunn describes as 'pure make-believe'. He goes on: 'the scout's picturesque costume, his 'patrol-animal' or totem, his secret signs, his 'spooring', all belong to a realm of facts and ideas queerly incongruent with the humdrum actuality of civilised life.' What the Scout learns, according to Nunn, is 'often far more valuable than anything he acquires from teachers in school.' This is because he draws 'spiritual and intellectual vigour' from 'the *atmosphere* (my italics) of make-believe.'

Returning now to the use of the term 'play', Nunn suggests that the practice of make-believe is to be displaced in school by its residual elements of 'power' and 'atmosphere'. The make-believe is to be implicit, releasing intellectual energy without the embarrassment of pretending. 'Overt making-believe' left behind, Nunn suggests:

> ...that the pupil's studies should be so shaped as to help him to be, in imagination and in anticipation, a sharer in those phases of human effort which have most significance for civilisation as a whole. His history and geography should look largely towards politics (in the wider sense) and economics; his science should make him a fellow-worker with men like Pasteur...'[9].

It seems that Nunn has picked up this conception, so clearly seen in the work of Finlay-Johnson and Caldwell Cook, of an overarching identity as a basis for pupil engagement with learning. Sadly he, unlike them, sees it as sufficiently potent – without actually involving the pupils in some kind of acting behaviour. For Nunn, any 'enactment' is to be confined to an attitude of mind.

In a following chapter (entitled 'The 'Play-Way' in Education, a title he acknowledges is borrowed from Caldwell Cook), he elaborates on the 'power' of make-believe. He gives an example of the 'heuristic method' of teaching science: 'Since the professed object of the method is to place the student as completely as may be in the position of an original investigator, wrestling for knowledge as the man of science wrestles, it is clearly in principle a play-method.' By his final chapter he is claiming that the aim in the teaching of science should be[10]:

to make our pupils feel, so far as they may, what it is to be, so to speak, inside the skin of the man of science, looking out through his eyes as well as using his tools, experiencing not only something of his labours, but also something of his sense of joyous intellectual adventure.

This notion of pupils' identifying with the 'joyous intellectual adventure' of an expert both echoes Harriet Finlay-Johnson and anticipates Dorothy Heathcote's later work.

Thus 'implicit' or 'metaphorical' [my terms] role-taking allows Nunn to argue for a particular form of Senior Education. He sees the possibility of applying the 'play' concept to vocational education, an education adapted to 'fit the young man or woman for some specific role in the great play of life'. Instead of ranging widely over curriculum subjects the imagination is now 'centred upon a chosen plot.' Nunn's use of theatrical imagery here and, indeed, throughout the book, is another example of keeping the 'make-believe' metaphor going without having to resort to that activity. His ambivalence clearly emerges with: 'Interest comes to close grips with the details of actuality, and making-believe is present only in so far as the student antedates his entrance into the calling of his choice.'

'Play' as part of classroom practice

By way of contrast to Sir Percy Nunn, we will now attempt to outline a rationale, drawn from Child Psychology, or, rather, from that branch of child psychology influenced by Freudian theory, that acknowledged child make-believe as having learning potential and seemed to advocate make-believe play as part of a young child's school day. The seminal writings of Susan Isaacs will be examined to this end.

Pre-Freudian Psychology had already registered interest in make-believe play activities and their connections with the art form of drama. In 1896 James Sully published his *Studies of Childhood*.[11] He saw a lack of audience combined with self-centredness as the two principal factors separating child play from 'fully art'. Joseph Lee (1915), an American Psychologist, recognised the importance of what he called 'impersonation' in learning: '...his (the child) instinct is to grasp the whole, to enter by one sheer leap of intuition into the heart of the object of his study and act out from there.'[12]

A few years after the publication in 1920 of Sir Percy Nunn's seminal work, Mrs. Isaacs[13] (nee Fairhurst) began her long-term project of observing infant behaviour at 'The Malting House School', Cambridge.[14] For the first time a 'progressive' institution was to come under 'scientific' observation. Susan Isaacs became regarded as an authority on child development[15] and her published observations included detailed accounts of children at play, and her theoretical conclusions about developmental outcomes of play activity, including 'imaginative' play activity.

Long influenced by Froebel and Dewey, in the 1920s she became interested in the theoretical works of Piaget (who visited 'The Malting') and Freud. She countered Piaget's view of logical development in the child by pointing out that a child's intellectual powers are variable, achieving, a relatively higher level through spontaneous play. She demonstrated to Freudian purists that play was a means of living and understanding life, not simply the 'embodiment of an unstable shifting imagery of unconscious erotic impulses'. Psychoanalysis nevertheless influenced the way she viewed children's behaviour years later (1933) in *Social Development in Young Children*.

Isaacs' record and study of Child Play gave authoritative approval to the introduction of 'play corners' in the infant classroom. Thus the more rigid recital of action songs and nursery rhymes were displaced by freer activities belonging to the child rather than the teacher. Unfortunately, her experience as head teacher of an experimental school did not take her sights beyond the infant school. The older age group taught by Harriet Finlay-Johnson did not immediately benefit from Isaacs' work. And yet, Isaacs provided a rationale for relating dramatic activity to learning that could have been applied to older children.

Isaacs' classification of make-believe behaviour
She divides 'imaginative' play according to its functions. The first is circumstantial, when make-believe 'may at any moment slip over into genuine enquiry, and it offers many occasions for the furtherance of skill.' The second is conative, a source of 'symbol-formation'. Isaacs shows her respect for Melanie Klein's work: 'The psycho-analysis of young children by Klein's play technique has shown that engines and motors and fires and lights and water and mud and animals have a

profoundly symbolic meaning for them, rooted in infantile phantasy.' Isaacs explains that 'Their ability to concern themselves with real objects and real happenings is a relative (Isaacs' italics) matter'. In such play children can work out their inner conflicts, thus 'diminishing guilt and anxiety'. She goes on: 'Such a lessening of inner tension through dramatic presentation makes it easier for the child to control his real behaviour, and to accept the limitations of the real world.' Isaacs' third function of play is within the field of cognition: it is a hypothetical function. She writes eloquently: 'The ability to evoke the *past* (Isaacs' italics) in imaginative play seems to me to be very closely connected with the growth of the power to evoke the *future* in con-structive hypothesis, and to develop the consequences of 'ifs'.' She goes on in a way that could well satisfy any theory of alienation in Brechtian theatre: 'and in his [the child's] make-believe, he takes the first steps towards that emancipation of meanings from the here and now of a concrete situation, which makes possible hypotheses and the 'as if' consciousness.' Isaacs sees make-believe as an act of 'construc-tive imagination', a process of breaking away from the particularity of the here and now in order, to turn to Finlay-Johnson's terminology, to grasp 'the fitness of things'.

For many theoreticians this is the distinguishing feature of theatre where, as Bruce Wilshire puts it: '...there can be no enactment without typification and generalisation...'[16] These quotations may suffice to underline my point that the very language in which Isaacs, in 1930, couches psychological purposes connected with imaginative play anticipates the conceptualising of theatre experience adopted by many theorists writing in the second half of the century.[17] I suggest that Isaacs has opened up a language pertaining to child play that could have simultaneously embraced the meaning of theatre. The opportunity was there to formulate a generic basis for the two activities.

Susan Isaacs is searching for a theoretical vocabulary that will adequately describe the different purposes of young children's 'imaginative play', which, in summary, promotes 'enquiry', 'develops skills', lessens 'inner tension' and creates a basis for 'hypothetical thinking'.[18] Although Isaacs did not often appear in print explicitly to promote drama in schools,[19] in outlining a framework within which 'imaginative play' might be discussed, she is tacitly providing teachers interested in classroom dramatic activity with a rationale for adopting it as a methodology.

Indeed Isaacs was the 'authority' the Drama and Theatre Sub-Committee of the National Under-Fourteens Council turned to in 1947 to write a Foreword to their publication, devised by one of its members, Mrs. E.M. Langdon[20]. Susan Isaacs' Foreword is generous in its support:

> I HAVE READ Mrs. Langdon's booklet with great interest and pleasure. It is an excellent account of what can and should be done in dramatic work with children from five to fourteen. The rich and varied technique suggested for the teacher is given its proper basis in the natural and dramatic instincts of children at successive ages. Mrs. Langdon carries the whole matter over from general principles to the concrete details of what and how and why...

Here we have an esteemed psychologist giving support to drama as something that 'can and should be done'. (Indeed the above preface to Langdon's book is the first instance [and perhaps the last?] of a leading figure in the world of educational psychology appearing to lend support to a drama education text.) Drama is to be approved as a proper school activity with a respectable lineage in child play. What amounts to an explicit affirmation of the classroom practice of Drama seems to supersede the position adopted by Isaacs' colleague and head of department, Sir Percy Nunn, of using play as a metaphor for progressive teaching. Now, apparently, 'Natural dramatic instincts' are to be seen as providing the 'proper basis' for dramatic work.

However, we have seen that Isaacs, while recognising the existence and power of 'natural dramatic instincts', fails to argue to any serious extent for harnessing those 'instincts' in the direction of the curriculum, in the direction of older pupils or, indeed, in the direction of theatre. One is left to muse on why this leading figure should become so close, but not near enough, to supporting drama as a medium for intellectual and emotional development. It may be that her own position as a female educational psychologist, in a field dominated by intelligence measurement, prevented her from exploring further the impact of her child play theories on curriculum innovation; it may be that her own interest in psychoanalysis took her into the more therapeutic aspects of play; or it may be that growing confusion over the identity of drama as a school activity dissuaded her from taking part in active experimentation. Some of the strands which contributed to this confusion will be investigated in subsequent chapters of this section of the book.

Dramatic Work with Children, a publication by E.M. Langdon (1948)

This is the first publication in England sponsored by a Committee out of a desire to establish a developmental pattern in relation to children's dramatic activity in school. As the chairperson of the national Under-Fourteens Council put it: there was 'an urgent necessity to formulate, at least in outline, children's needs of drama in relation to their own nature at various stages of development' There appear to be a number of assumptions behind the Committee's invitation to Mrs. Langdon: that dramatic activity was now seen to be part of the curriculum of non-selective schools; and that some kind of authoritative guideline was needed on the kind of drama suitable for each age group. Hence Langdon's division of her book into 'five to seven years', 'seven to eleven years' and 'eleven to fourteen years', and the Committee's decision to invite an educational psychologist to write the preface.

From Mrs. Langdon's first sentence, 'First let us look at play itself', one might conclude that her developmental account of school drama was to be rooted in child play. Indeed she appears to reinforce Isaacs' classification by affirming that the play of young children is about making 'imperfect knowledge really his own' and resolving conflicting emotions. In this she appears to be adopting Isaacs' 'enquiry' and 'therapy' categories.[21] She sees these functions reflected in two kinds of dramatic play, which she labels 'realistic play' and 'imaginative play', the former usually demanding a degree of presentational realism evoking familiar surroundings and people, the latter offering a chance to 'escape the actual world'. Mrs. Langdon seems not to intend any difference in status in respect of these contrasted kinds of content, accepting that '...play itself is so fluid and varied that all attempts to place it in separate categories must be to some extent artificial.'

The phrase 'making knowledge really his own' also reinforces the notion of 'ownership' of knowledge which was earlier suggested as characteristic of Finlay-Johnson's dramatisation. This early emphasis in her book, however, turns out to be somewhat misleading. Mrs. Langdon's is not to be an account of how school children might use drama to relate to aspects of the curriculum, nor is it to guide teachers in how to handle therapeutic aspects of dramatic play. The 'enquiry' purpose Isaacs attached to make-believe play, while remaining as an occasionally acknowledged feature in the background of Langdon's text, is overtaken, (or, rather, 'upstaged') by other matters, especially theatre form.

In setting out to describe what she sees as the defining features of 'realistic' and 'imaginative' play of 5-7 year olds, Langdon seems, in view of her claim to be examining 'natural play', too ready to point out apparent shortcomings. Her comments relating to perceived fragility of plot, indeterminancy of beginnings and endings and unreliability of commitment clearly stem from a theatrical stance which Finlay-Johnson and Caldwell Cook, working with older pupils, of course, would have shared.

Mrs. Langdon also appears to be addressing a theatre-minded readership whose tolerance of free-play needed to be secured. It is an activity to be 'watched' rather than 'directed', she advises. But even 5-7 year olds, she assures, need an alternative to run concurrently with 'dramatic playing'. By the fourth page of her text, Langdon inserts the following heading: *Plays for children of five to seven years. 'We're Pretending' becomes 'We're Acting'*. She goes on: 'At some point the children begin to enjoy dramatic work of a more specific kind'. She divides the 'specific kinds' into impromptu dramatisation of nursery rhymes (popular, as we have seen, in our infant schools from the beginning of the century) and plays the children make up themselves. She adds: 'At this time a stage is not needed, and a small audience is best, but the children do sometimes want to 'do things for the rest of the school to see' in School Assemblies or at a Christmas Party.'

Thus children aged 5 to 7 years are to experience three kinds of class-room drama, the traditional 'action rhymes', the 'play-corner make-believe' and 'plays the children make up'. It is the conceptual difference between the last two which is of interest to this study. Both are made up of spontaneous actions and talk, but Langdon insists that whereas one kind of activity is 'pretending' the other is 'acting'. She does not attempt to explain the difference, as though she could assume her readers would know what she meant. The distinction seems not, essentially, to lie in observable behaviours. Indeed she is at pains to minimise, with this young age group, changes in expression such as the artificial slowing down of speech, for example, as though she sees the advantage with young children of retaining as far as possible, the qualities of actions belonging to the 'make-believe game'. The essential difference, then, appears to lie in a conceptual shift, to be understood, tacitly at least, by both pupils and teacher, from process to product, from 'playing', an activity presumably not accessible to repetition, to 'a play'[22], something to be repeated and improved upon. Langdon does not, herself, use the terms, 'process' and 'product', but she does imply such a differentiation in her grammatical usage, in speaking of the activity of child play as a verb: 'Let's pretend' and taking the noun form when she refers to the alternative to 'let's pretend' as '*a* play'.

This seems to require, not necessarily a change in behaviour but rather a change in *responsibility*, which includes sharing 'the artefact', or, (to use her phrase) 'giving the play' to others who may be just fellow classmates or to the assembled school. Mrs. Langdon is using the term 'acting' then for a make-believe context in which something is made, that *potentially* may be repeated, reshaped, tidied up, dressed up, and projected to an audience.

Langdon recommends ways of easing the pupils from process to product, based on their readiness. What begins as typical Junior group's robust playing, (presumably, as for Susan Isaacs, out of the classroom, although she does not actually say so) for example, may 'sometimes... crystallise out into a sketchy play-form and require an audience ultimately, as for instance, a Red Indian play, a Pirate play, or, in the case of younger children, a fairy-tale play' The modest level of 'public' exposure of such informal play-making is neatly summarised as: 'They do not give a play so much as 'play it out' with an audience there' – a hybrid form of acting behaviour that combines Langdon's 'pretending' and 'acting', retaining, as it were, the verb, while purporting to give attention to the noun.

Langdon follows Susan Isaacs' wording very closely in describing junior age group playing, but whereas Isaacs seeks to reinforce the notion that such play allows the pupils to absorb their wider knowledge, Langdon's interest is in how it may become material for 'a play'. As I have already suggested, both lecturers fail to pursue the 'enquiry' potential of the material as Finlay-Johnson did. Langdon claims that this is the age when the children themselves discover the need for some technique: 'and their dramatic play can become at one and the same time a creative experience, an expression of their emotional needs and an outlet which is satisfying to their critical powers.' These are not, of course, 'critical powers' associated with Isaacs' intellectual development or enquiry, but ability to be critical of dramatic form, even of plays written especially for children. In writing of older juniors she suggests that the hybrid form of 'playing it out with an audience there' should be superseded by a sense of responsibility towards 'the rights of an audience' – the 'public' dimension of the product becoming unambiguously established. She goes on to argue for the social value embedded in playing to others: 'The social value of the experience lies in the bond of union, the giving and sharing, and the sense of participating together in a common purpose.'

Langdon sees carefully rehearsed performance as a regular part of Junior school life. Such a commitment leads her to consider a besetting problem of Western theatre that became, as we shall see, of central interest to the Amateur Theatre movement and of particular concern to advocates of School Drama. The perpetual question posed at all levels of theatre was (put simply): Do actors before an audience feel 'real' emotion or do they apply their craft to simulating it?[23] Langdon feels obliged to discuss the extent to which Junior school pupils should be expected to 'act with real emotion', although she is reluctant to sound dogmatic. She tentatively suggests: 'It seems true that children do 'feel' their parts, and sometimes they act with real emotion.', but she goes on with greater assurance as she draws on her knowledge of theatre: 'But, just because their experience of life and emotion is limited, they do not yet create a real character.' She adds: 'They may show quite acute observation of people in their acting, but true characterisation has to wait for the fuller development of later years.' Thus if performing to an audience was to be seen as a peak in developmental achievement, 'true characterisation' was to be regarded as the final summit. We shall find that 'characterisation' is to become a defining feature of sophisticated acting in most educational literature on school drama, and that a way of distinguishing children's from adult acting was to apply this 'characterisation' factor.

The pupils in the Junior School are to be taken through the whole gamut of audience experiences, from unrehearsed 'playing for themselves' to 'playing it out with an audience there' in the intimate classroom; from informal to formal, rehearsed productions for the entertainment of adults. She is not intent, however, in turning Junior pupils into smaller versions of amateur actors. Even with the 11-14 age group she is at pains to retain some of the impromptu characteristics of dramatic play, especially where there is a need, related to immaturity, learning difficulties[24], or a desire to 'let go' etc. She is keen is satisfy the contrary pull of two relatively new doctrines. In education, received wisdom pronounced that 'education of the emotions' was as important as 'education of the intellect' (she refers her readers to the authoritative figure of Herbert Read[25]); in theatre (she refers to the Russian maestro, Constantin Stanislavski[26]), improvisation became the fashionable route to in-depth characterisation. The climate was ripe for both freedom of expression and learning a craft. For the secondary child she wants teachers to consider a broad front:

> Is there not sometimes a place for spontaneous improvisation and dramatic play? Does not the adult sometimes help the children to take their first unsupervised version of a play a stage further? Do the children not enjoy reading or producing a play from the field of literature, whether they or the adult, or both together, carry out the production? And through a series of well-chosen dramatic experiences do the children not grow to appreciate drama as an art? It is surely true to say that there is room for several kinds of dramatic work, and that often many types of work are needed in the same age-group.

Conclusions

While Percy Nunn (1920), disappointingly from our point of view, saw make-believe play merely as a temporary compensation for an inadequate sense of reality in the young child, his vision of education as a Scout movement-like project in which participants may behave according to an agreed code, thus adopting the *spirit* of make-believe, anticipates Dorothy Heathcote's later conception of 'Mantle of the Expert'. By contrast, Susan Isaacs (1930) saw the activity of play itself as contributory to cognitive development, but failed to see the implications of her theory for classroom practice. Nevertheless she lent respectability to the notion that drama in the classroom was to be seen as *deriving from* child play. Mrs. Langdon (1948) attempted to embrace Isaacs' theory, showing how in practice, drama could be developed for children aged 5 to 14, attention to proscenium theatre form gradually superseding free, formless improvised playing. Distinctions between 'playing' and 'acting' and between 'playing' and 'a play' were introduced, if somewhat loosely. The pinnacle of mature achievement in dramatic art was identified as 'creating a character', something which she saw young children as unlikely to achieve. Indeed one could summarise the underlying attitude to classroom drama inculcated by Langdon as one of tolerance for shortcomings. Children's drama may develop from child play, but theatre was to be its model.

Notes

1   Courtney, Richard (1968) *Play Drama and Thought: the first examination of the intellectual background of drama in education* Cassell London

2   Nunn, Percy (1920) *Education: Its Data and First Principles* Edward Arnold London

3   Groos, Carl (1899) The Play of Man Appleton Press

4   Hall, Stanley G. (1904) *Adolescence* Appleton-Century Crofts

5   Nunn refers to Schiller's Letter 15 (See, for example Friedrich Schiller's *On the Aesthetic Education of Man* by Elizabeth M. Wilkinson and L.A. Willoughby, published by Oxford University Press in 1967, in which the authors collect and provide a commentary for Schiller's 27 published letters). It is the fifteenth letter that contains Schiller's much-quoted paradox: '...man only plays when he is in the fullest sense of the word a human being, and he is only fully human when he plays.' [Wilkinson and Willoughby (1967) *ibid* p.107.

6   This piece of wisdom is, in fact, a pithier version of Schiller's own words, also in the fifteenth letter. [Wilkinson and Willoughby (1967) *ibid* p.107]

7   Nunn, P. (1920) *ibid* p.92. This comment by Nunn is in striking contrast to the view later expressed by the woman who was to become his colleague at his own invitation, Dr. Susan Isaacs.

8   Nunn, P. (1930) *ibid* p.95. Note that Nunn's view of make-believe play as a 'biological device' is in keeping with Karl Groos' theory [*The Play of Man* (1989) Appleton Press]

9   Nunn, P. (1920) *ibid* p.99

10   Nunn, P. (1920) *ibid* p.247

11   Sully, James (1896) *Studies of Childhood* Longman Green London

12   Lee, Joseph (1915) *Play in Education* Macmillan New York p.110

13   Isaacs, Susan (1930) *The intellectual growth in Young Children* Routlege and Kegan Paul London

14   The post required her, according to her biographer, D.E.M. Gardner [Susan Isaacs (1969) Methuen, London], 'to conduct education of a small group of children aged 2-7, as a piece of scientific work and research.' Gardner D.E.M., p.54

15   She was appointed in 1933 to set up a new Department of Child Development at the London University Institute of Education

16   Wilshire, Bruce (1982) Role-Playing and Identity: The Limits of Theatre Metaphor Indiana University Press Bloomington p.105

17   One example of a theorist and practitioner in theatre from the first half of the century was, according, to Lars Kleberg, Nilolay Yevreinov, a Russian who believed theatre to be derived from child play. [Kleberg, Lars (1993 edition), trans from Swedish by Charles Rougle, *Theatre as Action* Macmillan P 55]

18   Of course there were those who could not accept her view of the importance of play. For example, three years after Isaacs' *Intellectual Growth in Young children*, Robert R. Rusk, a Principal Lecturer in Education in Glasgow writes: 'The view that fantasy is the primary mental activity of the child has little psychological support' (Rusk, Robert R. [1933] *A History of the Infant School* ULP London p.84/5) and adds 'Psycho-analysis has taught us the dangers of pandering to the 'pleasure' principle of Freud'.

19   She, likes others before her, saw connections between make-believe play and art. She writes: '...his play is a starting point not only for cognitive development but also for the adaptive and creative intention which when fully developed marks out the artist, the novelist, the poet.'

20   Langdon, E.M. *An Introduction to Dramatic Work with Children Theatre* in Education Series by John Andrews and Ossia Trilling (Eds) Dennis Dobson Ltd London 1948. Other members of the Committee included Lady Mayer (chairman), Mr. John Allen, Administrator, Children's Theatre Ltd. (Glyndebourne), Mr. Andrew Campbell, Publisher of Theatre in Education, Miss Cobby, Essex County Drama Adviser and Robert Newton, Middlesex County Drama Adviser.

21   However, she makes no mention of dramatic play as practice in thinking hypothetically.

22   Froebel drew a similar distinction between 'spiel' (play) and 'spielen' (playing).

23   The classic argument began with Diderot's publication: Diderot Denis, (c.1773) *The Paradox of Acting* translated by Walter Haries Pollock, Chatto and Windus, London [1883].

24   Langdon uses the label of the period: 'backward boys and girls' p.47.

25   Read, Herbert (1943) *Education Through Art* Faber and Faber London

26   Stanislavski, Constantin (1933) *An Actor Prepares* Theatre Arts London

CHAPTER FOUR
ACTING AS AMATEUR DRAMA

This chapter will seek to demonstrate how the popularisation of the notion of *training* the amateur actor provided enthusiasts in amateur theatre with an entrée into schools. Frances Mackenzie's (1930) text will be examined for a flavour of such training. E.J. Burton's publication (1949) will be used as an indication of how the amateur training approach could be translated into the Drama or English teacher's classroom. Four selected skills related to acting will be analysed. Where appropriate we will draw upon authors whose publications sought to make a specialisation of these skills.

Introduction
Amateur theatre, according to Mary Kelly (1939 and 1946[1]) can be traced back to Mediaeval times, but, after Puritan restrictions on theatre, it was not revived until the 20th century. There were two distinct early 20th century movements: development of theatre in the cities (many to become known as 'Little Theatres') and a much slower development in rural areas. Most of the city development took place in the north and a number of prestigious amateur companies were well established by the 1920s.[2] The early part of the century saw new local energies for reviving village drama sprouting in places as far apart as Grasmere in Westmoreland, Wells in Somerset and West Hoathly in Sussex, but it was only after the First World War, through the auspices of the Women's Institute,[3] the Village Drama Society (started by Mary Kelly herself in 1918) and the British Drama League (started by

71

Geoffrey Whitworth in 1919) that isolated revivalists could be in touch with each other – forty years of 'training programmes' followed.

A leading figure in the training schemes, and of particular interest to this study, was Frances Mackenzie, for many years on the full-time staff of the British Drama League, as 'Organizing Director of Drama Schools'. Her publication in 1935, *The Amateur Actor*, became a handbook for teachers of amateurs. The notion that adult amateur actors were trainable caused a rush of publications in the 1930s. Commitment, intelligence and a sound knowledge of theatre crafts were to mark the new amateurism. I will now look at her publication in some detail as an example of the attitude to training popularised by her in the pre-War period.

The Amateur Actor[4] by Frances Mackenzie (1935)

For the amateur, Miss Mackenzie represented not only a source of professional theatre expertise, but also a new kind of mentor: an authority on what amateurs needed to know. Many amateur actors were, of course, elementary and secondary teachers[5] for whom amateur acting was a hobby, and such teachers simply wanted to share their love of doing theatre with their pupils when they tried to apply Miss Mackenzie's 'common-sense' approach to acting[6] to their school drama.

Mackenzie is keen that the amateur actor should learn from the professional, although she recognises a gulf between them, expressed succinctly, if somewhat brutally, as: 'Broadly speaking, the professional does not act unless he can, while the amateur does, although he can't.' Nevertheless she believes:

> it would be an excellent thing if amateurs could sometimes watch professionals rehearsing. They would realise what an enormous amount of detailed and careful work goes to build up an effect, which probably in performance appears entirely spontaneous and casual.

For Miss Mackenzie technique in acting is a matter of creating a calculated effect. Such an effect is marred if the actor treats a line of script too intellectually, or relies overmuch on expressing himself 'naturally'. Mackenzie writes:

All acting is artificial; it is a fine art; according to Coquelin, almost an exact science. The amateur must rid himself of the idea that he is in any way fulfilling the functions of an actor by simply 'being natural'...the function ... is not to be natural, nor even to give an imitation of nature, but to give a representation of certain aspects of nature, interpreted in terms of his own personality, and having artistic form and significance.'

Nor should the actor indulge in feeling the emotion of the part as he plays it. Mackenzie explains:

The actor brings his emotional and imaginative faculties most fully into force when he is forming his first conception of the part; he then, in rehearsal, translates it into terms of technique, but, in performance, he re-informs it with a representation of that emotion which he experienced when he first studied the part. He uses what Wordsworth would describe as 'emotion recollected in tranquillity', intensified by the corroboration of his intellect, and stimulated by the presence of the audience.'

Drama in schools is not directly Frances Mackenzie's concern, but she does acknowledge that, exceptionally, lack of technique may have its own attraction:

One does occasionally see, in plays acted by quite inexperienced village players or children, an emotional performance which is entirely spontaneous and artless, but which moves us profoundly by the force of its sincerity. Such performances are rare jewels... But the sad thing is that these lovely performances can so seldom be repeated. They have their own value, but it is not that of acting.'

'Lovely performances', but 'not that of acting' confirms a distinction drawn by some amateur and professional instructors between what an adult might achieve through practice and performances by children. From this viewpoint, what children do on stage, provided it is untarnished by technique, does not qualify for the term 'acting': children's stage behaviour is to be seen as 'artless', and 'real' acting, in contrast, as 'artfully' working to achieve a calculated and repeatable effect. Such a view is in contrast to recommendations made by Mrs. Langdon, writing 13 years later, who, as we saw in the last chapter, urged teachers to recognise that even pre-adolescent children are ready to learn technique and consciously respect 'the rights of an audience'

Publications such as Frances Mackenzie's in the 1930s not only opened up the question of what acting entailed and the possible difference between professional, amateur and children's performances, but they also introduced the idea, no doubt derived from professional theatre-schools, of a training scheme embracing cumulative, performance-enhancing 'exercise' activities independent of rehearsing a play. I have underlined this notion of exercises as part of a training scheme, for, although Mackenzie is not writing her scheme with schools in mind, it not only gave authoritative advice to teachers seeking a model on how to improve techniques in acting, it solved the problem of what to do in a drama lesson when a school-play was not in the offing. It had more serious conceptual implications too, for whereas hitherto the notion of 'practising' was related to learning a script or 'practising one's part', the amateur theatre, following professional theatre training, now introduced the idea of practising acting itself, rather like a pianist practising scales.

Most of Mackenzie's book is devoted to providing the amateur student with exercises both to improve acting skills in, for example, use of voice, use of gesture, effective projection, sense of timing, and stage falls; and to acquire stage-management and production techniques in such matters as rehearsal organisation and general 'show' management.

The influence of the amateur drama movement on the school classroom

Those enthusiasts for theatre with a vested interest in schooling seemed to have fallen during this period into four categories:

(1) those who simply wanted better quality school plays.[7] Drama would not appear on the school timetable.

(2) those who want to see Drama in Secondary Schools as a time-tabled subject, to be taught by the English teacher [or, possibly, the Speech specialist or the trained actor[8]], turning the front of the classroom into a stage area for an *active* interpretation of scripts in contrast to the traditional reading aloud of texts from the classroom desks.

(3) those who wanted to evolve a developmental theory of Drama relating the natural expression of play to the craft of theatre. Drama would be in place as a school subject, mainly devoted to inventing dramatic scenes.

(4) those who subscribed to the notion of a course of training in Drama, a course made up of exercises, independent of scripted or unscripted 'play-making'. The performance of a play is not the immediate target. Drama would be time-tabled as a subject devoted to performance skills.

The above classification is crude and may be misleading, especially in respect of educational objectives which practitioners across the categories may hold in common. Nevertheless, it does draw attention to broad trends, which, if set alongside the contrasted approaches described in each chapter of this section of the thesis, contribute to the wide spectrum of drama activities out of which, or even against which, Peter Slade began to evolve his own particular theory and practice. Perhaps it is category (4), the notion of using graded exercises as a basis for training young people in drama skills, that had such a ready appeal to teachers interested in Speech and Amateur Theatre. The Speech bias, which was usually regarded as part of teaching English, we shall be examining in detail in the next chapter. For the remainder of this chapter, we shall concentrate on training in other acting skills most commonly included in publications of the time. These are 'emotion', 'characterisation', 'mime' and 'improvisation'. The writings of four leading figures will be used as illustrative of the kind of thinking about these topics that was prevalent in this period. They are Frances Mackenzie and E.J. Burton (already mentioned), Irene Mawer and Robert G Newton.

Acting Skills

Practising emotion

Both Mackenzie and Burton created classroom exercises relating to emotion, but whereas Burton[9] was concerned to give his secondary pupils practice in emotional expression, Mackenzie wanted to give her adult classes practice in emotional representation. They are worth examining in some detail for what they reveal about how acting was perceived in that period. Of particular interest is the assumption they make that expression or representation of emotion is something that can be practised out of the context of a play. Let us begin with an exercise from Mackenzie who recommends the following

> Two people start walking across the room towards each other; after a few steps they stop short in surprise at seeing each other. After the pause of amazement, continue the meeting, registering (a) delight, (b) anger, (c) fear, (d) embarrassment

In this exercise the participants are invited to *register*[10] emotion, but E.J. Burton, writing in 1949, explains that 'Acting is largely a matter of 'letting out', and not, as so many seem to think, of 'putting on' attitudes, airs and different clothes. Good acting will depend on the feelings that come from within the children.' But, as for Langdon, Burton holds that 'acting' is more than (just) 'pretending' and the audience must be catered for. To feel is not enough. He goes on to advise his pupils: 'If we act, we have to let the audience know what we are experiencing and what we feel about the things that are happening to us.' The young actor, then, has the responsibility of both feeling and communicating those feelings. Burton then proceeds to set up a classroom exercise in 'letting out the feeling'. He divides the class 'into two sides, one to act, the other to watch'. The first 'emotion' exercise is as follows:

> Here is the situation. You are going to meet an old friend whom you have not seen for many years. As you walk along the road to the station you think you see him. That is the start of a feeling of joy. As you go further, you become more certain that it is your friend. Lastly, you actually meet him – the joy reaches its climax. Try to live that experience. Think of a real friend. I will describe the various stages to you as you walk slowly down the stage together.[11]

The teacher, in this case, the author, proceeds to narrate 'plot' and 'emotional' instructions while half the students advance across a stage area. Clearly he believes that the atmospheric quality of teacher-narration will provide an effective stimulus for the 'release' of his pupils' emotions – and that these 'real feelings', obligingly, will be 'released' in keeping with the teacher's timing.[12] Burton seems to see this imposed structure as an advance on what he calls 'ham acting', which he defines as '...going through outward appearances, striking certain attitudes and so on, without really feeling the situation at all.'

Mackenzie, by contrast, straightforwardly trains her classes in the technique of showing emotion in a way that is disciplined and effective. Indeed the major part of Miss Mackenzie's book is taken up with 'production' exercises, in which she gives a brief, four to six-line 'practice' script and then, through elaborate notes, proceeds to 'coach' the trainees through their lines, dealing particularly with matters of appropriate emphasis, timing, eye-direction, position on stage, use of gesture and, above all, how to convey an emotion to the audience.

As Burton moves in his book to more advanced exercises in releasing emotion, the discipline of holding an audience's interest becomes paramount. The 'teacher' is to write a list of emotions on the blackboard from which groups of pupils are to create a scene based on the selection of one of the list. Burton gives advice:

> 'Fear may be shown by a whole party who are sheltering from gunfire. If there are several 'releasing' the feeling, each one must be an individual character, with a slightly different reaction from that of each of his comrades. For example, the coward will show abject fear in every word and movement; the braver man will reveal his fear only by increased alertness, watchfulness, and a tenseness of the body.'

He then, significantly adds: 'Now prepare your little scenes. We will mark them and see which team does best.'

Thus Burton, in a book that became regarded as an authoritative text,[13] introduced what may appear to be two rotten apples into the barrel of drama education: (1) a conception of classroom drama as '*little* scenes', with all that implies of 'juvenile', 'not important', 'not to be taken seriously' and (2) the notion of *competitiveness*. Indeed, one might wonder how such a drama of 'fear' could be taken seriously, and one may have doubts about Burton's assurance that this kind of experience is truly about 'releasing' emotion. Do the pupils themselves, stimulated by a list of emotions on the classroom blackboard, and spurred on by the approaching contest between teams of actors, believe that they have really experienced fear?

There appears to be an ambivalence in Burton's position that is not apparent in the unambiguously technique-focused approach of Mackenzie. Such a contradiction may be but part of a comfortable, belittling attitude to 'little scenes' – 'comfortable', because such an attitude allows teacher and pupils alike not to invest too much of their serious selves into their drama work, belittling, because they are dismissable as unimportant. If this is the case, Burton cannot be loaded with the blame for this educational deception – he was writing for a readership who no doubt found the contradiction acceptable and indeed embraced the rhetoric of 'true feelings' while reducing the activity to a none too serious classroom competition.[14] One is reminded again of Tomkinson's warning that 'In grasping at the substance you have even lost the shadow'.

Training in Acting – through 'Characterisation'
In Burton's 1949 text, the term that most often crops up in the 'Let's Act' section is 'character' or 'characterisation'. After the first exercise, Burton addresses the lower secondary participants with the question: 'When the climax came, did you act as the character you represented – or as yourself? Think before you answer. What should you have done?' and, in his 'Notes for the Teacher', he affirms: '...the first lesson of acting may be learnt: the necessity of remaining in character.' As we have seen in the last chapter however, Langdon (1948), in writing of the 7-11 age group comments: 'They may show quite acute observation of people in their acting, but true characterisation has to wait for the fuller development of later years.' For Burton, 'sustaining a character', however one dimensional, was an essential first step with pupils of 12 years

These authors, like many others, were simply following what appeared to be a theatre law. For any drama to get started, an actor is required to 'adopt a role', 'play a part', 'take on a character'. 'Building a character', from Stanislavski,[15] became the in vogue phrase, suggesting a sophisticated long-term process of craftmanship, which amateurs could barely hope to emulate. Nevertheless, however inexperienced the actor, the only available entry into secondary drama was seen to be through characterisation. Whether with a view to rehearsing a play or, more relevant to this chapter, as an exercise to improve acting ability, 'playing a part' defined the activity as drama. Not until John

Hodgson[16] published in 1966 was an attempt made seriously to adapt professional actor training to an educational context. Hodgson sought to bring a degree of sophistication to 'building a character' as a central plank of a student's creativity.[17]

Training in Acting – through Mime

Tomkinson's (1921) shrewd observation about 'even losing the shadow' may have even greater application to the popular practice of mime. We shall see that what aspires to the heights of refined spiritual expression on stage becomes commonplace when it is reinterpreted for the classroom. And yet it is arguably more prevalent as classroom practice than any other form of drama between 1930 and 1960. I have chosen to analyse the publication by Irene Mawer (1932),[18] who was the leading figure in mime education in this country, pre World-War Two.

Silent acting, dumb-show or 'Mime' as it was generally called developed as a feature of classroom drama from the 1930s. Many of its exponents properly emphasise the physical basis of this form of expression and for this reason, it may seem logical to include it in the later chapter on Rhythm. Certainly, classroom mime activities, especially when accompanied by music, might well have resembled the movement work of Emile Jacques-Dalcroze, Rudolf Laban or A.L. Stone, whom we will be discussing later, but it seems that most school miming did not derive from the 'dance' basis from which these exponents developed their methodology. Indeed, Jacques-Dalcroze,[19] as we shall see, viewed Mime as an inferior, reductive form of expression.

Mime as an art form, (as opposed to classroom mime) however, does indeed share the same roots as dance in ancient forms of expression. Irene Mawer, the first Mime artist and educationist to publish a seminal history of mimetic movement from its primitive and religious origins declares[20]:

> Thus, before man paints or carves, he cries and beats his breast in impotent sorrow; he sings and leaps in rejoicing, embraces in love, or kills in hate. Thus gesture and expressive movement are born from the natural instincts of humanity.

She gives a well-documented account of the use of meaningful gesture in the rituals and festivals of China, Japan, India, Egypt, Greece and Rome; and she shows how Mime or 'Pantomime',[21] as Dr. Johnson called it, featured in dramatic genre such as mediaeval religious drama and Commedia dell' arte.

The middle section of her book is devoted to 'The Technique of Mime', which includes expressive exercises for each part of the body including facial expression and this is followed by 'Teaching Mime', for, as she explains, Mime is to be regarded as 'an educational force'. Such objectives as 'mental control', 'alertness', 'sympathy', 'imagination', 'individuality' and 'personality' are placed alongside '...physical fitness, muscular control and nervous sensitiveness in every part of the body.'

Part One of Irene Mawer's book is about the collective impulse of humankind to express its elemental meanings. Parts Two and Three move onto a plane of skill-training that appears to be detached from primitive roots. Part Two, no doubt invaluable to the new kind of stage entertainer, the Mime Artist,[22] is packed with training exercises. From Part One to Two there has been a conceptual shift from a collective, spiritual dynamic to individualistic, histrionic refinement. Part Three is Miss Mawer's attempt to transfer these performance skills to the school classroom, a further conceptual shift from exquisite artistry of the individual to the occupational miming of a class, an activity she justifies as 'thought in action'. She herself warns: 'In teaching children we must remember that we are not training professional mimes, but rather developing expressive personalities, and are, at the same time, aiming at the unity of mental and physical control.' In carrying out this aim, the 'teacher must have a clear progression in mind throughout.'

The exercises are to be simpler versions of the 'body' and 'control' routines of Part 2. 'Relaxation' is to be harnessed; imagination is to be stimulated. On emotion, Mawer, in contrast to Burton, has this to say: 'It is seldom, if ever, wise to teach emotional expression to children.' The children (she does not specify an age group) are to be taught how to create a 'Mime Play', by giving them practice in Stage movement, particularly entrances and exits, gesture, crowd-work and character study. She gives some specific examples.[23] She includes actions to various nursery rhymes, practice in walking like 'Kings and Queens' and a number of 'scenes', one of which is described as giving the children an 'Historical sense and Characterisation':

> The queen enters and is sailing along with queenly dignity in her farthingale and high Elizabethan ruffle (every one has seen a picture of Queen Elizabeth!) when she finds a patch of muddy road before her. She says, 'We cannot cross this'. Sir Walter Raleigh advances gallantly...

This prosaic exercise seems a long way from the aspirations expressed by Irene Mawer in her introduction to the book:

> Mime is of every age, of every people. Her heritage is as great as that of Dance, or of Drama, her fellow-pilgrims. What in days to come shall it be said that this age has made of her? A shadow, with a voice mechanical? Rather let us give to her new life in bodies freed and minds new-lit. It is our duty and our honour to live courageously, to the full power of mind, of body, and of soul.

It seems that the courage of her own stage creations as an artiste, found little expression when she tried to translate her vision into the classroom. Unfortunately, the high regard with which she was held turned her book into an educational classic and exercise in Mime became legitimised as classroom drama practice,[24] a view reinforced by such a prestigious leader in the field as Richard Courtney, who, before he left to take up his career in Canada, published a guide on the teaching of drama which included the following[25]:

> Mime Improvisations; these can be based on occupations (a group at a fruit farm, and the rest guess what fruit they picked) or occupations[26] (half-a-dozen different characters put together in the situation, and the rest have to guess who they are and where they are)...As the children get older, the mime becomes more detailed: the class as a whole now might spend twenty minutes discussing and miming exactly how to make a cup of tea, or the actions involved in washing your face.

I am not suggesting that Mime is necessarily an inappropriate form of dramatic behaviour – we shall see in Chapter 5 how miming actions to poetry helped Marjorie Hourd's pupils gradually to understand the poetic spirit of a text, and there are many instances of children's own play and of dramatic play-making when children purposefully 'mime' actions instead of handling real objects. It is the use of Mime as training in Drama which may be objected to, partly because it tended to be translated into pedestrian 'occupational exercises' seemingly a long way behind 'new life in bodies freed and minds new-lit', and partly because training in drama seemingly detached from the making of drama falls far short of the drama-making adventures of Harriet Finlay-Johnson's and Henry Caldwell Cook's classrooms.[27]

Training in Acting – through improvisation

Whereas by the 1930s terms such as 'Mime', 'Movement, and 'Dance' were well established as part of a theatrical or dramatic vocabulary, 'Improvisation' was in its infancy. To the professional theatre, in England, the concept smacked of indiscipline. Although the word was occasionally used by educationalists,[28] no-one took the term seriously enough to make more than a passing reference. The term 'improvising' had more common usage, referring to something being made up on the spur of the moment, but the noun, 'improvisation' presented problems, its meaning varying according to its purpose. Cecily O'Neill has demonstrated the complexity of the concept in her doctoral thesis and subsequent publication.[29]

The one British writer in the 1930s to take a firm grip on the genre was Robert G. Newton. His two publications warrant a close analysis for their author is using his knowledge of professional theatre to invent a form of dramatic activity that he knows from experience has an appeal to amateur adults and hopes from his observation of school drama that it will have a place in the classroom.[30]

It is indeed Newton's particular experience, during the 1930s slump, with a special group of amateurs, the 'working-class unemployed', that spurred Newton to find a way of doing drama that catered for such a group of novices in theatre. Thus behind his particular usage of the term 'improvisation' lies an image of a group that may not readily respond to the words on paper of a printed text, who may not have much tolerance for sustained rehearsals, a group who need to learn techniques of theatre within a less cumbersome form than a set play, and who need an opportunity to discover their own originality and inventiveness, a group for whom 'speaking learnt lines', even their own, may kill lively acting. Newton rarely makes these deficiencies explicit, occasionally, merely referring to the special needs of 'beginners'; he tends, rather, to look for positive aspects, for example[31]:

> The spontaneity of Improvisation reveals resources in players which no other method could bring out and which will colour the inventiveness of their acting. Again, the degree to which Improvisation will 'get over' to an audience is helped by the imaginative concentration of the players; it is the intensity of their imagination which almost hypnotises the audience into following with ease what is happening on stage. The more freedom actors are allowed, the more invention and imagination they will bring to their work.

Unconstrained spontaneity is not what Newton wants, however, and the rest of his book argues for a subtle combination of spontaneity and form. 'Form', according to Newton, is a central concept of all theatre-making, including Improvisation. In his 1949 publication he discusses it as follows[35]:

> Now every theatrical moment must be sympathetically related to the one which precedes and to the one which follows it. Attention has to be paid to the way in which they merge judiciously from one to another. The clear-cut and vivid presentation of a single theatrical moment is a vital factor in theatre experience, but even more important is form which is, in general terms, a harmonious, truthful, and compelling relationship between such moments...the theatrical moments must be contrasted and linked together in truth and should have in their relationship some of the grace and sensitivity that is found in music as it modulates from one theme to another.

Cecily O'Neill (1991) comments on Newton's insistence on a 'sequence' of 'theatrical moments' as innovative practice, anticipating, to some extent, the kind of structure built into what in the 1990s became known as 'Process Drama'. Indeed he sees a 'scenario' as a base-line, giving shape to spontaneous exploration by the actors, who, he claims, can only learn about 'form' (that is, elements of suspense, contrast, mood and climax etc) and 'appreciate the importance of Invention, Clarity, Economy, Breadth, the Theatrical Moment' from within the security offered by such a foundation.

Implicit in Newton's work is the presence of a director, club-leader, or teacher whose initial task is to select the material, and then negotiate its interpretation and transformation into theatre-form with the players. 'Negotiation', a term which was to be popularised in Drama education circles in the 1970s,[33] characterises this first attempt in Great Britain to publish the kind of question and answer interaction of a leader and group operating as co-dramatists. The author offers his group a 'mountain rescue' story (significantly to be performed in what Newton calls 'dumb-show';[34] his class are not to be burdened with the responsibility of finding dialogue with such intense material), and a discussion takes place on the crafting of the scenes and the details of the staging, covering such items as sky-cloth, cut-outs, curtains, improvised shelter and traverse curtains.

This kind of negotiation could well have taken place in Caldwell Cook's classroom: a problem is set; the task is to translate an incident (with Caldwell Cook the material was often a legend or myth) into formal and scenic elements. The latter for Caldwell Cook related to the Elizabethan stage; for Newton it was the picture frame of the proscenium arch.

The comparison with Caldwell Cook founders perhaps in respect of overall context. Caldwell Cook's pupils were set this task within the identifiable parameters of the 'English' lesson; Newton's young adults, subjects of a politically contrived 'do good' context defined by the government as 'recreation', no doubt needed the motivation of a public performance, not just the task itself. Thus, for Newton 'Improvisation' is scenario-based experimentation within a rehearsal context aimed at giving an audience, as Newton puts it, 'its money's worth'. The second half of Newton's book (1937) is devoted to examples of scenarios for improvisation, with and without dialogue, suitable for what he calls 'Concert Party' or Variety' programmes, but he has a broader vision of its usage. He is aware of its application to the training of actors, professional and amateur, and has aspirations for its inclusion in the 'emotional and imaginative education' that he suggests educationists are beginning to understand.

Newton's enthusiasm for improvisation as a vehicle for theatrical expression is sustained throughout his career, but a change of heart can be detected in later publications in respect of his own emphasis in the practice of improvisation and, more importantly, in relation to improvisational work in schools. Whereas in his 1937 publication he confidently claims: 'The spontaneity of Improvisation reveals resources in players which no other method could bring out...', by 1949 he is writing: 'In fact spontaneity tends to evoke stereotyped rather than true emotion.'

Newton's 1937 publication expressed an optimism about the use of improvisation in education that gradually faded. By 1948 he expresses a distinct hostility towards school improvisation. In an early issue of the first drama journal, Theatre in Education (1948), he wrote[35]:

> Recently the 'making use of drama' has shown new characteristics which have tended to confuse the whole conception of its educational value, and these characteristics have shown themselves chiefly in the field of drama for children of the primary school age group.

> The root of the difficulty seems to be largely connected with improvisation. I have for many years been an advocate of this, and may, in a minor way, have contributed towards its development. Today, however, in certain circles improvisation, or free expression, seems to have acquired such significance that many regard it the be all of theatrical experience, particularly the theatrical experience of the young. In my own Acting Improvised I stressed the point that 'there is nothing like Improvisation for teaching players to think of material *in terms of Theatre* as well as in terms of everyday life.' The italics do not appear in the printed text, but I fear that that particular phrase would cause many of the present supporters to shudder and feel concerned lest their children be tainted by too much contact with that terrible thing – The Theatre.

This was written almost immediately after what became known as 'The Bonnington Conference', a landmark in Drama Education idealism. Whereas, as we have seen in our account of Mrs. Langdon's publication, some attempts were made to find a bridge between the conflicting demands of 'natural' play and theatre, the Bonnington Conference served to reinforce a growing rift between interested parties. For the first time in Drama Education history the traditions of classroom acting based on amateur and professional theatre were openly challenged by a spokesman for a form of drama based not on theatre but on play. That spokesman, a relatively new arrival on the drama scene, was Peter Slade who clearly saw in 'improvisation' the possibilities of unfettered personal expression. Robert G. Newton's 'improvisation' was a disciplined, ensemble, proscenium stage performance. Perhaps it is typical of the history of drama teaching that two leaders in the field could both use the same term but with antithetical intentions.

Notes

1 Kelly, Mary (1939) *Village Theatre* Nelson London.

(1946) *Group Play-Making* Harrap London

2 Mary Kelly, sometimes described as the 'first national pioneer' of amateur drama began her village drama in Kelly, Devon at the beginning of the century. [Ref: Griffiths, David *The History and Role of the Drama Adviser* an unpublished dissertation, University of Durham, 1970]

Examples were: Sheffield Playgoers; Huddersfield Thespians; The Leeds Industrial Theatre; Bradford Civic Theatre; The Stockport Garrick Society; The Unnamed Society, Manchester. A few southern societies were founded, notably Citizen House, Bath and three London groups. Perhaps the most influential of all these was the Madder Market theatre in Norwich, an amateur company employing, from its inauguration in 1911, a professional director, Nugent Monck. Its uniqueness lay in its purpose-built architecture, modelled on the design of an Elizabethan theatre.

3 The W.I. was brought to England from Canada by Mrs. Alfred Watt.

4 Frances Mackenzie was the first of many professional actors and directors to be appointed to train amateurs in theatre-craft. Whereas some were appointed to organisations such as the British Drama League (Miss Mackenzie), the Village Drama Society (Miss Mary Kelly) and the National Association of Boys' Clubs, others were appointed to geographical regions – for instance Miss Lyn Oxenford in Newcastle upon Tyne and Robert G. Newton in Berkshire, both of whom were appointed in the 1930s to promote drama with the unemployed. See Griffiths, David (1970) *op cit*

5 In the *Drama in Adult Education Report* by the Adult Education Committee of the Board of Education (1926) Paper No. 6 HMSO London p.97, the authors refer to attendance by London teachers at a series of lecture recitals: 'The large audience of teachers of all types that these have attracted testify to the width and intensity of the interest in drama in the educational world'.

6 John Bourne in a review of Mackenzie's book writes:'The most sensible, informative and readable treatise yet published'.

7 In his introduction to School Drama (1938) The British Drama League appointed a School Drama Committee which, under the joint editorship of Guy Boas and Howard Hayden, both English teachers in Grammar Schools, published in 1938 a

collection of chapters separately dealing with all branches of school drama from 'The Dramatic Play of Young Children' by Jeannette Hennessy to 'Religious Drama' by Mona Swann. (Boas, Guy and Hayden, Howard (1938) *School Drama: It's Practice and Theory* Methuen London)], Guy Boas confines his remarks to the public performance.

8   Howard Hayden contributed a chapter to his jointly edited book [Boas, G. and Hayden, H. (1938) *op cit* pp.32-47] entitled 'Drama in the Classroom' in which he assumes, as did Caldwell Cook, that if drama is to occur in a classroom, then a stage area (for performance of a script) should be simulated. Hayden advises: 'The class should have fair notice of all acting lessons....Where space is available a standard-size stage should be marked out on the classroom floor with tapes.' The classroom was to become the place for learning about the craft of acting scripted scenes.

9   Burton, E.J. (1949) *Teaching English Through Self-Expression* Evans London. Burton is described in this book as 'master in charge of Speech Work and Drama'; he later became head of department at Trent Park teacher-training college. His work bestrides all four of the categories listed above. His interest in practical theatre and drama sprang out of his professional interest in the teaching of English. I have specifically included him under 'acting skills' because he appears to be the first classroom practitioner in English and Drama to introduce a training scheme of acting exercises for his pupils. However, his passionate devotion to making theatre accessible to his secondary pupils was to be life-long pursuit. See Burton, E.J. (1993) *Drama in Schools 1930-1960· Some Footnotes* St. Radigund Press, p.5, a pamphlet published by himself (when he was in his mid-eighties) in reaction to what he saw as the absurd rift between drama and theatre in schools. In his own church he has the status of Bishop, and, since retirement from teaching, he has adopted the title of Very Reverend.

10   As late in the century as 1972, a research document was published in America which recorded a procedure for testing elementary pupils' ability in 'characterisation': Smith, Louis M. and Schumacher, Sally (1972) 'Extended Pilot Trials of the Aesthetic Education Program: A Qualitative Description; Analysis and Evaluation' in *Beyond the Numbers Game* by Hamilton D., Jenkins D., King C., Macdonald B., and Parlett M. [1977] Macmillan Basingstoke p.318

Following instructions from a 'Creating Characterisation package', 'the first three children were sad, happy and surprised in turn. The sad girl rubbed her eyes, commenting 'Oh I'm so sad; the happy boy exuberantly jumped up and down and commented 'Oh, I'm so happy. The sun is out.' Later, anger and fright entered the parade.'

A British example occurs in a 1965 publication by Richard Courtney [*Teaching Drama* Cassell London]. In the sub-section of his book entitled Mime Courtney includes the following instruction in one of his exercises: 'Face: be angry, happy, sad; glance to show that you think there might be a ghost behind you...' (p.51)

11   Burton E.J. (1949) *ibid* p.172

12 A more extreme version is included by Burton on the following page (p.173): 'You are asleep in Bethlehem on the hills outside the town. It is the first Christmas night. You wake to hear the angels' song. Then you see the heavenly host. Finally, you hear their proclamation that the Messiah is born.' Additionally, he expects that his pupils will simultaneously be able to 'let the audience know what we are experiencing.' p.171.

13 It reached an eighth printing by 1967.

14 We shall see in the following chapter on Speech training that much of the communal growth of in interest in school speech and drama from 1920 onwards took the form of competitive Festivals. Both Mackenzie and Burton had a hand in promoting this kind of competition. Burton's suggestions for 'marking' to find out the best team would not seem to his readers to be out of place.

15 Stanislavski, Konstantin S. (1949) *Building a Character* translated by Elizabeth Reynolds Hapgood, Theatre Arts Books New York

16 Hodgson, John and Richards, Ernest (1966) *Improvisation* Eyre Methuen London. John Hodgson, who started his career as a Birmingham teacher and subsequently moved to the training of professional actors at Bristol Old Vic, where he was Vice-Principal, was well placed with his background to establish a prestigious Drama Department at Bretton Hall, the leading institution for training teachers in Arts education in the country. Hodgson educated a generation of talented Drama teachers whose influence is apparent today.

17 It is perhaps of interest to note here that Dorothy Heathcote's influence was later to replace 'Building charactisation' with 'Building belief' as the drama teacher's shibboleth.

18 Mawer, Irene, (1932) *The Art of Mime: Its History and Technique in Education and the Theatre* Methuen London

19 Jacques-Dalcroze, Emile (1921) *Rhythm, Music and Education* trans. by Harold F. Rubenstein Chatto and Windus London p.192

20 Mawer, Irene (1932) *ibid* p.3

21 The term 'pantomime' goes back to Roman times and has retained its original usage, (actions without words or actions to music) in North American, while, in the UK, it seems to have become associated with Christmas vaudeville entertainment..

22 On Page 112 is a photograph of Joe Grimaldi and his father as a monkey and clown.

23 Mawer, I. (1932) *ibid* pp.226-231.Curiously, she has a foot-note about her examples: 'These scenes are copyright and must not be produced in public without permission.'

24 Hence, the sub-title of Burton's first publication [*Teaching English Through Self-Expression*) is 'A Course in Speech, Mime and Drama'

25 Courtney, Richard (1965) *Teaching Drama* Cassell London p.51.

26 This appears to be a misprint in Courtney's text: 'occupations' should here perhaps read as 'characters' or 'personalities'.

27 It should be noted that a more imaginative form of mimetic work has been retained in some quarters throughout the century. See, for instance, 'Mime in the classroom' by Pat Keysall in *Scottish Drama Spring* 1995, Issue No 3.

28 The HMSO publication *Teaching of English in England* (1921), for example, refers on one occasion (p.317) to 'happy improvisations'. Even as late as 1955, E.J. Burton in Drama in Schools in his one reference to 'improvisation' (Footnote, p.65) feels impelled to place the word in inverted commas, and to use the term 'charade' as an alternative.

29 [1] O'Neill, Cecily C. (1991) *Structure and Spontaneity: Improvisation in Theatre and Education* Doctoral thesis, Exeter University and [2] O'Neill, Cecily, C. (1995) *Drama Worlds: a framework for process drama* Heinemann New Jersey.

30 Robert G. Newton (1937) *Acting Improvised* Nelson London and (1949) *Magic and Make-Believe: An essay enquiring into the relationship between theatre experience and improvisation* Dobson London

31 Newton, R.G. (1937) *ibid* p.15

32 Newton, R.G. (1937) *ibid* p.20

33 See, for example, the School's Council Report (1977) Learning Through Drama, in which 'negotiation of meaning' became a motif.

34 'Dumb-show' is meant by the author to convey a freer form of presentation than conventionalised 'mime' [See p.7 of Newton R.G. (1937)].

35 Newton, R.G. (1948) 'Let's Enjoy Drama' in *Theatre in Education Journal* No 7-8, March-June pp.24-5.

CHAPTER FIVE

DRAMA IN THE ENGLISH-TEACHING CLASSROOM

Acting as training in Speech
Acting to understand the Text
This chapter will discuss two major publications relating to the teaching of English. The first, the 1921 Ministry of Education Report, gives detailed guidance to teachers on how Drama could be taught through Speech-training; the second, published just after the Second World War, offers a theoretical framework for the inclusion of Drama within the teaching of literature which remains unsurpassed at the end of the century. Its author was Marjorie Hourd who would have qualified as a pioneer for this study had she chosen to pursue the interest she showed in 1949 and allowed herself to become associated with Drama teaching rather than creative writing in which she ultimately gained reputation as an authority.

Drama in the English-teaching classroom:
acting as training in Speech
In the last chapter, 'Acting as Amateur Drama', it was established that the notion of training in acting as part of a course was introduced in the 1930s, so that it became possible for a school to have 'Drama' on the timetable without the activity being seen as a 'rehearsal'. Whereas the concept of 'acting exercises' was new in an educational context, one aspect of acting-training, 'speech' had a much longer history. Of course speech-training was not regarded as training in acting, but as

91

'personal development'. Nevertheless its established practice no doubt made it easier to introduce related acting skills as drama became established as a subject.

Teaching of English in England (1921) an HMSO publication[1]
Astonishingly, for there is no evidence that drama featured as common practice (rather, the reverse), more space is given to what the Report terms 'Drama in Education', than to any other aspect of English teaching. Perhaps it is the optimistic spirit of the immediate post-World War One times that prompts its writers to declaim[2]:

> It was in no inglorious time of our history that Englishmen delighted altogether in dance and song and drama... It is a legitimate hope that a rational use of the drama in schools may bring back to England an unashamed joy in pleasures of the imagination and in the purposed expression of wholesome and natural feeling.

Only occasionally, however, do the writers return to this rapturous note. The tone is mostly that of practical advice sprinkled with occasional warnings about pitfalls to be avoided. Fully aware of the range of activities embraced by 'drama in education', the Report introduces the major section on the subject with a classification: 'For the purposes of school work the Drama may be considered in three aspects: (1) as something to be written; (2) as something to be read; and (3) as something to be acted.'[3] The writers even recognise that 'acting' requires further subdividing[4]:

'(a) the performance of scenes or pieces in class,

(b) the public performance of plays by pupils,

(c) visits by pupils to professional performances of suitable plays.'

It is (a), of course, that is of central interest to this book. The very phrasing of (a) betrays the kind of activity intended. The term 'performance' is being used in a straightforward, unambiguous way, readily understood in this period as young actors entertaining a passive audience. In this report there are no indications, as in the work of Harriet Finlay-Johnson, that the audience might actively engage as note-taking critics, directors or text revisionists nor, as in the case of Caldwell Cook, that the performance might centre on Elizabethan staging, and certainly not that the participants see themselves as a company of actors. Such refinements, qualifying, as has already been discussed in previous chapters, the meaning of performance for Finlay-Johnson's and Caldwell Cook's young scholars, seems to have escaped the writers of this report. They do, however, on one occasion refer to 'happy improvisations' as an alternative form of performance to the presentation of scripts. It has already been noted that both Finlay-Johnson and Caldwell Cook (reluctantly) permitted this freer form very occasionally.

It is the word 'pieces' in (a) above that is of special interest, for its usage implies an acceptance of a mode of dramatic behaviour that was popularly called a 'recitation' or 'monologue', in which an individual entertained an audience with the presentation of a memorised poem or excerpt from a play. Where participants combined, it was called 'choral speech'. From further examination of the Report, it can only be concluded that the basis of the writers' conception of classroom acting was indeed a narrow one; they saw its educational purpose as the improvement of speech. 'Speech Training' and 'Oral Expression' not only earn separate sections earlier in the Report, but the whole chapter devoted to 'Drama in Education' makes continual reference to the need for improving articulation, voice production, pronunciation, and skills in reading aloud verse and prose, not solely for the sake of elocutionary correctness, but as a way of appreciating literature. The Drama section concludes with[5]:

> There will be no better opportunity for correcting them (speech faults) than the play read or performed in class. This, following on some instruction in the elements of phonetics and of voice production, ought to do much to raise the whole level of reading and speaking both of prose and verse. Their rendering of literature by the voice is not a mere matter of mechanical correctness, but is the final result of sympathetic entry into the spirit of the writer, and without it no education in letters can be complete.

Mention should be made here of the influential figure of Elsie Fogerty,[6] a 'witness' to the Committee, who founded the Central School of Speech and Drama, which included the first Speech Therapy School[7] in 1906, held the first conference, in 1912, on 'Speech Training in London Schools and Colleges', and formed the influential Society for

Teachers of Speech and Drama influence on the Committee Report is marked, acknowledging, as it does, the important place of 'phonetic symbols' in the 'scientific method of speech training', a method no doubt more accessible to London Schools (Elsie Fogerty's 'territory') than to other parts of the country. The Report avers

> It is emphatically the business of the Elementary School to teach all its pupils who either speak a definite dialect or whose speech is disfigured by vulgarisms, to speak standard English, and to speak it clearly, and with expression. Our witnesses are agreed that this can be done, provided that definite and systematic teaching is given from the outset.

Such an affirmation from an official document of the importance of Speech-training as part of the teaching of English, not only enhanced the reputation of Elsie Fogerty, the Institute for which she was responsible[8] and other similar academies of Speech and Drama,[9] but also gave a backing to the recently-formed British Drama League. The Report too gave unofficial blessing to the domestic Speech-training industry that was to spread rapidly during the next forty years throughout the British Isles.

As a result of this 'domestic enterprise' almost every town in England eventually had its 'teacher of elocution'. Sadly, it gave unwarranted attention to the value of drama as a solo performance – the words 'monologue', 'recitation', or, as in the Report, performance of 'a piece', became part of middle-class vocabulary – and the British Drama League, in introducing competitive Festivals, unwittingly gave support to this peculiarly British view of the performer in drama.[10] Mark Antony's oration over the body of Caesar, for many children, became either an address in private to an examiner across a table, or a competition fought in public against other 'Mark Antonys'. That some 'private' teachers were brought, often part-time, into the State schools, reinforced the expectation that a progressive view of English would include Speech and Drama and that any practice of drama in the classroom would be framed within a Speech-training course in which 'solo' performance of an excerpt from a play was not thought to be unusual.

Drama in the English-teaching classroom: acting to understand the text

In 1949, there appeared in published form a way of writing about classroom drama in the context of teaching literature that wrested it from the skill-based 'Speech-Training' approach adopted by teachers of English for the previous thirty years. It could be said that in this respect Marjorie Hourd's book was in the tradition of Caldwell Cook, but its pages reveal a determination to find a theoretical basis for understanding literature through Drama that went beyond Caldwell Cook's 'Playway' philosophy.

The Education of the Poetic Spirit by Marjorie Hourd (1949)[11]

Marjorie Hourd draws on T.S. Eliot's image of 'The paw under the door': she does not want 'the pocket torch of observation' (Eliot) searching out the literal meaning of the words in a poem, but the sensing of 'The paw under the door'.[12] She is aware of the powerful hold a teacher's reading of a story can have on her listeners. Hourd sees what goes on in the listener's mind as 'dramatic', a process of 'losing oneself to gain oneself', by which paradox she appears to mean that the very act of imagining is self-enhancing, that by temporarily moving away from oneself in the world one gains a firmer sense of oneself in the world. She adds, more practically: '...often dramatisation of a most powerful and mentally active kind can be taking place in a class-room where an untrained observer might only be conscious of passive listening.' Like W. S. Tomkinson (1921), Hourd concedes that: 'frequently class-room acting reveals a complete lack of any imaginative understanding at work.' For Hourd the solution lies, not in a dismissal of acting, but in harnessing its potential to express the unspoken, to glimpse 'the shadow', to be awake to 'the paw under the door'. Marjorie Hourd is the first British teacher to articulate what happens when a child turns poetry into action.

Hourd, in presenting a theory of teaching English for Expression, takes advantage of the recent impact on education of writers such as Sigmund Freud, Carl Jung, Jean Piaget, Herbert Read, Martin Buber and Susan Isaacs. Hourd explains: 'When I began to teach these children, like most teachers I did not set out with a psychological theory to prove or an educational philosophy to put to the test. It was only gradually that I realised that my findings were in line with many of those of Dr. Susan Isaacs, Piaget and the Gestalt School, to mention a few of the most outstanding sources of agreement.'

The issues raised by Hourd may be discussed under four headings: 'The paw under the door'; Psychological and aesthetic dimensions to creativity; Concepts of 'understanding' and drama; and the concept of 'naturalism'.

'The paw under the door'

Hourd maintains that dramatic action, usually simple miming while teacher speaks the narrative poem, can, through repetition, illuminate its more elusive meanings for both the actors and the rest of the class watching. Her theory is that by isolating (as we have seen miming does) the superficial meanings in the text, the spaces between them, that is, the 'deeper meanings' may be 'sensed'. Such a view enhances the worth of miming as an activity. Whereas Courtney, for example, sets the miming against an occupational 'standard' of, say, 'how to make a cup of tea', Hourd is juxtaposing the crude mimetic representations with elusive resonances of a text.[13]

Psychological and aesthetic dimensions to creativity

These two dimensions, Hourd suggests, may make for conflicting claims according to the stability of the personality. The early adolescent who is more interested in 'himself playing the part' than 'the part', is less ready for a public performance than the Junior child who unselfconsciously takes on a 'part' that may be beyond him in both understanding and artistry. He plays himself, while 'believing' that he is portraying a character. Late adolescence is the time when the two dimensions merge into a synthesis.

Concepts of Understanding and Drama

Hourd's use of drama in the classroom is to enhance understanding, for which she has an interesting developmental theory. She labels stages of development as 'knowing or not knowing'; 'knowing that you know or do not know'; 'knowing *what* you know or do not know'; and 'being able to *explain* what you know or do not know'. Drama, according to Hourd, helps a child intuitively to recognise that s/he has learnt something, that s/he knows something new. While satisfying the Junior School child, this unconscious grasp of meanings is not enough for the older child who, not yet ready to explain, what s/he knows, needs a degree of protection which acting may not provide.

Hourd relies heavily on what may well be a basic law of drama education or drama therapy – she consecutively (and sometimes, simultaneously) harnesses more than one medium of expression. At its most superficial, pupils read the text or hear a text read and translate those words into mimic actions; at its most sophisticated, having read the story, they *write* about which character they would choose to play and why or penetrate a difficult text through analogy. It is the act of *reinterpreting through a different medium*, whether from (to take examples emanating from my own and others' teaching) acting into drawing, or talking about feelings, or turning it into a story, or making a formal report, or recapitulating as a character etc. that generates the new understanding, even if derived from quite pedestrian 'acting'. Marjorie Hourd in this began an approach that became a central feature of Drama teaching in the final three decades of this century.

The concept of 'naturalism' in acting

Hourd, newly experiencing 'theatre-in the round', adopts the useful notion of '*being*' round in relation to the kind of acting required and she further recognises that this would be an equally useful way of describing the acting behaviour of children in the more informal 'minstrelsy' setting of the intimate classroom performance. Having said this she is keen to make sure her readers understand that the two contexts, while sharing the 'statuary' style of acting, nevertheless part company when it comes to artistry, for 'in-the-round', like 'proscenium arch' requires a degree of technique and craftmanship of which children are not capable. She does not want it to be assumed that 'theatre-in-the-round' is but a public version of children's 'naturalistic' classroom acting.

Common to both Hourd's and Caldwell Cook's classrooms, perhaps to a lesser degree in Hourd's, is the notion of pupils as craftsmen. The term 'craft' may be legitimately applied to the pupil's function as a 'dramatist' (as exemplified in both Hourd's and Caldwell Cook's classrooms) or as a 'stage-manager/director' as established in Caldwell Cook's classrooms, but not necessarily to the pupil's skill as an actor, which Hourd designates as lacking in 'perfected technique'. Hourd does not want to see the pupil/actor achieving 'artistry', for she reserves that term for the 'artifice' as does Frances Mackenzie, of rehearsing and reproducing emotional truths of the script, to make them '*tell*'. Caldwell Cook, on the other hand, while appearing not to train his pupils in 'acting techniques', nevertheless encourages them to match the 'bold, definite touch' of Shakespeare's words with appropriate actions. It seems then that by 'naturalistic' Hourd means 'acting that is unrehearsed and lacking in perfected technique'; it may, in its spontaneity, express complexities of emotion and meaning, but is without the technique to revive that emotion and meaning for an audience. However, is the kind of drama in Hourd's classroom justifiably regarded as 'natural'? It could be argued that 'Miming' is not lacking in artifice; that spontaneously acting the words of a script, even written by the pupils themselves, requires some performance skill.

Of relevance here is a form of acting behaviour for which Caldwell Cook has very low tolerance in the classroom. In Chapter Two, his arguments against the introduction into the classroom of what he calls 'realism' were noted, but it is now appropriate to return to them as, not only do they highlight contrasts with the Hourd approach, they also draw attention to a form of classroom practice that has featured increasingly from Caldwell Cook's time to present day, a representation of, to use Caldwell Cook's words, 'the incidents of everyday life'. This kind of acting behaviour appears to have a slight kinship with 'unstructured playing' of the Nursery School or playground, in that the staging, acting, shaping and the choosing of themes are regulated by the pupils themselves. For Caldwell Cook, it is the subject-matter of such drama that is its undoing: '...the incidents of everyday life, before they can become fit stuff for drama, have to undergo a process of refinement or sifting, and it is too much to expect this work of young boys.' Caldwell Cook is not dismissing the dramatic potential of inferior material, but rather placing it beyond the skill and maturity of his pupils.

It seems that Caldwell Cook is arguing against both 'realism' and 'naturalism', if the former is to refer to the familiar and the latter to a lack of theatrical style. E.M. Langdon acknowledges albeit reluctantly, the apparent need in some children for both these. When she writes in connection with the same age group as Caldwell Cook's pupils: 'Some groups of children will want endless improvisation, charades and quickly prepared group plays to perform to their club audience or class-mates', she is showing at least a tolerance for spontaneous presentation of 'everyday' material, an exercise in 'impressions and appearances' that was to become part of a regular diet of many English[14] as well as Drama lessons.[15]

When Marjorie Hourd uses the term 'naturalistic', however, she clearly is not referring to glib performances of everyday material. There is a sense, then, in which the Drama of Hourd's pupils might be regarded as '*non*-naturalistic' – in respect of its 'Romantic' material and in its kind of informal staging for an intimate audience. But, more distinctively 'non-naturalistic', a loftiness is achieved in the dialogue of the Junior pupils' own play-making, which is scripted from their close study of the literature. Hourd gives us an example, which includes a speech from Thetis before Zeus, on Mount Olympus:

Thetis: Promise me – O promise me, Father Zeus. Do as I ask I am sad and weary. O bow your head as a sure sign that you will give the Trojans victory.

(Zeus does not answer and there is silence)

This kind of stylised language from a Junior School child is far removed from the domestic 'sketch' or casual 'cops and robbers'[16] improvisation that Caldwell Cook determinedly checked in 1913, but was positively encouraged in schools by the 1950s. There was nothing casual about the spontaneous dialogue in Hourd's classroom. Here is another example:

Hera: Yes, my son, you are quite right, even if you are younger than your mother. (With a sigh.) I have still a great deal to learn.

It seems reasonable to regard this kind of dramatisation as 'non-naturalistic', but it may be more difficult to characterise the pupils' acting behaviour in their performance of Mime-Ballads. Hourd does not give a detailed account of the kind of gestures they made. It seems unlikely that these Junior girls adopted the artificial signing of Caldwell Cook's 'Miming', as no mention is made of any kind of train-ing. It may indeed be the case that for the most part her pupils' actions were simple imitations of actions described in the poetry although the following anecdote points to heights of achievement:

> ...the perfection of some of the acting is such that it is not within the power of a grown-up to recapture it any more than he would be capable of writing children's poetry or painting their pictures. One such moment of completeness is vivid in my mind. The class was miming the mediaeval version of the Orpheus and Eurydice legend. The fairy procession with Eurydice in their midst was passing by the spot where Orpheus was playing his lute. He looked up just as she moved by and a recognition took place, perfectly timed, and at once remote and near; whilst the look of tender despair on their faces afterwards was exquisitely penned that I do not think I have ever been more deeply moved.

No doubt the quality was variable, but even minimal achievement in acting, (i.e. the loosest 'sketching' of obvious actions), in this kind of dramatisation, is juxtaposed against the reading (often adult) of the verse, so that the overall impact carries a 'non-naturalistic' effect.

Hourd claims that the trying and retrying of different ways of doing the actions enhances the chances of 'half-born thoughts' becoming expressed through the actions. It is, as has been observed earlier in this chapter, as if the act of translating the unfamiliar images of the poem into a different artistic medium releases unarticulated thoughts and feelings.

If the actions of these Junior School pupils can become charged with subtleties of meaning beyond 'impressions and appearances', then, at its best, as in the above account of Orpheus and Eurydice, this kind of acting behaviour could be said to be artistically expressive, that is, gesture and stillness combining to tell of 'the paw under the door'. In the next chapter, the term 'musical gesture' is introduced as the Eurhythmist's way of describing the poetry of action.

English has continued throughout this century to be a major vehicle for Drama, each period reflecting current Drama practice. The publications in the second half of the century of leading English teachers such as E.J. Burton (1949) Chris Parry (1972),[17] John Seely (1976),[18] Ken Byron (1986)[19] Peter Creber (1990)[20] all sought to include the most up to date approaches to drama within their English orbit. From 1986 onwards the Cambridge project newsletter, Shakespeare and Schools, edited by Rex Gibson,[21] rekindled interest in imaginative approaches to Shakespeare.

Notes

1   For a more detailed analysis of this publication, see 'A conceptual framework for Classroom Acting', an unpublished Ph.D thesis by Gavin Bolton, University of Durham.

2   *The Teaching of English in England* HMSO (1921) *op cit* p.319 Para 291

3   HMSO (1921) *ibid* p.310 Para 285

4   HMSO (1921) *ibid* p.315 Para 289

5   The Teaching of English in England (1921) *ibid* p.328 Para 298

6   H. Caldwell Cook is also listed as a witness.

7   The Speech Therapy Department of Central School of Speech and Drama was not officially recognised by London University until 1923, two years after the publication of this Report.

8   The Central School of Speech and Drama was primarily a training establishment for Professional actors, and like a number of similar institutions, it offered a course in the training of teachers as a lucrative 'second string'. Often regarded as 'second best' – what you did if you failed the audition for the 'acting course' – the teaching courses nevertheless accrued a degree of éclat not shared by the usual broad curriculum-based teacher-training institutions. To have been to a 'specialist' London Drama College added an expertise and glamour to one's teaching qualification. Many teachers, trained in this way, stayed in London to teach in the hope of the odd professional engagement. London County Council Secondary and Elementary Schools tended to appoint directly from these institutions, no doubt with a view to bringing the whiff of grease-paint into their classrooms. Gwynneth Thurburn, John Allen and Robert Fowler were among later Principals of this distinguished School.

9   Professional theatre-training institutions, especially those linked with training professional musicians, such as Guildhall School of Music [founded in 1880], the Royal Academy of Music founded in 1822], Trinity College of Music [founded in 1872], and London Academy of Music and Dramatic Art [an amalgamation of four Music Colleges, the earliest of which was founded in 1861], opportunistically set themselves up as Examination Boards in 'Elocution' (later to be called 'Speech and Drama'). Graded examinations for solo performers, from six-year olds to adults, were introduced country-wide and their teachers were entrepreneurs, setting up their 'businesses' in their own homes, attracting large numbers of middle-class families who wanted to have the speech of their offspring improved. By the time Trinity College, for example, celebrated its centenary in 1972, it recorded 20,000 Speech and Drama candidates (throughout the world) in just one year. [Page 50 of Trinity College of Music: *The First Hundred Years* by Harold Rutland (1972) Trinity College of Music] A typical textbook supporting this private industry was Frank Ridley's *A Manual of Elocution for Teacher and Student* (1924) Samuel French London

10   Also a colonial view – many 'speech' teachers emigrated to South Africa and Australia etc and well-established commonwealth countries, such as India, South

Africa, New Zealand and the West Indies have continued the practice throughout this century of inviting examiners from England to supervise their Diploma or Licentiate Examinations. For instance, David Griffiths, a highly respected North-Eastern Inspector of Drama, since his retirement has visited, on behalf of Trinity College Examining Board, South Africa, India, Australia and New Zealand.

11 Hourd, Marjorie (1949) *The Education of the Poetic Spirit* Heinemann London

12 'Paw under the door' is a line taken from T.S. Eliot's *Family Reunion* and is part of Agatha's speech quoted more fully by Marjorie Hourd as a preface to Section Two of her book, Page 72.

13 It should be stressed that Courtney, writing in the 1960s, was not the only exponent of unidimensional actions in drama. Patrick Creber [Creber, J.W. Patrick (1965), *Sense and Sensibility* ULP London] publishing in the same year as Courtney, included in his book on the 'Philosophy and Practice of English Teaching', a chapter on Drama in which he states that accuracy should be a criterion of 'expressive movement': 'After the children [he is writing of Secondary pupils] have worked as a class on simple individual mime exercises, they may be asked to assess each other's efforts – to estimate how adequately John conveyed the idea that it was a hot day, or Gill that she was fed up with homework.' pp.. 89-90

14 Frank Whitehead, in his 1966 publication [Whitehead, Frank (1966) *The Disappearing Dais: A study of the principles and practice of English teaching* Chatto and Windus London p.126] writes enthusiastically of "free' or 'creative' or 'improvised' drama' as part of an English teacher's responsibility. 'Local market-place on a Saturday afternoon' and 'a crowded beach on a hot summer day' seem far removed from Cook's concept of 'Play Way' and Hourd's 'Poetic Spirit'.

15 The term 'sketch' might fit here, for a drama that aims at accurate reporting, but does not go 'beyond impressions and appearances'. The North American equivalent is 'skit'.

16 Writing in 1965, Creber (*op cit* p.87) suggests that teachers trying out drama for the first time might want 'to combat at the outset the superficiality of 'cops-and-robbers'. On the previous page Creber admitted that 'in some cases what masquerades under the name of free drama may be little more than superficial, exuberant tomfoolery.'

17 Parry, Christopher (1972) *English Through Drama* Cambridge University Press

18 Seely, John (1976) *In Context: Language and Drama in the Secondary School* OUP

19 Byron, Ken *Drama in the English Classroom* Methuen London

20 Creber, P.(1990) *Thinking Through English* Open University Press Milton Keynes

21 Gibson, Rex (Ed) (1986-) Shakespeare and Schools, The Newsletter of the 'Shakespeare and Schools' Project, Cambridge Institute of Education. See also Gibson, R. (Ed) (1990) *Secondary School Shakespeare, Classroom Practice*, A Collection of Papers by Secondary Teachers Cambridge Institute of Education and Aers, L. and Wheale N. (1991)

CHAPTER SIX

ACTING AS RHYTHM

The speech-training and the enactment of ballads etc. discussed in the last chapter appeared to have connotations beyond that of a practical way of teaching English. That a physical dimension, however modest, was being introduced into the teaching of an academic subject was in keeping with and an example of the gradual breaking down of subject divisions. For instance, a new way of regarding possible interrelatedness among time-tabled subjects led to the 1931 version of the 'Hadow' report's[1] tentatively opening up the possibility of links between Physical Education and Music. Drama and Dance were also mentioned in the same report as having aesthetic qualities in common with Drawing and Games. At one point in the report Physical Education was linked with Music and Drama. Significantly, in its section on 'Drawing and elementary Art', the following comment is made: 'It is generally agreed that all children should feel and recognise the joy of colour, and the pleasure of rhythm and harmonious pattern' and it is further explained: '...rhythm is as much felt in such activities as pattern making, weaving and stitchery as in dancing, verse speaking and singing.' Thus (albeit, towards the end of their report) the 1931 Committee urge the place of 'rhythm' as a basic component of those school activities that require some kind of physical expression or manipulation. Through 'rhythm' such diverse activities as stitchery and verse-speaking were to be linked. Rhythm was to be seen as a synthesising human characteristic, and, as such, basic to growth.

To slip in at the end of a document a fundamental conception of human development after previously mentioning rhythm only twice (in connection with music, but not linked with physical development), may suggest either a lack of conviction or an uncertainty about its reception. Such tentativeness seems at odds with the known views of the committee's chairman, the vice-chancellor of Sheffield University, Sir W.H. Hadow who, ten years earlier, in 1921, had written an introduction to the first translation of *Rhythm, Music and Education*, a seminal publication based on 'Eurhythmics' in which he writes of Emile Jacques-Dalcroze as having 'done more than any man living for the study of rhythmic beauty...' Sir Percy Nunn, too, as was seen in Chapter 3 of this study, acknowledged Jacques-Dalcroze's influence in his own 1920 publication. Professor J.J. Findlay, in a footnote on Page 24 of his 1930 publication[2] referred to *Rhythm, Music and Education* in the following glowing terms: '...in my opinion this book is one of the greatest contributions to education in our era, but neither the musicians nor the physical trainers treat it seriously. If Dalcroze had been a man of science his name would stand side by side with Einstein.'[3]

Thus educationists such as Findlay, Nunn and Hadow paved the way for the possibility of two aspects of the curriculum, Music and Physical Education, hitherto seen as unconnected, becoming linked in the minds of some British teachers of these subjects. The connection was to be epistemological, founding a 'new subject', called 'Eurhythmics'.[4] The introduction, from the 1920s onwards of 'Eurhythmics' into British educational vocabulary, had repercussions, not only for teachers of Music and Physical Education but for the other Arts, especially Dance and even Drama.

For this reason it will be useful in this chapter to refer to Jacques-Dalcroze's philosophy. This will be followed by a discussion of an account[5] of an experiment in a Birmingham primary school during the 1940s of a form of integrated education based on expressive movement. No such discussion can take place without reference to the arrival in Britain in 1937 of another continental teacher[6] whose career was dedicated to the 'Art of Movement': Rudolf von Laban.

Rhythm, Music and Education by Emile Jacques-Dalcroze (1921)
This is an unusual book in that it is made up of a series of separate, dated lectures, previously published in journals on the continent. They spread from 1902 to 1919, representing not only Jacques-Dalcroze's twenty years of teaching, but also a twenty-year development, including self-confessed contradictions, in his thinking about the subject. Not until the later years does he begin to make connections between his philosophy and Drama.

The major purpose of Jacques-Dalcroze's publication is to promote the idea of Eurhythmics as a basic subject of the school curriculum. It is not appropriate to this thesis to outline in detail how teachers experimented with his methods. Suffice to say that a view of movement education as providing a dynamic opportunity for uniting 'all the vital forces of the individual' had some impact on the way a number of Primary Schools devised their curriculum. It not only affected how some educationists and teachers saw Drama, through its emphasis on rhythm it provided art educators with a basis for arguing a generic theory of the arts, a theory that became politically critical in education in the last three decades of the century.[7] Edmond Holmes, as we have seen, sought to separate drama from the other arts as a 'sympathetic faculty', to be functionally contrasted with the 'aesthetic faculty'. For the remaining half of this chapter we shall see how drama along with other arts and crafts becomes but an off-shoot of movement.

The only references to do with acting in Jacques-Dalcroze's lectures are related to the stage, and, more specifically, to opera, dance and classical theatre. He introduces the concept of 'musical gesture' in acting. He invites us to see acting as moving sculpture or architecture, primarily meaningful in the way it penetrates space.

He points out that a gesture on stage may be indicative of degrees of specificity, miming being 'reductive' and concrete, while classical gesture achieves a quality of musical expression. Scenery, stage properties and all actions should also fulfil this basic law of abstraction, so that, for instance, for a dancer to gather flowers from a stage or a classical actor engage in precise, simulated actions, would be to confuse two forms of expression. We have already seen that Caldwell Cook's educational instincts were to eschew a high degree of specificity or naturalism. Perhaps a way of talking about his pupils' attempt to match Shakespeare's eloquence with non-naturalistic gestures in a non-naturalistic stage area is to place their acting part way towards Jacques-Dalcroze's 'musical gesture' end of the continuum of abstraction. Using this kind of classification, Marjorie Hourd's pupils' efforts to mime actions against the background of a well-read poem, might be regarded as close to Caldwell Cook's actors, whereas Langdon's occasional tolerance for what she calls 'spontaneous improvisation' no doubt qualifies as an example of extreme concreteness.

Just as we selected Marjorie Hourd's seminal work, published in 1949, as an example of a poetic/dramatic approach to the teaching of English, we now look at a slender, but significant account, published in the same year, of how a Birmingham Primary School came to Drama through experimentation with movement.

The Story of a School by A.L. Stone (1949)

The difference in practice between Harriet Finlay-Johnson and A.L. Stone could not have been more marked and yet they both shared an interest in freedom of expression through the arts. Trained in Physical Education, Stone spent ten years at Steward Street School, Birmingham, before becoming a Physical Education Organiser for the West Riding of Yorkshire, under the mentorship of Alec Clegg, Yorkshire's charismatic Chief Education Officer who devoted his career after the Second World War to promoting the Arts in the School curriculum.

'All the arts have a common beginning in movement', writes A.L. Stone, echoing Emile Jacques-Dalcroze, in his account of experimentation at Steward Street Primary School.[8] This is the first (and perhaps the only) record in England of the Arts taking precedence over the 3 R'S. Such was the success of the experiment that the Ministry of Education undertook the publication of Peter Stone's[9] account. It was not the case that this headmaster undervalued the 3R's. As he wrote: 'I believe... that there are things of much greater importance; the development of the personality of the child, his growth as a whole, demand greater attention than the three R's.' Thus what was taught under the heading of 'Reading' 'Writing' and 'Arithmetic' was dictated by whatever naturally emerged from the art experiences – and Movement was to be the central dynamic.

A.L Stone does not refer to Jacques-Dalcroze, but acknowledges the influence of Rudolf Laban whose theory and practice we need to look at before examining Stone's account in detail.

Rudolf von Laban

Rudolf von Laban, born in Hungary and a refugee from Germany where he had his own dance company, came to live in England in 1937 at the age of 58.[10] That an association, 'The Laban Art of Movement Guild', together with the biennual publication of a journal, was formed round his name by an influential group of women Dance and Physical Education specialists just a few years after his arrival is one indication of the admiration a nucleus of teachers had for Laban himself and for his artistry. During his exile in Italy at the beginning of the war the famous Laban Dance Notation was conceived. Once in England this notation was seized upon by educationists and industrialists.[11] From Dartington Hall, his first destination in England, where he briefly recuperated after his ill-treatment in Germany, he moved with Lisa Ullmann to London where they gave the first of what became known as 'Modern Dance Holiday Courses', which ran each year for twenty one years. By 1942, significantly, it was decided to change the name to 'Modern Educational Dance'.[12] Laban began to apply his practice and theory to the British Education system, or, rather, to that aspect of the system amenable to the influence of women educators (men were away at war) – to the primary school and to girls' physical education. Laban's reputation overtook the relatively flimsy support Emile Jacques-Dalcroze derived from the 1931 Hadow report.[13]

Perhaps this was because Laban's interest in movement was broader-based than that of his predecessor. Whereas Jacques-Dalcroze's pursued his theory from piano playing to stage dance, Laban moved away from stage dance to an examination of how humans move in their everyday actions. In doing this he discovered a universal pattern based on *efforts*[14] which he, in turn, re-translated into an art of dance suitable for schools. Such a conception, however, was to remain rooted in personal and social expression as an end in itself. Laban writes[15]:

> The cultivation of artistic taste and discrimination in general can-not be furthered better or more simply than by the art of movement. Yet the dances which are produced must never originate from the

wish to create outstanding works of art. Should such a miracle occur once, everybody will be pleased, but in schools we should not attempt to produce external success through effective performances.

A detailed analysis of the work at Steward St. Primary School, Birmingham

Although an indirect influence[16] of Jacques-Dalcroze and Laban may be detected in Stone's work, his experimentation in movement belongs to him and his staff and Story of a School is a modest, honest account of their discoveries. The marked contrast between the teaching contexts of Harriet Finlay-Johnson and Henry Caldwell Cook has already been noted. Stone's professional environment appears to have little in common with either of theirs. Faced with 240 inner city school children, aged seven to eleven, roughly 50 to a class, Stone was aware of the ugliness in their lives. He did not know what to offer; he was prepared to wait and watch. He saw his professional responsibility as discovering priorities and only then giving a strong lead. He concluded that these deprived children could not learn anything until they could be freed into expressing themselves. The Arts seemed to open up a possible avenue.

Thus, tentatively, this headteacher learnt how and what to teach. Early ventures in paint, crayon and clay revealed an uneven capacity among his pupils in respect of interest, concentration and imagination, qualities which, he noticed, also varied from activity to activity. These three criteria were to become the yardsticks by which he measured the experience of each pupil, the experience claiming priority, in his view, over the results. Stone was aware that for these city children to develop, they must first become 'free' and 'For a child to be free, the first essential is that he should move easily.'

With charming honesty Stone admits that he did not know how to do this, drawing, mistakenly at first, on his own experience of country dancing and then abandoning that rigid course for something akin to 'Modern Dance' derived from Laban, which he describes as having limitations but 'infinitely better' than anything he had introduced so far. He and his staff realised, not unlike Jacques-Dalcroze, that children needed to find their own basic rhythms and patterns through 'natural movements of walking, running, skipping, jumping, hopping etc.' A break-through appeared when his pupils were able to build on Laban's 'efforts', making them their own and gaining in confidence as a result. The gradual improvement in the pupils' ability to express themselves uninhibitedly through movement affected everything they did, socially and educationally. Stone finally reaches the following pedagogical conclusion:

And soon it became obvious that the creative urge expressed in all the arts comes from the same source. Although the way it is expressed in each particular art is somewhat different, all the arts have a common beginning.

That common beginning is movement – movement, something primitive and fundamental, so it seems to me: not movement for expressing emotion or ideas, which becomes Dance: not movement which makes us feel we want to say something, which is Drama: not movement for developing bodily strength or skills, which is Physical Training: but movement for movement's sake, the starting point of all the arts.

This conception of movement as an identifiable component on which all the arts can be based is not far removed from Jacques-Dalcroze's own thinking. What is different here is that Stone is setting his conclusions in a school context. He selects the three school subjects which might be expected to include movement – Dance, Drama and Physical Education – and argues that there is a form of movement-training independent of but also nurturing of each of these. His thesis is that such training provides the foundation for all the arts in general and for other 'movement' subjects in particular.

This publication, which amounts to no more than a pamphlet, marks the beginning of a view of Primary Education that for the next twenty years held considerable currency among a select group of Her Majesty's Inspectors, in certain localities of England.[18] It seems likely that HMI saw the Steward Street experiment as an early interpretation of Laban's philosophy.

The pamphlet also had influence on the way Drama was to be viewed, for its central thesis required Drama to be seen as but one of the three 'movement' subjects and, along with Physical Training and Dance, dependent on a foundation of rhythmic movement. This 'movement' approach to Drama was to become a central feature of Peter Slade's work. Historically, it also marks the beginning of determined opposition to the 'Speech-training' approach described in the previous chapter.[19]

It would be misleading to suggest that Stone set out from the beginning of his time at Steward Street to test out what I have called his 'central thesis'. Indeed it is more likely that his views were not articulated until he came to write the pamphlet, for the account he gives of practice represents a journey of following a hunch rather than implementing a hypothesis.

In the early days at the school Drama was regarded as 'Mime', but it becomes clear from Stone's descriptions that 'Mime' at Steward Street was not the practice of rigid, occupational mime introduced by Irene Mawer. Just as Jacques-Dalcroze saw Eurhythmics as musical expression, so Stone seems to have linked Miming with Music. It took place against a background of carefully selected music, so that the children's actions no doubt at times appeared to be an extension of the sounds emitted from the gramophone or the piano. Stone gives two significantly contrasted accounts:

> I remember in a mime of the nativity in which the whole school participated the difficulty the children had in making a slow entrance. The angels walked down the hall to the music of Roger Quilter's 'Children's Overture', blowing imaginary trumpets. How these youngsters waddled, as they tried to keep their steps in time with the slow beat of the music and play their trumpets at the same time!
>
> ...Two years later, when they had more experience of movement through dance and effort training, we revived the same Nativity mime, and their awkwardness in moving to a slow time was gone. ...
>
> In the first instance, much of the spontaneity had unavoidably been killed by constant practice in trying to achieve a certain balance. In the second instance... spontaneity was not killed by constant repetition.

There are a number of things to be noted from this anecdote. Whereas most teachers using Mime assumed the classroom was an appropriate place for its practice, Stone's Mime, conceived of as movement in space or (to use Jacques-Dalcroze's terminology) 'musical gesture', required a hall space, a space that could be filled with sound as well as bodies. All Stone's examples in his pamphlet seem to include having a group of pupils moving to music across from one end of the school hall to the other. Whereas in the first instance above, the pupils suffered from the imposition of a slow beat, in the second instance, they were freed to make the music their own. In respect of Jacques-Dalcroze's levels of abstraction, the above examples are illustrative, the first, 'trying to keep in step to the music' veering towards the specific, compared with the second attempt in which the pupils captured the quality of the music, finding the 'musical gesture'.

Also implicit in Stone's description is the assumption that a Mime is a 'Composition', devised mainly by the teachers. A repertoire of stories and accompanying music could be built up by a teacher, so that, as in this example, it could be taken out and reworked two years later. Seen as a created event for a large number of pupils, 'constant practice' did not seem out of place.

It should not be assumed, however, that this was the normal 'constant practice' of rehearsal towards a public event, as Finlay-Johnson, Caldwell Cook or Langdon might have understood it. Certainly the Mime was to be shared, but as a communal experience within the school. The 'constant practice' did no more than fulfil an understood obligation to do something well. Stone is quite firm on the point:

> ...I am quite sure that when the child is miming and using this medium as a purely creative art an audience has a detrimental effect on the sincerity and value of this medium of expression – only very privileged people were allowed to see drama in school, and only a few at a time.

This choice of expression, 'pure creative art', should be noted. Stone himself contrasts it with 'interpretative art', giving life to a written play. This distinction was to feature significantly in the theoretical writings of Peter Slade and others for more than a generation after the publication of Stone's pamphlet. It should be noted, too, that both forms of expression, the 'creative' and the 'interpretative', were to be regarded as art. Stone does not appear to consider 'inner reflection', as Jacques-Dalcroze does, of the creator becoming, in the act of creating, 'both actor and spectator of his own composition.' He may well have been aware of this as a psychological concept, but not felt it necessary to write about it in a short publication.

Stone and his staff discovered that the movement training began to affect the children's art (including Marion Richardson hand-writing) and their creative writing. Music as a time-tabled 'subject', however, seemed to remain at an uninspired level. Stone wonders whether this was because it was approached as an 'interpretative art'. He reinforces his point with: 'The only spark of real creative work developed when we composed our own rhyme and tunes for our dramatic work.' Stone finally [and perhaps mistakenly] arrives at a developmental formula: (a) The 'repetitive' stage; (b) The 'expressive' stage and (c) The 'communicative' stage. Significantly, he does not attempt to align this sequence with any age grouping.

By the 1940s teachers were beginning to require a special kind of space for doing drama, as well as a special place on the time-table. If drama was to become part of a Physical Training programme as it was for A.L. Stone, then the School Hall was the kind of space it needed. It certainly affected what acting could be. The 'amateur actor' pupil could utilise the stage end of the school hall – but not if he was stripped for P.E.! and Marjorie Hourd's pupil would no longer find an intimate niche for 'the paw under the door'.

And yet Stone, like Hourd, was seeking a poetic style. We have seen that Jacques-Dalcroze was conscious of an incongruity of styles in the example cited above when a dancer picks up a 'real' flower from the floor of the stage. Stone has his own anecdote that makes a related point:

> In the story of Arthur and the Knights of the Round Table, I gave the Archbishop a gold tinsel crown with which to crown Arthur. Of his own desire, he preferred to crown Arthur with an imaginary crown. It was, he said, a much better crown than the one I had given him.

For us to be satisfied that this was indeed an improvement we need to have it confirmed that the child's crowning of Arthur was to be something more than mimetic, that it expressed the poetry of Jacques-Dalcroze's 'musical gesture'. If the latter, then, one might wonder, to raise an issue Stone tended to be dogmatic about, whether the presence of an audience would have made any difference. Of course, it is likely that Stone, along with Jacques-Dalcroze, would have argued that the work fails when such gesture is aimed at pleasing an audience. Both claimed that what was created was art and that it would 'speak' to sensitive onlookers.

Notes

1   Board of Education (1931) *The Primary School Report: Report of the consultative Committee on the Primary School* HMSO

2   Findlay, J.J. (1930) The Foundations of Education Vol 2 ULP, p.24 (footnote)

3   Some years earlier Findlay had written a brief account: 'Eurhythmics'in *Educational Movements and Methods* (1924) by John Adams (Ed.), D.C. Heath London pp.63-72 of Jacques-Dalcroze's 'Eurhythmics' in a collection of essays edited by Professor John Adams. Inspired by its philosophy, Findlay, as an educationist, hastened to translate 'Eurhythmics' into curriculum terms, locating it between Physical Education and Music. He puts it as: 'the rhythms of the body' in an intimate relation 'with the rhythms of sound.' (p.68)

4   Whereas some teachers no doubt were impressed, others were threatened. One Physical Education expert, writing a chapter in Professor John Adams' The New Teaching in 1918, gives a laconic warning: '...no amount of Eurythmics, however graceful and fascinating, will teach a child the best way to jump a ditch or climb a rope.' [Campbell, Guy M. (1918) 'Physical Education' in *The New Teaching* by John Adams p.367

5   Stone, Peter (1948) *The Story of a School* HMSO

6   A third influence from the continent in the early decades of this century was Rudolf Steiner who saw education as of the spirit, '....a spirituality which comes to expression in the physical image of man.' [Steiner, Rudolf (1971) *Human Values in Education: Ten Lectures given in Arnheim* (Holland) July 17-24, 1924, Translated by Vera Compton-Burnett for the Rudolf Steiner Press London p.46]

7   *The Arts in School* (1982 Caloustie Gulbenkian Foundation London) is an example of a theoretical exposition relating to Arts education founded on a generic base for all Arts. David Best [as in, for example, 'Generic Arts: An Expedient Myth' in *Journal of Art and Design Education* (1992)] is the key figure opposing such a theory.

8   An unpublished play written in 1993 by Peter Wynne-Wilson celebrates the work of the school during the 1940's. It is called *Heads or Tales* and was given a school

tour by 'Big Brum' theatre company during Autumn 1993. John Somers of Exeter University has been engaged in research (so far unpublished) on Steward Street.

9   He was known as Peter Stone by colleagues and friends, although his initials were accurately recorded as A.L.

10 Olive Moore wrote: 'Unable to continue working with the Nazis, who saw in this theory of freedom and fulfilment through rhythm re-education a threat to their own harsh indoctrination practices, Mr. Laban came to England with some of his pupils.' [in 'Rudolf Laban' by Olive Moore in the Special 75th birthday number, December, 1954 of *The Laban Art of Movement Guild Magazine*.] Laban's first publication in English was *Effort* (1941) Macdonald and Evans Ltd London. His better known book was *Modern Educational Dance* (1948) Macdonald and Evans London.

11 In 1942 Laban collaborated with F.C. Lawrence, a Manchester industrial consultant. Between them they invented 'The Laban Lawrence Test for Selection and Placing', a means of identifying the kind of machine most suitable for each worker, based on an operative's natural movements. It is interesting to note that this industrialist became vice-president of the Laban Art of Movement Guild [See Olive Moore (1954) *ibid* p.39].

12 See Thornton, S. (1971) *A Movement Perspective of Rudolf Laban* Macdonald and Evans London, p.9

13 Herbert Read, publishing in 1943 before Laban became known outside a small coterie of admirers, identifies Jacques-Dalcroze as the true interpreter of Plato: 'It is extraordinary that we should have had to wait for a Swiss music master to rediscover the truths so eloquently proclaimed by Plato' Read, Herbert (1943) *Education Through Art* Faber London p.65. On an earlier page, however, Read regrets that '...successful as the Dalcroze movement has been, there is no disposition on the part of educational authorities in Europe or America to make it the basis of the whole educational system.'

14 'Effort is the common denominator for the various strivings of the body and mind which become observable in the child's body' (p.18 of Modern Educational Dance). Laban classified his 'efforts' (See Laban R. and Lawrence F. C. (1947) *Effort* Macdonald and Evans London) into Floating, Gliding, Wringing, Punching, Dabbing, Slashing and Pressing.

15 Laban, Rudolf (1948) Modern Educational Dance Macdonald and Evens London p.50

16 An example of a direct influence on a English and Drama teacher at Secondary level is Alan Garrard who records his indebtedness to Laban. [Wiles, John and Garrard, Alan (1968) *Leap to Life: An Experiment in Youth and School Drama* Chatto and Windus London

17 Ruth Stone, Staff Inspector of Physical Training for Girls, Jim Gill, HMI in charge of Teacher-Training, and John Allen, HMI for Drama, for example, were to become devotees of the method and helped turn a 'thesis' into an official 'policy'. I can recall a certain growing preciousness associated with movement education.

On one occasion I was taking part in a workshop for teachers conducted by Peter Stone. When it was over I moved to ask him a question, but Jim Gill intervened by explaining 'You have just witnessed a great artist at work; he now needs to be left alone'.

18 Particularly Birmingham City and the West Riding of Yorkshire, to which authority A.L. Stone was appointed, after his headship at Steward Street, as Organiser for Physical Training .

19 Stone makes the following comment on Speech-Training: 'Speech training as such had little value, I discovered, with these children, but when they spoke, as a result of their emotional interpretation through movement and mime, their speech was clear and well enunciated and could easily be corrected...we achieved a certain level of clear and well-enunciated speech throughout the school without making any laborious effort to supcrimpose another language, which so often happens in speech training.' p.21

20 Stone A. L. (1949) *ibid* p.18

SECTION THREE
SLADE AND WAY

CHAPTER SEVEN
PETER SLADE

A brief summary of Peter Slade's professional work:
'a professional of that new profession of Drama Adviser'[1]
Having been a free-lance actor and director, story-writer, radio script-writer and presenter, Peter Slade in 1943 at the age of 31 took up the newly created post, intended to bestow status on *amateur* drama.[2] The terms of reference of his appointment required that he should train leaders, advise on choice of plays and raise standards of production. Slade, in his publications, makes it clear that he had rather different ideas about what the 'new profession' should entail: he succeeded in becoming the first 'professional' in drama *education*, concerned with enlightened practice with children.

His partially autobiographical publication, *Experience of Spontaneity* (1968), includes fascinating anecdotes of his early observations of himself in different kinds of make-believe play from boyhood to manhood. They read as though the self-spectator in Slade, even as he played, recognised a significance he was predestined to tell others about. The excitement, genuineness and spiritual vigour of spontaneous dramatic group activity was the message he devoted his life to passing on to others.

He had established his first company (simply called 'The Children's Theatre Company) in 1932, always seeking new ways of getting his actors to break with a proscenium arch tradition. He had seized opportunities to do drama with disturbed young people and those with

119

learning difficulties. Interested in the therapeutic and preventitive potential of Child Drama,[3] he had contacted the medical profession for advice and started a clinic. He took on free-lance lecturing engagements and consultations and became an unofficial adviser to educational institutions and local authorities. He joined the staff of the BBC as 'the youngest uncle on Children's Hour'.

Becoming a full-time County Adviser, however, gave Peter Slade a more solid platform from which he could expound his philosophy of child education – and extend his own practice in school. But it was the appointment to the City of Birmingham Education Committee in 1947, the most prestigious position related to drama education created in Britain to date, that allowed Slade to become a public figure – and the leading authority on all matters to do with drama and children. In keeping with his and Drama's new status, it was fitting that he was invited to broadcast on the BBC Midland Home Service, 15th July, 1948.[4] He began:

> These days Drama is almost in the air. Everyone seems to be talking about it, you hear of conferences everywhere; and all this goes side by side with a general recognition of Drama as an important part of Education, and this in turn has ultimately led to the appointment of Drama Advisers under local Education Authorities... But when you come to schools...you quickly find that the approach to children in this subject should be very different indeed from that which used to be considered right for adults.

When Slade claims, optimistically, that 'everyone seems to be talking about it', he is responding to an undoubted change of attitude towards Drama since the war. Conferences were held,[5] journals were published,[6] courses for teachers were run,[7] and, perhaps the key event of the period, an Examining Board was set up for leaders in Youth Drama.[8] Peter Slade's influence was pivotal in all these activities, but of special significance was that the Ministry of Education, in setting up its first Working Party (1948) in Drama education, invited Peter Slade to be one of it members. Its draft report, written by George Allen HMI in February 1951 was never published, but nevertheless it allowed a Ministry policy to emerge.

That policy included the recommendation that in future the teaching of drama may well 'involve jettisoning much of the existing theatre tradition.'[9] and that, at least until the Secondary age group, Drama was to be perceived as 'a natural activity, not a 'subject'' Also, teachers should be wary of 'dramatisation' in case, through lack of 'artistic output', imaginations were merely to be 'singed' rather than 'kindled'. A further major plank of their policy was that language was to be seen as a natural development from movement.

Now, we shall see that the above recommendations drawn from the Ministry of Education document could very well serve as a summary of Peter Slade's own Child Drama ideology. It may not be going too far to say that the Working Party *relied* on Peter Slade to help it evolve a philosophy it was ready to believe in, drawn from a practice it knew little about. What set Slade apart from others on the Working Party was that he was already practising the new approach and had been doing so, unreported, for many years. The members of the Working Party no doubt had before them evidence of the four strands of development in drama we have discussed in the previous section of this thesis. According to their chairman,[10] they were united in opposing the 'school play' approach and the study of Shakespeare as 'a mine of useful knowledge'. It seems that what I have called the 'Amateur Drama' trend and 'English as textual study' dominated the overall scene. The negative attitude of the professional theatre towards 'creative' drama also generally prevailed. Respected theatrical entrepreneurs such as Harley Granville-Barker, a supporter of Caldwell Cook, challenged the very concept of the young actually acting a play[11] and were even more opposed to the notion of 'self-expression' in school drama. George Allen suggests the Working Party members were clearer on what they did *not* want than what they did want.

Peter Slade's concept of 'Child Drama'

For Slade 'Drama' was the word that best described the 'Art of Living'. It stood for any spontaneous activity generated by the child him/herself in pursuit of 'doing'[12] and 'struggling' with life. Slade does not attempt to justifiy this broad usage of 'drama'; he simply draws our attention to a phenomenon: 'This book is about a very wonderful thing which exists in our midst but is as yet hardly noticed.' With such an arresting claim (and all Slade's writing for the next forty years continues in this vein of having discovered something so important that he has to share it) Slade demanded of his readers that they look more closely at the children engaged in Play and that they reappraise their expectations of Drama.

Drama is to be everything that is good in life and is even to embrace the other arts. Whereas, as Slade explains, '...Play with dolls and toys, I would call drama of the obvious kind', he adds, '...as a creative form of 'Doing', Art is Drama of the less obvious kind.' In a footnote on the same page Slade avers that 'Where climax is intentionally brought in and enjoyed, Music might be said to be bordering on Drama.'[13] and he takes the point even further in a personal note to me in January, 1995: 'Music with no drama-thinking in it would be very dull and makes bad use of timing, pause, quietness and climax.'

Slade intends, through this 'hard sell', to put Drama at the centre of living and, consequently, at the centre of education, and, more specifically, at the centre of all the arts. From now on, he believes, the quality of a school would be determined by its Drama, and, indeed, the quality of home-life for the pre-school child. The 'sensitive' parent and 'sensitive' teacher are to carry the same kind of responsibility to the child's make-believe play.

Slade's theory of Personal and Projected Play

From his close observation of children over many years, Slade evolved a developmental theory of Child Drama, arguing that at each stage of development[14] the healthy child will engage in a balanced diet of two distinct forms of play, although for the very young child Play will be predominantly projected. 'The true distinction in Play is that of personal Play and projected Play'. He elaborates:

> Personal Play is obvious Drama; the whole Person or Self is used. It is typified by movement and characterisation. We note the dance entering the experience of being things or people.

Projected Play is Drama, too; the whole mind is used, but the body not so fully. The child stands still, sits, lies prone, or squats, and may use chiefly the hands. The main action takes place outside the body, and the whole is characterised by extreme mental absorption. Strong mental projection is taking place.

This categorisation of play is unlike that of any previous play theorist. It appears, at first sight, to be based, not on structure, nor function, nor content of Play, but on the extent to which the body is critical to the activity. Slade gives a list of associated activities, so that the reader might understand the distinction:

> Out of personal Play we may expect to develop later: running, ball games, athletics. dance, riding cycling, swimming, fighting, hiking. These are forms of acting. To these should be added Acting in the full sense.

The 'whole' body is to be used. Notice also the claim that 'These are forms of acting'. So keen is Slade to establish that Play and Drama are one and the same thing he logically follows his own thesis through by referring to these commonplace physical activities as 'acting'. But, no doubt aware of an absurdity here, he deftly invents an 'Acting' with a capital 'A', presumably to represent that kind of play behaviour characterised by impersonation, leaving acting with a small 'a' to cover all action.

He proceeds to give a similar list for 'Projected Play':

> Out of projected Play we may expect to develop later: Art, playing instruments, love of freshwater fishing, non-violent games (from snakes and ladders to chess), reading, writing; observation, patience, concentration, organisation and wise government. To these should be added interest in puppets and model theatres, and, in the full sense, Play Production.

These activities too are to be seen as Drama, but, once more, there is to be a 'full sense' of 'Play Production' with a capital 'P'. He then re-affirms the 'physical' basis for his classification, adding a sound dimension:

> In personal Play the tendency is towards noise and physical exertion on the part of the person involved; and if noise is not employed, exertion is. In projected Play the tendency is towards quietness and physical stillness; and if there is not quiet some physical stillness is there.

For Slade, 'noise' and 'exertion' represent something more than crude instances of assertive behaviour; they are also the raw material of aesthetic expression. Moving to an aesthetic frame, one may see 'noise' and 'exertion' as points along two of the three basic dimensions of theatre: sound/silence and movement/stillness respectively.

That there appears to be some overlap in Slade's theorising between psychological and theatrical explanations, however, is no accident. It was not whimsicality that prompted Slade to insist that all these play activities should be called 'drama'. His perspective on how children behave was focused through the lens of his theatrical experience, for one of his realisations was that previous authoritative studies of children had largely ignored their theatrical impulses. His claim was that you can look fully at the development of a child only if you perceive the whole child, including the child as artist, and as a theatrical artist in particular. Any observation he makes about the psychology or sociology of child behaviour, therefore, tends to be finally expressed by Slade in artistic terms. When he writes, for example, of young children's typical satisfaction in 'banging things', Slade interprets such experimentation as the development of 'rhythm and climax'. Thus a *psychological* phenomenon, 'satisfaction from banging' is seen as having an *aesthetic* potential.

There are many facets to Slade's complex philosophy. I have here selected two for detailed discussion: his concept of acting in *space* and *sound* and his concept of *sincerity*.

Acting in Space and Sound

Peter Slade is fond of describing Child Drama events as 'beautiful'. For example, '...and a very clear, exceedingly beautiful piece of theatre is acted out before our eyes. The climax, so beautifully timed, is of high realms of Drama and Music.' and later: 'There does, then, exist a Child Drama, which is of exquisite beauty and is of a high Art Form in its own right.' To the casual reader these kind of comments may sound like affectation, but they nevertheless reflect Slade's theory. Children's acting behaviour is to be viewed in terms of an aesthetic dimension, specifically a spatial/musical dimension in relation to Personal play. Formal meaning is to take precedence over content, to such an extent that, for example, how a group use the available space, in a drama about 'finding a mysterious box' might be, in Slade's view, of more immediate concern to both teacher and participants than the reason for its being there, or, indeed, what is in it!

This attending to form as a way of making expression significant has a respectable pedigree in aesthetic education, dating from Friedrich Schiller (1788), who describes the disposition eloquently[15]:

> Uncoordinated leaps of joy turn into dance, the unformed movements of the body into graceful and harmonious language of gesture; the confused and indistinct cries of feeling become articulate, begin to obey the laws of rhythm, and to take on the contours of song. If the Trojan host storms on to the battlefield with piercing shrieks like a flock of cranes, the Greek army approaches it in silence, with noble and measured tread. In the former case we see only the exuberance of blind forces; in the latter, the triumph of form and the simple majesty of law.

Slade too is disposed to perceive in children's own drama the 'harmonious language of gesture', the 'law of rhythm' and the 'contours of song', but, Slade would have us understand, their achievement of 'high realms of drama' is to be largely unconscious. Indeed it is the very lack of contrived artistry that contributes to its beauty. Within each child, Slade claims, there is a Child Drama that intuitively seeks beauty of form, a form which, when expressed collectively, captures moments of theatre. For some of Slade's followers the connection between the 'Drama within the child' and 'Theatre' was no doubt elusive, for it was perhaps easier to assume that Slade intended an anti-theatre posture rather than try to grapple with a new conception of theatre.

Slade's regret is that so many teachers failed to see what is there. Even the most pedestrian improvisation may bear incipient spatial, aural, structural, or climactic indicators that enhance the creation. Because the teacher fails to see these possibilities, s/he is left wondering both how to build on the original and how to find theatre in an activity so indifferent to 'performance'.

Slade invites teachers to re-examine what is going on when children play and to see it as 'art'. He wants them to understand that when children and teacher work together as artists in the classroom (or rather in the school-hall), they are creating theatre. The choice of photographs included in Child Drama, and the written references to background sound effects or music, to different levels, to 'filling-space', to mood and climax, to shapes on the floor, to 'language-flow', even to lighting, betray a theatrical awareness on the part of the author when he watches a drama activity. Slade is looking for a new form of theatre embedded in Personal play. Many of his contemporaries, leading writers on drama education, sought to make bridges between a kindergarten and a proscenium arch: – imaginative, expressive dramatic exercises were invented by exponents such as E.J. Burton, in the name of 'free-expression' and drama classrooms became lively places. Peter Slade was not building a bridge, however; he was changing the template. 'Theatre' was already there in the kindergarten, but, of course, not theatre of the proscenium, nor theatre waiting to be directed by someone else, nor theatre setting out to entertain someone else.

Slade held his theatrical lens over the whole group; not just the few selected to 'act out at the front of the classroom'; his new conception of theatre was 'group' theatre, its formal elements described above dependent on broad strokes created in uncluttered space. He was also aware of the individual child as an actor in his own private space, not an actor striving for an effect, but an actor 'centred' within an enclosed 'circle of attention': 'They act outwards from Self all round the body.' This notion of 'a circle of attention', Slade acknowledges, coincides with Stanislavskian (1937) methodology which trained professional actors to concentrate, to the exclusion of anything or anybody outside the circle, on either 'inner', imagined objects or objects literally within the prescribed circle. When a child is acting spontaneously he is metaphorically drawing a circle round himself, isolating himself from distractions. Slade calls this 'acting-in-the-round', not the same as 'theatre-in-the-round', but these three-dimentional qualities of child acting should be passed on to the best kind of adult arena theatre. We have seen that Marjorie Hourd (1948) voices a similar point when she puts it succinctly: 'The round' is an inner quality...' requiring the actors, not so much to 'look round as *be* round.'

In 'acting-in-the-round' the child invades space with his whole body, moving in any direction, relating particularly to floor space and learning to respect the space of others: 'It is during this movement-at-will that the Child begins to cover the actual floor space in so interesting and beautiful a manner, filling the space as if it were a picture.' Thus Slade gives another glimpse here of his central thesis that drama embraces all the arts, that the child absorbed in acting is making a picture on a large canvas, or sculpting figures in three-dimensional space, moments to be caught by the camera or the observant teacher, and presumably, to be felt unconsciously by the children. This 'making space significant' [a feature we have already come across to some extent in the work of R.L. Stone (1949)] is, for Slade, an overriding characteristic of classroom acting.

The concept of 'Sincerity'

It seems that most writers about children's drama, Slade included, assumed that their readers know what is meant by 'sincerity'. And yet, it might seem ironical to apply the term 'sincerity', a word of high moral overtones,[16] to an art that is based on what Stanislavski calls a 'palpable lie'.[17] Nor does it make immediate sense to say of a child's performance: 'S/he played, say, a villain or a con man or a murderer 'sincerely'.'

I will begin this section by looking at how some writers on professional theatre use the term, in order first, to tease out how Peter Slade intended it should be understood in relation to classroom acting, and, secondly, to argue for a particular usage. Some authors see sincerity merely as a quality compensating for absence in technique: for instance, the authors of the 1926 Board of Education The Drama in Adult Education Report[18] wrote "Sincerity' of acting in amateur/ children's acting often atones in great measure for deficiencies in technique and finish'. This begs the question 'to whom'? To whom is 'sincerity' compensating for lack of technique? The authors clearly have an audience[19] in mind, an audience of adults who are counted on to adjust their 'normal' expectations of performance. Apparently child performers and untrained adult performers share this capacity for 'sincerity' without 'technique'.

The above comment by the 1926 Report writers does not explain what 'sincerity' is, unless it is meant merely to be understood as 'well-intentioned' or 'artless'. Such a view would deny a more positive usage applied by some authors in respect of professional actors. Stanislavski (1948), for example, expects of his actors that, through the 'creative if' (an expression also adopted by Slade) an imagined truth will command a 'sincere belief'. Linked with *belief* in this way, 'sincerity' represents the HIGH point on a 'belief barometer' – the lowest point presumably reading 'disbelief' or 'cynicism'.

Thus, on this basis, there are three qualities: (1) 'lack of sincerity', because of insufficient or intermittent belief in what is imagined [to be found in the untrained and trained alike] (2) 'sincere acting', meaning adequate belief in what is imagined [to be found in both untrained and trained] and (3) 'sincere acting combined with performance techniques' [to be found in the trained only]. Keeping to this 'sincerity as belief' metaphor, there is a fourth category, for the trained, described by Peter Brook (1968)[21] as follows: 'So he [the young professional actor] searches for technique: and soon he acquires a know-how. Easily, know-how can become a pride and end in itself. It becomes dexterity without any other aim than the display of expertise – in other words, the art becomes insincere,' Thus 'insincerity', in Brook's usage, is different from 'lack of sincerity', the former representing a trap for the trained actor only.

This kind of simple categorisation, into 'without sincerity', 'sincerity', 'sincerity plus technique' and 'insincerity', still does not tell us enough about sincerity in acting. For instance, it fails to explain how anyone can be 'sincere' in an action of 'pretence', or as Peter Brook puts it[22]: '...he (the actor) must practise how to be insincere with sincerity and how to lie truthfully'. The answer appears to require, as we shall see, a conceptual adjustment, a displacement or overriding of 'pretence' and 'lie' with the notion of capturing a 'truth'.

Other theoretical writers on theatre adopt this latter, more positive view of sincerity in acting, and in so doing take us nearer to what Peter Slade understood by 'sincerity' in Child Drama. They tend to write in terms of 'truths' created by the fictional act. For instance, Charles McGaw (1964)[23] writes: 'The actor's imagination allows him to abstract the essence of truth from the familiar and the everyday...' Such an observation matches[24] the philosophical position adopted by Cassirer (1953): '...reproduction never consists in retracing, line for line, a specific content of reality; but in selecting a pregnant motif...'. The actor, it seems, abstracts from reality. Is 'sincerity', then, to be linked with the meaningfulness of that abstraction? Slade does not attempt within his extensive publications to define how he is using the term, but when I sent him a draft of my doctoral thesis, he wrote comments, suggesting he thought that the 'belief' metaphor applies to an audience situation, for sincere acting is that which has 'believability' *for the audience*, in spite of 'lack of attack, poor diction, clumsy foot work and letting the scene down'. He goes on to suggest, however, that what he calls 'the best child's creation' (presumably to be found in classroom drama and, perhaps, exceptionally in 'performance drama') is 'truth' – for it is, as Slade puts it, a 're-testing and a deep proving of something the child has experienced in real life, being played out before us.'

In the above explanation Slade is connecting with two sources commonly assumed to be contributory to imitation – the present reality of the world and past personal experience. He seems to be linking 'truth' and 'imitation' within the concept of 'sincerity'. Let us first look at imitation specifically in Piaget's study of Child Play. After watching a near two-year old girl play with her dolls Piaget concluded, 'When real scenes are reproduced in games with dolls, imitation is at its maximum, but there is also a transposition for subjective ends...'[25] On the previous page Piaget gives an example of what he means:

At 2;7 [2 years, 7 months] she made up by herself a long game of washing, drying and ironing her dolls' sheets, then gave all the dolls a bath, which was very well imitated in detail.

In this illustration, Piaget has selected make-believe play at its most realistic; although, the child was not, in actuality, washing, drying and ironing sheets: her actions could be said to meet an acceptable level (acceptable, apparently to both the child and the adult observer) of realism. Piaget himself does not acknowledge the possibility of a conventional signing of reality, but concedes the possibility of 'a transposition for subjective ends'. That he is disposed to comment on the impressive degree of accurate detail suggests that he might have seen the episode as exceptional. Indeed many of his examples of child play include but token imitative actions. From this it may be concluded that the meaning of a make-believe event may not be dependent on an intention to imitate accurately, if 'imitating accurately' refers to external features of the model. There may, instead, be a form of engagement with the model relating to some aspect for which selected external features may be but a point of reference. For instance, Piaget cites the example of a near two-year old sliding a shell down the edge of a box while explaining 'Cat on wall'. Piaget further refers (echoing

Slade's 'a deep proving of something') to examples of symbolic play that 'liquidate a disagreeable situation by re-living it as make-believe..', one example being the child who, afraid of the tractor in the field next to the garden, puts her doll on an imaginary tractor. Now the tractor, in this kind of instance, does not have to resemble a tractor, nor is the child required to do accurate 'steering-a-tractor actions'.

Thus Piaget follows McGaw in seeing make-believe as an abstraction from reality rather than a pure imitation of it. They have, however, distinctly different ends in mind. Whereas Piaget sees accuracy of imitation undermined by an egocentric subjectivism, McGaw perceives what is abstracted as a more penetrating truth. Piaget, examining child behaviour, sees the child in play distorting reality; McGaw, analysing stage behaviour, sees the artist commenting on it. Both may behave independently of verisimilitude.

It seems that in enactment therefore, whether in play or on stage, imitation as copying appearances is almost irrelevant, but identification[26] is paramount. It is the degree and quality of identification that partly determine the choice of abstraction. The last child's intensity of identification with the tractor is unmistakable – she was afraid of it – but the intellectual quality of the identification was perhaps superficial, maybe based on no more information than that there was a monster over the garden fence. Whatever the level of identification, it could be said that it was 'true for the child'. It can be argued, then, that imitative actions in play are consequent on the meaning the child is abstracting from reality as s/he understands it. The child abstracts a 'truth' from the situation as s/he sees it for the purpose of representation. What is represented is the child's understanding of, not a facsimile of, a reality. In adult acting the 'actor's understanding of a reality' may not always be enough to satisfy a public notion of that reality, but what is created is nevertheless based primarily on the actor's identification with the world. 'Identification' is related to the degree to which the child or actor successfully represents that 'truth'. It will be necessary, in my final chapter, to take the relevance of this conclusion in respect of child play a little further, more precisely indicating *what kind* of 'truth'. If the concept of child make-believe play is to have any relevance at all in a dramatic framework, a fundamental shift is needed beyond the received wisdom of most play theorists.

McGaw adds an additional responsibility for the actor expressed as 'unexpected significance' which Slade would urge as outside the scope of children: 'The actor's imagination', writes McGaw, 'allows him to abstract the essence of truth from the familiar and the everyday, and give it new form which will command our attention and make us vitally aware of its significance.' We, the audience, are to have our attention arrested into seeing something afresh. Anthony Frost and Ralph Yarrow[27] add a further dimension to the stage actor's art: disponibilité, that experiential condition of being 'open to the moment'. That 'moment' is to include the audience in a spontaneous, existential sharing. This is to describe a stage performance at its best. Child Drama at its best is also of the 'existential moment', but in 'contented privacy'. Responding with 'openness' to one's fellow participants while retaining the integrity of what one is representing may well be another aspect of 'sincerity'.

If, according to Peter Slade, teachers attempt too early in their pupils' development to train them for adult theatre instead of their own drama, then a great deal of harm can be done. Asked from the floor of his lecture hall: 'Why is acting on a normal stage bad for young children?', Slade answered:

> Because it destroys Child Drama, and the Children then merely try to copy what adults call theatre. They are not successful in this, and it is not their way of playing. They need space, and don't need to be embroiled in the complicated technique of an artificial theatre form. It makes them conscious of the audience, spoils their sincerity and teaches them to show off.

As we have seen, some of Slade's contemporaries were already trying to break away from a rigidly held view that drama in schools should replicate adult theatre. The work of Mrs. Langdon and E.J. Burton, for example, challenged preconceptions about children's drama, but their innovatory suggestions sprang from an idiom of the proscenium stage. Slade was a true innovator in the sense that he changed the idiom of theatre. Consequently his message was rarely understood at first because he challenged educationalists to see differently, to teach differently, to judge differently.

Many of Slade's followers, not surprisingly, in reading the kind of answer about young children and adult theatre quoted above, jumped to the conclusion that Child Drama was anti-art and anti-theatre. This, as we have seen, was far from the case. On Page 105 of *Child Drama* Slade writes: 'First...let me reiterate that *Child Drama is an Art in itself, and would stand alone as being of importance* [his italics].' Thus he has identified an art of drama that is shot through with the magic of theatre, and yet he could not call it 'Child Theatre', for had he done so he may have unwittingly reinforced the very 'Beginners Please!' mentality he was struggling to oppose. He had to find a terminology that conveyed the development of the 'whole child' through Art, for ultimately, it is the child as a liver of life of which Art is an important part, that Slade wants us to look at.

Child Drama in Practice
From the 'trends' followed in Section Two of this study, it seems that a number of leading practitioners sought to promote particular lines of practice: dramatisation, textual study, speech, dramatic play, movement, mime, play performance etc. Against these kinds of specialisms, Peter Slade's approach could be described as eclectic, for within the pages of his various publications there appear examples of his own practice that spread across a whole spectrum of activities. He is as comfortable with a class of adolescents in Social Drama and with Dance Drama with Adults as with 'backward and disturbed' six to seven year olds, making up a story to play out Such eclecticism appears to defy any attempt to characterise Child Drama in terms of specific kinds of activity.

It is more likely to be defined in terms of 'freedom' and 'encouragement': 'freedom' from teacher interference, from the need to entertain an audience, from authoritative judgment and from moral pressure. 'Making up a story to play out', however, marked a distinct break with any of the methodologies associated with the four previous trends.

There was, too, a physical feature to his teaching, a characteristic that became known as 'exploration of space'. Given a choice between a classroom and a school hall, Slade would always opt for the larger space, for freedom from the normal clutter of a classroom. The most regularly used teaching space at Rea Street Centre was the central hall. His work was nevertheless adaptable to classroom constrictions.

Exploration of space is both liberating and constraining; interacting with other members of the class and using different levels of rostra, offer both stimulation and limitation. Slade, conscious of these contrary pulls, although occasionally permitting uninhibited playing, tended to employ one of two kinds of artistic constraint: (1) a story (mentioned above) made up by the teacher from the children's own ideas, to be enacted as the story was retold in a way that was flexibly open to innovation by the children or (2) some kind of sound stimulus or music, a selected record, percussion or, occasionally, piano accompaniment to which the class could either (a) move freely and spontaneously or (b) interpret in a prepared Dance Drama. Both these, (2a and b) were conceived of as 'Natural Dance', in which each person has the chance of developing personal style, a freer form of expression than the more structured interpretation associated with the Laban system of Movement.[28] Accompanying these artistic constraints were social constraints, such as beginning with the class spread out individually and equidistantly[29] and putting hands up to give suggestions, one at a time. Here is an example, in the first year of the Junior School, of both aesthetic and teacher control:

SELF: 'When I put the music on, I am going to suggest some funny things to you (*note, not 'I want you to'* [Slade's italics]). I'm going to make quick changes, just to see how quick and clever you are at getting into things. Ready?'

I put music on (*not forgetting to have put volume down -always-before starting, so no unwanted scrape or odd sound destroys the atmosphere*). I bring up some cheerful quick jazz.

SELF: 'You are someone in a hurry to do shopping. Off you go'. (*I often give a quick clap here so that people know **exactly** when to start. It avoids a lazy beginning and keeps a good strong control from the start. I hate to see a class that is not in hand. It is bad for discipline. The clap, in starting improvisation in these circumstances, is almost the parallel of the rise of the curtain in adult theatre. Everyone knows: **Now we begin**. When there is no curtain, there has to be something else and, to obtain the best work, it must be precise.* [Slade's italics and emphases])

Although he does not explicitly comment on it, Slade was no doubt aware of the ambiguity signalled by these architectural and pedagogical arrangements. To the children (and, no doubt, to their teachers) the association with Physical Training of being placed equidistantly in a school hall must have been overwhelming in the early days when Slade started his experimentation. A tradition of stripping down to vest and shorts for Drama dated from this time, not that Slade himself encouraged it, but those in the teaching profession, particularly Her Majesty's Inspectors who wanted imaginative, physical expression of this kind to be seen as an enlightened form of physical education, pressed for Drama as an extension of basic Laban movement – and, as such, 'vest and shorts' became the required attirement.[30]

Slade may have sensed that the physical exercise setting offered both the security born of familiarity[31] and the potential for physical freedom when the class were ready. Indeed Slade's maxim was 'beginning where people reveal they are in life.' His choice of physical setting and tight lesson structure combined with teacher-controlled, short, sharp commands requiring a series of instant, physical responses[32] may have seemed at odds with a creative activity, but the manner adopted by Slade of gentle, quiet tones[33] no doubt smoothed down the harsh edges of instructions, giving them a quality of an invitation. Slade wanted children to 'reveal where they are' when they were feeling safe. 'Space on their own' combined with teacher-instruction represented the familiar out of which freedom might burst. Some teachers, it seems, allowed the physical conditions to dictate a heavily imperious, 'physical instruction', style. Occasionally, Slade came across the following kind of lesson, with rapid changes of activity in too quick succession. The teacher's instructions with a class of 42 seven years old ('Turn yourselves into big fat frogs'; 'Now little baby frogs'; Now all asleep'; 'Now show me how your father walks' etc. etc. until they in turn represent horses, wheelbarrows, clowns, chariots, crocodiles and trees – all within a few minutes) draw Slade's tactful comments to the teacher: 'But you are using this as a P.E. period too, aren't you, when taking it at this speed? It is all right so long as you only suggest what to do not how to do it.'. Slade is only too aware that a series of instructions taken at this rate is merely a way of establishing a surface discipline not an invitation to creativity, resulting in an equally surface level of involvement.

It is instructive to see how Peter Slade himself treads delicately between teacher imposition of ideas and children's suggestions. The following suggestions to teachers are for an infant class of five and six years:

> ...try making a noise and saying, 'What does that sound remind you of?' 'What does it make you want to be or do?' Sometimes you may get little response, particularly at the beginning, before children fully understand that they are allowed and are encouraged to use their imaginations. Response at first may be rather traditional... You then may have to say what it reminds you of... you will be helping them to open up, to widen their vision. It also helps them to see how far they may go and give them rails to run on. They will learn that you will not deflate them, or laugh at them for saying imaginative things.

This brief quotation exemplifies principles of teaching that many 'progressive' classroom practitioners, especially in the arts, attempted to adopt. Slade recognised that children sometimes needed to be persuaded to be imaginative and to take risks. Thus what may sound like teacher imposition, is supplying them with a temporary track to run on, creating a mood of fun and freedom from which their imaginative ideas may spring. When the children, faced with this stranger's first question, are non-plussed, he might share with the class (and one can imagine how tentatively) what the sound reminds him of – not as a teacher who knows what needs to be done next, but as a 'fellow traveller' intrigued by a shared problem. Peter Slade has recaptured the vision of Harriet Finlay-Johnson of teacher and class as 'fellow-workers', prepared to be 'fellow-artists'. When they do take risks, his pupils discover that he accepts their wildest imaginings – and trust is established.

Slade, then, attempts to create (within the limits, it should be noted, of the 'once-a-week' Drama or P.E. lesson, or even worse, the 'one-off' occasion of his visit) an atmosphere of trust and happiness in which children might play, but it takes place, as we have seen, in an environmental and pedagogical context that militates against the kind of child play activity from which his philosophy derives.

A whole class are simultaneously required either to respond to teacher's or a fellow pupil's suggestion by springing into appropriate actions, which continue until the teacher decides on the next instruction or question, or builds a whimsical story for re-enactment. This appears to be far removed from child play and to make a mockery of an art form. In terms of education it appears to be no more worthwhile than if an art teacher asked his class rapidly, in succession, to draw cartoon figures.

However, one of the problems for a reader of Slade's accounts of particular lessons is that the mood of the pupils and the general atmosphere of the lesson cannot be grasped from the printed page. It is not possible to 'read' the (presumed) warmth of the response from children or young people to this smiling, friendly stranger, sounding more like an ally than a teacher, inviting them to venture into fantastic, silly, funny, nonsensical, unschool-like games. The invitation extended to them to shed their school selves was undoubtedly disarming. At a period in our educational history when the majority of schools followed a formal tradition, one can only assume that Peter Slade's judgement was sound and the method successful. In a formal school, children present their formal selves – they are well-practised in leaving their personalities, imaginations, feelings, opinions, guesses and humour at home. To expect them, perhaps just once a week, to be creative in a group, to be playful in a setting that inhibits play, appears to be asking the impossible. It seems that Peter Slade found a way of achieving just that.[34]

Slade's recipe for success seems, then, to have relied on whimsicality, what Peter Slade describes as 'a sort of poetic romanticism',[35] combined with a gentle but firm physical exercise type of control. There was another feature, however, that may have had something to do with the extraordinary attraction of his teaching style: his approach suspended the normally expected deference to 'meaning'. The meaning of anything created did not have to be sensible, worthwhile, significant, moral or useful. That such epithets rarely appear in Slade's practice or theory is one of the features that marks his work apart from that of his predecessors. Harriet Finlay-Johnson constantly referred to the usefulness of the knowledge acquired through dramatisation. While Henry Caldwell Cook held a high degree of tolerance for 'din and clash and horrors', he continually stressed learning 'to appreciate literature in its highest form.' Slade's emphasis too seems far removed from the 'poetic spirit' of Marjorie Hourd's literature-based dramatic method. Slade, of course, recognises the potential in dramatisation for learning, including the learning of school subjects and the learning relating to children with special needs, but such learning, during periods of what he calls 'pure Child Drama' is to be incidental, spontaneous, and not to the fore of the minds of either the pupils or the teacher. That he is alert too to the poetry of children's expression is seen in his obvious delight in what he calls 'language flow'.

Slade's approach freed pupils from an immediate obligation to learn directly from whatever the content happened to be, a sine qua non of most curriculum subjects. Thus Drama's kinship with physical education was not only a matter of physicality and lesson structure: both subjects were to be seen as *experiential*, as valuable in themselves. Slade persuaded his followers that the 'doing and struggling', the life-learning through Drama[36] was all-sufficient. The 'life-learning' was broader than specific content. As Slade expressed it in his private correspondence (1995): 'They learned other things ...that they might not learn in any other way – about space, self-expression, cooperation, tidy movement, clearer speech and communication.'

Acting behaviour in Slade's approach

Signing
Child Drama is essentially based on the concept of self expression, and yet at the moment of a teacher's instruction, pupils are required to find an instant, communicable response. It could be argued that Child Drama is dependent on a kind of acting unerringly related to 'conventional signing' or 'stereotyping'. Such an argument certainly appears to challenge Slade's theoretical rhetoric.

A way of containing the apparent contradiction is to accept the notion of two phases to the acting. If the pressure on the child to find a conventional representation is regarded as both temporary and protective, no more than a means of entry into true creativity, then it is conceivable that the conventionally expressed role or action of teacher's story becomes the individually expressed role or action when the child is ready. It is as if Slade is opening a safe, conventional door for the children to go through at their own pace, using whatever stereotype, if any, they need. Once through, they are free (and the lesson structure usually allows for it) to break-away into 'true' expression, which may or may not be understandable to an observer and which is independent of any need to show off to the teacher.

If we look at a typical Sladian story,[37] built up from suggestions from the class of 'blue hat', 'food' and 'umbrella', we can see how the stereotypic control implied in the tale offers the young children a high degree of safety:

> Once upon a time there was funny old man and he lived in a funny old house over there in that corner, and there were two things which he wanted very much in the shops over there... he shuffled out of the house and down the winding road... and by the road were trees which bent towards him as he passed, saying, each in turn, 'Good morning, old man good morning.' But when he got to the shops...

and when the story has finished he invites: 'Now, we'll act it, and you shall add some more ideas.' The class are required to follow a set course, stereotypically signing each event until they are ready to break away into a quality of acting that belongs to child play, in which conventional signing is contingent on the child's freedom to choose. Slade generously praises a Birmingham teacher's lesson which is a good example of this transformation into what he perceives as child theatre. With a class of 5 year olds the teacher, using piano accompaniment at first, gives a sequence of instructions to be slavishly followed by the young children, but then changes her strategy so that Slade is able to describe the new phase of her lesson in these terms:

> Two or three boys became postmen. The teacher saw that she had created the right atmosphere for Child Drama, and ceased to guide the class. She backed quietly into a corner... [*The class, spread across the hall in naturally formed groups, become different kinds of transport etc*]...

> This was the supreme moment of real Child Theatre... Lorries were driving towards the train between the tea-parties and behind the postmen; inter-crossing waves of six and six aeroplanes were weaving a snakewise dance in the only space left, their arms outstretched and banking as they ran... I longed for a gallery to see from. This is what we should realise. The Child creates theatre in his own way, own form, own kind. It is original art of high creative quality.

Content

The activity is nevertheless markedly different from self-generated child play, in that even the new ideas introduced freely by the child are logically determined by the teacher's story structure. It seems unlikely that there might be an input from individual children equivalent in personal concern and intensity to the child in Piaget's example, referred to above of repeatedly playing the 'monster tractor', although the occasional child might use any fictional context as an escape into his/her own obsessions. (Such is the openness and tolerance of Child Drama that this kind of personal indulgence can be accepted and contained.)

A curious mixture of serious and non-serious, or rather, 'tongue-in-cheek' serious and whimsey seems to characterise Slade's approach to content. Most of his examples verge on fantasy. For example, the lesson mentioned above with first year Junior children continues in the following vein:

SELF: (*seeing the hasty shoppers have started off well, no doubt moving round the space anti-clockwise*) 'You see an amazing hat in a window. The hat whizzes out of the door to meet you. Put it on and start to feel posh.'

(*Not too satisfied, I don't criticise by saying things like 'Oh, come on, you are not looking posh at all. When we are being posh we spread ourselves out like this, don't we?' **Don't show**. be patient and **watch**)*

'Feel even posher...yes, posher still...Throw hat(s) away; you are a jumping kangaroo

(*they jump for a short time*); you are an ogre with a bad leg; you are suddenly a nice person – but with an ugly face. Be as ugly as you can. Now be horrid and pull a face at people near you as you pass by.'...

'A Wizard put a spell on you and you are very beautiful. yes, aren't you nice? Not too cissy, though. (*I had noticed one or two boys mincing on purpose.*) Better get conceited, so you are now a Dinosaur. (*this will probably show some ingenuity among them*) ...

The pupils in this example, switching rapidly from shopping to hats to wizards, seem to have been rendered totally dependent on the teacher's whims. One might wonder at the level of creative potential in such an exercise: – supposing, on hearing 'shopping' a child invents his own image of a 'do-it-yourself' shop, to be discarded, within seconds, in favour of the teacher's 'amazing hat'?... and, having visualised a hat, supposing the same child has a distinctly promising image of, say a 'fireman's helmet'...to be superseded by the requirement 'to be posh' etc. etc.?

Note the language in which the following example is couched[38]

> You can read a story and then get the children to act it; they can mime to a story or poem while it is being read; better still they can make up something entirely of their own – you may have to give them an outline such as – a bad man is trying to get money from an old woman, he watches her in the bus. There are too many people in it to try anything so he follows her off – then *bonk*! When he has bonked her what happens?...

To contemporary ears this 'story' sounds shocking and offensive, and yet Peter Slade himself would be equally shocked at our seeing it that way. Part of an address to an audience in 1948, there is an assumption that no-one is going to take the ideas of 'bonking' seriously, any more than the drowning of the Scottish lairds in the ballad of Sir Patrick Spens would be expected to be taken as a tragedy by young pupils in an English literature classroom. Such an attitude, however, has implications for how Drama in Schools was to be conceived. It may be that the authorities, the public and the children themselves needed to be reassured that, ultimately, the content of dramatic material would be of a non-serious nature. Whatever the reason, it seemed that if Drama was to have a place in Education it was to have kinship with the lighter side of literature. We have noted this possibility in discussing E.J. Burton's (1948) work and, of course, W.S.Tomkinson's (1921) complaint was related to what he saw as the inadequacy of drama as a vehicle for making poetic meaning available to school pupils, and no doubt the earliest attempt at the acting of Nursery Rhymes did not expect pupils to be upset by Jack 'breaking his crown' and Jill 'coming tumbling after'.[39] Classroom drama, and indeed most school-play performances, by tradition, veered towards the 'playful'. Peter Slade knew this very well and, to some extent, nurtured it. His reasons, one suspects, are complex. There is to some extent an adherence to the kind of public attitude to Drama I have described in this paragraph, but Slade's choice of language in the above 'old woman' story is his way of capturing something of the cruel humour of the child. The style of telling represents Slade's identification with a mask of heartless detachment sometimes adopted by young people of his day, to hide a deep, unarticulated concern.

When children were observed to reach the phase of shedding their initial need to 'show' stereotypic representation and when they rose above this tongue-in-cheek tradition of not taking the content too seriously, then 'absorption' and 'sincerity' no doubt came into their own. It is noticeable that Slade's usage of these latter terms tends to coincide with the the the end of a lesson, as though, some pupils were only then ready 'to go through a door' (a metaphor to which Peter Slade responded with warmth).

Collective Art

But it is the collective enterprise that Peter Slade is finally looking for: when there is a mutual sharing, spontaneously occurring; when the whole is more than each actor's contribution; when the space is unconsciously used as an aesthetic dimension; when a collective sense of timing brings about climax and denouement. Theatre is created, 'sensed' rather than contrived by the pupils.[40] This, too, occurs, if at all, in the later phase of the lesson. Such 'golden moments' prompt the following kind of observations from Slade, who has obviously felt privileged to have been a witness: 'It is the type of acting not seen under any other conditions, and is an experience no one should miss.' and, on another occasion, 'I felt the light dying. If not of a real sun, it was the light of 'real theatre' when a great scene comes to a close.'

Slade's emphasis on the actions of narrative, however, no doubt contributed to a limited assumption held by a generation of teachers and pupils of Drama *as* a narrative form. The 'what happens next' of a story-line' became the guiding structure of many Drama lessons and the base-line for dramatic form. Acting became *temporally* biased, that is, anticipatory of the *next* action of the story rather than exploratory of the present moment.[41] It is difficult to sustain Slade's emphasis on 'spontaneity', a concept bound up with immediacy and impulse, with a responsiveness to and anticipation of teacher-instruction.

Comments

Slade's new philosophy embraced the belief that within every child there was a Child Drama [along with Child Art] needing continual expression. The lucky child found this opportunity in playing alone or with others before the school age. Slade wanted schools, for the sake of their pupils' growth, to harness children's capacity for play by bringing their natural Drama into the classroom. Within the formality of the school setting, this opportunity for each child to engage in a 'retesting and deep proving of something the child has experienced in real life', should be fostered and nurtured by a benign teacher, especially with children whose capacity for playing had been neglected. Slade saw the hitherto rigid format of the physical education lesson as the one aspect of the curriculum mould that was open to revision when he started teaching, for Rhythm as a basis for both physical development and the arts was beginning to enter the educationist's vocabulary. Most of Slade's practice was concerned with how best to adapt the physical training style of teaching to stimulate freedom of expression. It is a mark of his genius that he achieved this.

Slade's conception of child play at times seems narrow compared with the many functions of enquiry, skill development, conation and constructive hypothesis identified by Susan Isaacs. Whereas Isaacs, perceived the easing of 'tension' and 'diminishing guilt and anxiety' as but *one* function of play, Slade sometimes confined his view of play [as Piaget tended to] to Freudian functions. Piaget, does not, of course conceive of child play as an activity that could be adapted for the classroom. Indeed he is at pains to ensure that his readers do not confuse symbolic play with 'parts acted in a play',[42] for he saw play as egocentric and drama as decentring.

For Slade, classroom drama was to cater for self-expression, in a form that qualified as child art. In the conceptual framework in the final chapter, I shall extend the notion of art, dramatic art, that is, to all forms of classroom drama without, however, supporting Slade's perception of Child Drama as a unique form of self-expression.

Notes

1   It should be noted that the Slade archive material is housed in the Theatre Department of Manchester University. Private correspondence between Peter Slade and Gavin Bolton, some of which is referred to in this book, is held in the Drama Archives in the School of Education, University of Durham.

2   The early 1930s had seen the appointment by the National Council of Social Services of two regional Drama Advisers, one of whom was Robert G. Newton whose experimentation in Improvisation we have discussed in Chapter 4. Their remit was to promote Drama with the unemployed.

3   An example of this interest is in the pamphlet published (undated) for him by the Jungian Guild of Personal Psychology, entitled *Dramatherapy as an aid to becoming a person*, a title evocative of Carl Rogers' 1954 publication *Becoming a Person* Oberlin Ohio.

4   The text of his broadcast was subsequently published in Creative Drama (undated, possibly late 1948), the *Magazine of the Educational Drama Association*.

5   The most famous was the Bonnington Conferece, 'a water-shed' according to Slade, January 1948. See Coggin, Philip (1956) *Drama in Education* for an assessment.

6   The first was *Theatre in Education* started in 1946 and devoted to 'Drama in University, College, School or Youth Group', but, about the same period, the first journal specifically relating to schools, sprang from the Birmngham-based Educational Drama Association and was entitled Creative Drama. Peter Slade became the 'Permanent Director' of this association in 1948.

7   Slade's own annual Summer School course, started in 1961, was perhaps the first to attract international interest in Drama. (Rudolf Laban's summer courses were already well-established in Modern Dance.)

8   The full story of important events during this period still needs to be told. Of particular interest is the work of the Drama Board, which under the guidance, first of Leo Baker and then Peter Husbands, conducted examinations for the next thirty years. As it moved into drama in schools as well as youth clubs, it became the most effective national body for raising standards in drama teaching. The callous dismissal of the enterprising Peter Husbands, by the Department of Education and Science, when the Drama Board was taken over by the Royal Society of Arts in the early 1980s is a shameful incident that has never been fully recorded.

9   Ministry of Education *Drama Working Party Report* (unpublished), p.12. A copy of this report written by George Allen, HMI is housed in the University of Durham Drama Archives.

10   Private letter to Gavin Bolton (1995) *ibid* pp.3-4

11   Granville-Barker (1944) writes: 'For having well studied a play, they really should have gained too much regard for it to be *ready to defame it by crude performance.*' [my italics] Granville-Barker, H. (1944) *The Use of Drama*. He wrote: 'Study of the drama, indeed, should properly begin for the adolescent not from the self-expressive, but from the exactly opposite standpoint.' [Granville-Barker, H. (1922, 2nd edition) The Exemplary Theatre Books for Libraries Press New York, p.1]

12 'Drama is doing' was to become the catchphrase of progressive drama teaching for the next generation of leaders in the field [See, for instance, Chris Day's *Drama for Middle and Upper School* (1975), p.3]. By appealing to its etymological origins [from the Greek, Dron, meaning to do, to act or to make] advocates were able both to dissolve barriers with seemingly non-artistic activities such as play and games and even claim a kinship with John Dewey's 'Learning by Doing' aphorism. Such a deconstruction of the term 'drama' allowed other theorists in the *theatre* (but outside education) similarly to widen the term 'performance' to embrace a range of social activities from play to ritual and from everyday greetings to celebrations [See, for example, Richard Schechner's *Performance Theory* (1977 Reprint 1988 p.40)] Both child drama advocates and Performance theorists pursued the breaking down of conceptual barriers between the arts and other human activies. Both groups saw themselves as examining the 'Art of Living', but the very choice of terms, 'personal play' and 'performance', predisposed them to look through different lenses. (Schechner Richard (1977; reprinted and revised 1988) Routledge NY; Carlson, Marvin (1996) *Performance* Routledge New York).

13 For example, of one school he visited Slade commented: 'This is a happy school. I have never heard a cross word from teacher or Child. The school accepts the principles of Child Drama and develops all work from this starting-point.' [Slade, P. (1954) *Child Drama ibid* p.205]

14 It should be appreciated that this study, focusing as it does on classroom acting, cannot do justice to the breadth of Slade's thesis of Child Drama. The psychological phases necessary to healthy growth, for example, are among a number of aspects which, although important to his theory, appear to have little bearing on acting behaviour. Also much of his work was devoted to Children's theatre, for which no place is given in this study.

15 Schiller, F. (translated 1967) *On the Aesthetic Education of Man op cit* 27th Letter, p.213

16 Peter Brook nicely captures such overtones: 'Sincerity is a loaded word: like cleanliness it carries childhood associations of goodness, truth-telling and decency.' [Brook, Peter (1968) *The Empty Space* Atheneum New York p.116-117]

17 Stanislavski, Constantin (1948 translated by J.J. Robbins) *My Life in Art* Theatre Art Books New York p.467

18 Board of Education (1926) *The Drama in Adult Education: A Report of the Board of Education*, being paper No. 6 HMSO London

19 Harriet Finlay-Johnson, as we have seen in Chapter One, refers to 'crude action from the adult's point of view', but does not apply the term 'sincerity'.

20 Stanislavski, C. (1948) *My Life in Art ibid* p.467. It should also be noted that although Slade acknowledged the usefulness of Stanislavski's term 'circle of attention', Slade had observed this phenomenon before Stanislavski's publication was available in English.

21 Brook, Peter (1968) *The Empty Space* Atheneum New York pp.109-120

22 Brook, P. (1968) *op cit* p.117

23 McGaw, Charles, J. (1964) *Acting is Believing* Holt, Rinehart and Winston New York p.47

24 It also echoes Caldwell Cook's concern that '...boys have not the experience to go beyond impressions and appearances' [Cook, H. C. (1917) *op cit* p.271].

25 Piaget, Jean (1951 translated by C. Gattegno and F.M. Hodgson) *Play, Dreams and Imitation in Childhood* Routledge and Kegan Paul

26 Juliana Saxton and Norah Morgan were the first educationists to recognise and categorise 'identification' as the prime dynamic of all forms of acting behaviour. [Morgan, N. and Saxton J. (1987) *Teaching Drama* Hutchinson Education pp.30-36]

27 Frost, Anthony and Yarrow, Ralph (1990) *Improvisation in Drama* Macmillan Basingstoke pp.152-3

28 See Pages 51-55 of *Natural Dance* (1977) for Slade's sympathetic comments on Laban and what he was trying to do. Slade is critical of some of Laban's interpreters, especially Physical Education specialists who reduced Laban's vision to a training scheme. Slade writes: 'Laban himself told me he despaired of this [when they do Labanesques all wrong], and of what some physical education specialists had done to destroy his work. At the last he (Laban) implied that he regretted ever getting involved with education. He said he should have stuck to theatre.'

Clive Barker (1977), a self-confessed disciple of Laban, convincingly argues that the fault lay not with Laban's 'method' but with those who, instead of teaching movement, rigidly taught 'the system'. [p.46 of *Theatre Games* Eyre Methuen London]

29 In what I hope was a gently mocking vein, I have referred to this as 'space on your own' drama. [See my keynote address to the University of Bergamo, Italy, 'Una breve storia del classroom drama nella scuola inglese. Una storia di contraddizioni.' (1994) in *Teatro Ed Educazione in Europa: Inghliterra E Belgio* a cura di Benvenuto Cuminetti, Guerini Studio.]

30 This tradition of changing into special clothing for Drama ('gym strip', as it was often called) lasted for almost a generation. When I (employed as an LEA Drama Adviser) first went into schools in the North-East of England, in the 1960s and asked to do Drama with a class of children, it was automatically assumed by teachers (and their pupils) that undressing would be required.

31 The instruction: 'find a place alone' precedes each of the early lessons illustrated in the Board of Education's 1933 *Syllabus of Physical Education*. From the 1950s onwards, for many teachers, the practice of Drama was dependent on a similar instruction. Even as late as 1972 Drama was associated with 'a space on the floor' [King, Colin (1972) *A Space on the Floor: a planned approach to teaching drama* Ward Lock London].

32 It should be remembered too that class-size during this 1940-1960 period typically could be 40-50 pupils.

33   I had the privilege of seeing Peter Slade teach a class of Secondary pupils in the
      mid-fifties.

34   As has already been observed, Peter Slade was among the first professional drama
      educators to teach classes that were not his own. We have already commented, in
      Chapter 6 on R.L. Stone's early struggle to introduce creative movement into
      Physical Education. Stone found that to be an uphill task at first, even in the
      context of regular lessons, often taken by Stone himself as headmaster, linked
      with other art forms and language work and with the staff working as a team,
      backing each other's experimentation. Slade was expected to 'make things
      happen' for a 'one-off' visit.

35   It is difficult to find one word to describe Slade's style – there is something of the
      magician who, fully in tune with his fellow creators of magic, is ready to spring
      into an adventure. The phrase, 'a sort of poetic romanticism', was suggested by
      Peter Slade in his private correspondence with Gavin Bolton (dated 30th January,
      1995) after reading a first draft of this manuscript.

36   This phrase, 'life-learning through Drama' was kindly suggested by Peter Slade
      in the private correspondence referred to above.

37   Taken from 'Starting Improvisation' in *Theatre in Education* No. 7-8, March-June
      1948 pp.. 6-7

38   Slade, P. (1948) 'Starting Improvisation' *op cit* p.6

39   This assumption no longer holds for the end of the century. In a recent videoed
      discussion with teachers on 'Chamber Theatre' Dorothy Heathcote describes how
      a presentation of 'Jack and Jill' by 8 year old pupils took a frighteningly serious
      turn in spite of her attempt to offer an alternative interpretation. [Dorothy
      Heathcote's visit to Birmingham Polytechnic's MA in Drama Education class,
      20.5.91 – David Davis' students.]

40   It is certainly contrived by the teacher. See, for example, the instruction to
      teachers quoted above: 'The clap (by the teacher, that is) in starting improvisation
      under these circumstances, is almost the parallel to the rise of the curtain in adult
      theatre.' [Slade, P. (1995) *ibid* p.73]

41   The acting required of Brecht's 'Epic Theatre' is also 'temporally biased', but in
      the opposite direction, towards the past. The actor is saying: This is how it was'.
      See, for example, his essay 'Street Scene' translated by John Willett in which
      Brecht instructs: 'The street demonstrator's performance is essentially repetitive.
      The event has taken place; what you are seeing now is a repeat.' Brecht, Bertolt
      (1968; first translated by John Willett, 1949) 'Street Scene' in *The Theory of
      Modern Stage: An Introduction to Modern Theatre and Drama* by Eric Bentley
      (Ed) Pelican Harmondsworth p.86

42   Piaget, J. (1951) *op cit* p.112.

CHAPTER 8

BRIAN WAY

An Introduction

A close friend and protégé of Peter Slade's for many years, it is not surprising that Brian Way was Slade's choice of editor for *Child Drama* (1954). In his introduction to this book Way writes: 'Whilst with the West Country Children's Theatre Company... I continually sensed a chasm in educational thought; that chasm has now been filled by the writing of this book, and my own and the hopes of many have been fulfilled.'. They shared a passionate interest in children's theatre.[1] Like Slade, his experience and knowledge in this field represent a major aspect of his professional work, and any attempt at a full account of Brian Way's influence would necessarily place that work as central. Children's theatre, however, is beyond the scope of this study, but his free-lance work took him into schools and teacher-training colleges to which institutions he became an unofficial adviser on classroom practice. It was, no doubt, his association with Peter Slade that gave his early work cachet and publicity. It may well be a comment on the confidence and adventurous spirit of the times that educational institutions so readily invited these two charismatic personalities from professional theatre[2] into their academic enclaves.

Although their classroom practice appeared to spring from a common philosophy, Way moved away from Slade's doctrine of a play-derived art form. As Hornbrook (1989) has expressed it[3]:

Way reinforced Slade's distinction between 'theatre' and 'drama', but largely abandoned his idea of Child Drama as Art in favour of a comprehensive theory of personal development.

Way seems to avoid using the expression 'Child Drama', appearing to eschew both its artistic and, as Margaret Wootton[4] points out, its child play connections. A drama/theatre dichotomy is clearly spelled out by Way: '...there are two activities, which must not be confused – and one is theatre, the other is drama.' He then goes on to define these terms:

> For the purposes of this book – that is, for the development of people – the major difference between the two activities can be stated as follows: 'theatre' is largely concerned with *communication* between actors and an audience; 'drama' is largely concerned with *experience* by the participants, irrespective of any communication to an audience.

Thus Way dichotomises, more explicitly perhaps than Slade attempted, a complex mimetic behaviour into either 'communicating' or 'experiencing', binary oppositions which the earlier pioneers, Finlay-Johnson and Caldwell Cook, would not have understood. In Way's writing the very term 'acting' is dropped; clearly its theatrical connotations were thought to place the term outside the new orthodoxy.

Way also overlooked Slade's broader concept of theatre. In the previous chapter on Slade, it was pointed out that Slade was always seeking to create a form of 'theatre' in an artistic sense, as opposed to theatre as a place where actors perform to an audience. It is the shared, unconscious achievement of a group of children who spontaneously create 'moments of theatre' that mark Slade's approach as art. Robinson draws our attention[5] to Way's curious dismissal of 'the arts' as offering too narrow a conception of personal creativity. In his teaching Way is not looking for opportunities to 'go through a door' (to use a metaphor introduced in the previous chapter), but the enhancement of specific personal attributes. As we shall see his emphasis on 'Drama as exercise' did not lend itself to development into the kind of shared moments of theatrical significance sought by Slade, although his choice of vocabulary, as we shall see, still tended to be that of the theatre.

No doubt the apparent arbitrariness of reaching Slade's 'magic moments' might well have bewildered Slade's followers, however impressed they may have been with his child-centred approach. Brian Way, in contrast, offered a conception of drama practice that seemed to reduce the risk of abortive creativity and provided a clearer recipe for lesson content. That the similarity of Slade's and Way's philosophy and classroom practice was largely superficial seemed at first to pass unnoticed. This may have been due to the common ground shared by their children's theatre work or it may be because Way appeared to adopt much of Slade's rhetoric. It is more likely, however, the continuation by Way of Slade's 'physical education' style of teaching that caused people to assume a deep professional similarity between the two men. Way appears to confirm Slade's methodology when he writes: '...the whole class is working at one and the same time, but each individual is working entirely on his or her own.' – and, as for the PT lesson, the pupils are to be equidistantly placed, poised for an action starting point.

Brian Way's theory of Education
The basis for Way's philosophical position is to be found in the circular diagram to be found on page 13 of his (1967) text. While emphasising the notion of the 'whole person', he develops a model dividing the personality into 'facets', relating to Speech; Physical self; Imagination; The senses; Concentration; Intellect; Emotion; and Intuition.[6] The planned development of these interconnected faculties through carefully graded practice is to Way the central purpose of education. Such a circular model is offered in deliberate contrast to the notion of linear development associated with the learning of disconnected subjects of a traditional school curriculum.

It is this model that provides Brian Way with a conception of Drama teaching marking a radical departure from the practice of his erstwhile friend and colleague. As Mike Fleming[7] has pointed out, there is a significant philosophical shift. Whereas Peter Slade, following his contemporaries in the visual arts such as Dr. Cizek,[8] writes in terms of 'The Aims and Values' of Child Drama, a heading implying an inherent worthwhileness in the activity itself, Brian Way subtly shifts this to 'The *Function* (my italics) of Drama', leaving the way open to a more purposeful interpretation and to activities directed specifically towards different points of his personality 'circle'. Determining selected goals was not of course new to Drama teachers – those following the Amateur Drama Route, the Speech route or even the English Lit. route tended to work to specific targets. What was new was that a non-performance orientated drama approach could be so explicitly purposeful.

Both men would claim that classroom drama was experiential. I have suggested in the last chapter that Slade's 'narrative/instructional' methodology distorted the experience away from the present in anticipation of the next instruction. Way, too, as we shall see, adopted this method at times, but in adding the 'exercise' dimension to the activity, he sometimes further distorted the 'experiential' towards 'practising'. This key to Way's methodology will be discussed below in greater detail.

The 1950s and '60s were times of innovation in professional theatre training too and it seems not unlikely that Brian Way, in breaking with the child-art approach to education of Peter Slade, was in part influenced by the new emphasis given to improvisation and spontaneity by innovators in the theatre. Margaret Wootton draws our attention to improvisational techniques used by Way, derived from Stanislavski, St Denis and, in particular, Viola Spolin, whose exercises for actors seem remarkably close to Way's. Wootton points out that whereas innovators such as Stanislavski worked with a clear theatrical end in view, that is, learning to act or act better, Way, in using similar techniques, 'pours them into an educational mould.'

And that 'educational mould' is to be of a particularly narrow kind, not the theatre craftmanship of Caldwell Cook, nor the deeper grasp of ballad poetry of Marjorie Hourd, not 'movement for movement's sake' of Peter Stone, nor the open-ended creativity of Peter Slade, but specific personal attributes such as concentration, imagination and sensitivity around which he built his graded exercises. The centre of the teacher's attention is to be the individual child – and the centre of the child's attention is to be himself as an individual. Way summed up his philosophy with his adage: 'drama is concerned with the individuality of the individual'. We shall see that such a holistic perception of the worth of the child, did not stand in the way of planned exercises for the child's separate faculties.

Brian Way's classroom practice

Way's 'work in a space on your own or in pairs' approach

'Find a space on your own' echoed through many schools following the dissemination of Way's methodology.[9] Pupils over many parts of the country engaged in exercises taken directly from the pages of Way's book. There were three kinds of such exercises: what might be described as direct, non-dramatic exercises (for instance 'listening to the sounds outside the room'), or as indirect and non-dramatic (recall the sounds of your neighbourhood), or as indirect and dramatic (recall the sounds of your own neighbourhood – and listen as though you were going to leave the neighbourhood and store up memories). There are three implications to be drawn from such exercises.

1. One is that for the first time in the history of drama teaching in this country a leader in the field is suggesting that exercises of a non-dramatic kind should be included in a drama teacher's repertoire and may even be dominant in the lesson. So important is the development of, say, 'intuition' that it did not matter to Way that no make-believe was involved. He saw his theory of development through drama as part of an all-embracing philosophy of education whose practice was basically concerned with human development. He set his sights beyond the promotion of drama; he was part of a larger 'personal growth' movement that was beginning to sweep the Western world, particularly North America.[10] That many of Way's exercises were non-dramatic appealed to operators in the fields of Gestalt and Group therapy, who shared his concept of 'the uniqueness of the individual'. The 'human growth' movement was not established to the same degree in the U.K., but the idea of being able to structure a Drama lesson without necessarily doing any Drama began to take hold in some quarters, a diversion also paralleled by the Laban movement which had such an influence on Drama teachers that a lesson purporting to be 'Drama' could be made up entirely of 'effort' exercises.

Way seemed not to make a distinction between dramatic and a non-dramatic exercise. He opens and closes his book with a recommendation that moving round a room with one's eyes closed might help to know what it is like to be blind. This may be the case, but Way offers this as an example of the function, not of sense deprivation, but of *Drama*. This conflation of two orders of behaviour betrays either a failure to mark their distinctive differences or, more likely, a vested interest in identifying common ground.

A further reason for including non-dramatic exercises in a training programme came from professional theatre. Nikolai Gorchakov's book,[12] published in USA three years before Brian Way's shows how Stanislavski was experimenting with such direct, non-drama, sense exercises during rehearsals. Indeed he set up the very same 'blindness' exercise in a particularly frightening way, causing the blindfolded 'victim' to burst into tears, at which, according to Gorchakov, Stanislavski triumphantly exclaimed: 'Now you know what blindness is like'. It is something of a coincidence that Clive Barker, writing ten years later,[13] uses a similar exercise to illustrate the *differences* between a game utilising sense deprivation (being blindfolded) and theatre (playing the same game, but *pretending* to be blindfolded). Barker actually sets up both experiences for his students so they, as participants or audience to both versions, can appreciate the chasm between the two. He claims that not until actors acquire the high degree of mimetic skill to be found in Peking Opera (the source for the exercise) can they without blindfolds convincingly behave as if they were blindfolded. Photographs nicely contrast the automatic difference in posture adopted by the respective 'game' and 'theatre' participants.

'Warm-ups' were also becoming very popular among acting companies as a mental and physical preparation for rehearsing. Brian Way must have been among the first educationists to introduce 'relaxation' into a teacher's repertoire.[14] As teachers took up the idea it became an unspoken law that no Drama lesson could start without its 'warm-ups', including a suitable period of 'relaxation'.

2. The second implication to be drawn from the exercise approach is that drama, far from being a social activity is, initially at least, to be as solitary as any pianoforte five-finger exercise. We have, of course met this with Slade's approach. Way offers some dubious theorising in support of his recommended sequence of starting with 'individual' exercises, moving on to work (perhaps weeks later) in pairs and then eventually into small groups and, finally (but exceptionally) the whole class[15]:

Human growth follows a similar pattern. The baby discovers and lives most happily in a simple form of isolation until it is about three years old; then it enjoys... sharing with one other person; then with two others and so into smaller groups. Integration within a larger social unit is a sophisticated and later stage of development, very much dependent on full opportunity for experiencing the other stages...

(One may feel some sympathy for humankind, isolated for the first three years of life!) It could be said that Way is here denying drama's essential characteristic as a social art.

Way, without Slade's passion for 'natural dance', does nevertheless use music or sound effects as a unifying medium. Notice, in the following extract from an exercise that takes up three pages of description, the care with which he instructs his readers:

He (the giant) bends down and picks up the stone – and starts to rub the mud off of it – and finds himself fuming and turning and turning – and as he turns he is getting smaller and smaller and smaller – until he becomes a very small bird (again *the slowly growing climax of sound for the spinning and the changing from one character to another – a final loud sound completes the change*). This bird has never flown before, so he hops around a bit – then discovers he has wings and stands very still and begins to try to use them – to practise flying....at last he is able to go soaring off into the sky. (*Again, a very, very slow, rolling climax of sound for the practice at using the wings, and finally for taking off – then with up and down rolling rhythms, the bird is helped to fly – and a slow de-climax brings it back to earth*) The bird finds itself by the pool and sees a yellow stone – and picks it up and starts to rub off the mud – and finds itself turning and turning and growing very tall and thin and stiff – growing into a puppet (*again the slow climax of sound for the turning and growing into a puppet – the repetition of the formula has many values of its own, including the class's growing readiness for what is coming, and beginning to spin almost the moment that they pick up the new stone*) – and the puppet enjoys dancing by the pool (*and gay rhythms on the tambour or drum help both the dancing and the 'stiffness' of the puppet – after a while we drop the volume of the sound, without losing the gaiety of the rhythm, so that we can be heard over the sound, with the dancing still in progress.)...*

Way believes that music adds to the depth of the drama experience, but his explanation is far from compelling[16]:

> ...experience of doing drama to music adds depth to the experience; but the same quality of experience might well be contained within the more concentrated passage of music the full duration of which is only four or five minutes; the microcosmic level is changed, but the experience can be very much the same, and what a play takes two hours logically to unfold, the passage of music will unfold, in no less logical terms, in a much shorter period...

Not usually obscure, Way has written a passage here that is almost incoherent. What both Slade and Way no doubt discovered, although they do not actually say so, is that music can effectively override the 'physical education exercise/space-on-your-own' mentality. While the teacher's instruction demands solitary practice, the accompanying music or sounds creates the illusion of group experience and possibly contributes to a general readiness for subsequent collaboration. Further, however pedestrian the pupils' actions, the music elevates indifferent miming to a sense of an artistic creation, to, perhaps, what Jacques-Dalcroze referred to as 'musical gesture'.

3. The third implication is the underlying 'exercise mentality' (this writer's expression) that the pupils bring to their pretend behaviour. Way seems to eschew Slade's occasional use of story-building from the children's suggestions, preferring to use a sequence of his own (often less whimsical and more imitative of 'real life'.) If we take an example in which Way recommends that the teacher instruct the pupils in what to do (not how to do it):

> One morning you are fast asleep in bed; the alarm clock rings, so you push back the blankets and sheets, put on your slippers and go to the bathroom; then you wash your face and hands – don't forget your neck and behind your ears; and then you clean your teeth...

One may conclude, as for Slade, that the resultant acting behaviour is likely to be qualitatively affected by this kind of quick-fire teacher-instructional context. A travesty of creative acting, it no doubt became fast practice in stereotypic signing. No activity appears to require sustaining beyond three minutes, often much less – one minute is typical. Whereas Slade, at the end of such a sequence would look for opportunities to let the class break out (using whatever grouping seemed natural to them) into freer 'playing', Way's rigid theory about individuals on their own only moving into pairs when ready can only lead to further exercises. The 'exercise mentality' pervades the drama lesson and gives rise to a new conception of what drama in the classroom might mean for both teacher and pupil. One aspect, however, that should be stressed is the undoubted all-pervasive atmosphere of fun that was generated.[17]

Class Drama

Even when Way does give attention to the final stages of his grouping sequence, that is a whole class involvement, he still persists in giving the experience an exercise orientation. The following example is taken from his chapter on improving 'speaking':

Stage 1
In pairs. Two factory workers are grumbling about conditions at work: long hours, bad canteen arrangements, low wages, dangerous machinery...

Stage 2
Each pair joins up with another pair. In fours, the grumbling continues and now includes discussion of what should be done about conditions, the main thought of which is that the manager of the factory should be forced to do something to improve them.

Stage 3
The groups of four begin to join up into larger groups, arguing about the best way of forcing action from the manager. Each group decides they should at once go to the manager's house and demand that he listens to their complaints and does something about them.

Stage 4

The first three stages are repeated, leading to the whole group walking to the manager's house and calling for him, perhaps reaching some kind of general chant, such as 'We want the manager, we want the manager', etc

Read as 'Drama' such a sequence can only be regarded as banal, but Way has intended the whole experience as a series of *speech* exercises. He extends the plot to:

...suddenly one of the workers picks up a brick and throws it at the manager(s); the brick hits the manager; the crowd are shattered and deflated by this as they did not want it to go so far – and they go back to work, talking in pairs or small groups about the incident.

and then explains: 'The additional circumstances [Way is referring to the brick-throwing] within such an episode do not take long to build and are enriching experiences, taking a simple intention of speech exercises to the kind of exciting and stimulating moment that creates further interest in the activity.' Late 20th century readers of Way's book might have expected that the stimulation of further interest from the pupils is referring to arousal of interest in the final scene as a piece of theatre or of concern for the outcome of the brick-throwing, but while acknowledging the dramatic potential of such a scene, Way's obsession with 'personal development' is paramount: 'Always this factor of creating further interest is important, not just for the possibilities of the drama that are thus realised, but because as interest grows so do responsibility and effort; there develops a conscious realisation that many personal factors – concentration, sincerity and maximum effort among them – are all basically concerned with the success of the scene.' The new awareness for Way's pupils is not to be theatrical or political but '*attribute*-centred', a conception perhaps paralleled in the theatre by rehearsals in Grotowski's Laboratory where it is not the character but the self that the actor is required to discover.[18]

There was a precedent for large group work, however, that Way occasionally followed. Uncomfortable as he appears to be with the idea of a whole class sharing a drama, he nevertheless occasionally gives a tighter structure to an approach first recommended by E.J. Burton (1948) who conceived of large group work, not as dramatic events to be faithfully followed sequentially, but as 'settings', as places where a crowd assemble, members of which may or may not be expected to mingle and interact.[19] Such settings, for Burton and Way, included 'a busy street', 'a busy railway station', 'street-market', and 'school play-ground'.

Way, in developing what he calls 'a crowd scene', sees such scenes of course as opportunities for practice in one or more segment of his 'Personality circle'. He did not attempt to work out a sophisticated methodology for sustained, thematic work with a large group. One suspects that such work was, in the main, out of his experience and out of the experience of his readers, who sought and were indeed satisfied with the simple exercises which make up the bulk of the book. He obviously sensed potential in an elaborate large group creation, but his suggestions for possible topics: 'mine disasters', 'a storm wrecking a market-place', 'earthquake', 'landslide' and 'avalanche' etc. betray a naive faith in children's ability to represent such violent, environ-mentally-oriented scenes with any degree of credibility, and indeed, in a teacher's ability to lead a class into such serious topics.

There is an assumption of course in my last sentence that the goal of such dramatic presentation as an 'earthquake' or a 'storm' is indeed *credibility*. These kind of 'disaster scenes' were played for decades from the 1960s onwards throughout the country in drama (Brian Way was but promoting a fashion that had already started). The HMI for Drama, AF Alington[20] who must have witnessed more of these scenes than anyone, appears to have a high tolerance for this kind of endeavour, provided it is treated *romantically*. He explains, echoing Caldwell Cook: 'Real life is one of the hardest things to portray convincingly.' He goes on to suggest that no attempt should be made to make, say, 'A Shipwreck' 'real'; movement and mime may be the appropriate means for children to create such a topic. Perhaps Jacques-Dalcroze's 'musical gesture' is a useful term here.

Way's approach to 'A Mining Disaster', however, reveals a more penetrating plan than his previous examples have led us to expect. For instance, so that his pupils are better informed, he suggests holding preliminary discussions and giving practice in relevant occupational actions. The general style of the performance, however, (for instance, a clash of a cymbal is to represent the sound of the disaster) is in keeping with Alington's conception of 'romantic' drama.

Way did occasionally include a 'dramatisation' approach reminiscent of Harriet Finlay-Johnson's work in which learning about the environment appeared to be a prime objective, but such examples are few and seem to be perceived by Way as final achievements in a lengthy programme of training. One can sense his ambivalence towards the dramatisation of history in the following comment: 'Inevitably, however, as an extension of the circle, the time comes when intellectual and emotional experience can be enriched by using themes and stories...side by side with reliving (re-enacting) events... that are part of the heritage of knowledge because they are known facts.' 'Inevitably', 'however', and 'the time comes' appear to give but tentative approval to the use of drama in the acquisition of knowledge. Way rounds off his point with typical rhetoric:

> Drama provides the unique opportunity for bringing immediacy to any situation, making what is knowledge of the past an actual discovery in the present. Drama helps the re-creation of human endeavour, and can draw on material from the beginning of time, making immediate what is now possibly dry information. Drama transcends information and makes of it living experience, significant to the heart and spirit as well as to the mind.

Way does try to provide a bridge between drama and theatre. He is aware that, eventually, pupils well-trained in 'all the many different points of the circle' and in a 'non-audience and uncritical framework' may be ready to create 'a kind of end-product' which he describes as '...a fully conscious drama, fully intended acts of creation...It is a deeply valuable experience to reach, affecting all facets of personality and life...', but this concession to polished work takes up but a page or two in a book almost totally devoted to dramatic activity that is to be spontaneous, short-lived and not for repeating.

C.4. Improvisation[21]

It may seem strange that in *Development Through Drama*, a book devoted entirely to improvised dramatic activity, Way should choose to include a separate chapter entitled 'Improvisation'. Indeed this lengthy chapter does lie uneasily within the book's conceptual frame for most of the chapter's content, in respect of both ideas for discussion and examples of practice replicates those of other chapters. One may speculate that Way was well aware that 'improvisation', the noun, was by the 1960s firmly established as part of the vocabulary shared by professionals, amateurs and teachers and that he felt obliged to establish his views of it as a genre rather than simply a disposition to spontaneity. Although the term was indeed shared by most people interested in drama, its applications were diverse to a point barely sustaining a common usage. There is very little in common between, for example, the improvisational theatre of Commedia Dell'arte and Stanislavski's intense use of improvisational exercises for characterisation development during rehearsals, or between the paratheatrics of Moreno's Psychodrama and Child Play. What these examples have in common, of course, is a quality of extemporariness or spontaneity; what in the main divides them is the critical presence or absence of an audience. It is likely that Way felt under some pressure to re-establish the position of improvisation in relation to his child-centred approach to drama.

We have seen that the first person to introduce the term 'improvisation' into education was Robert Newton (1937), and that later (in 1948) he expressed his regret that improvisation in the classroom was losing its connection with theatre. Most texts of the period [See for, instance, Alington (1961)][22] advocate pupils improvising scenes on their own with a view to showing them to the rest of the class later. Way, however, stolidly reinforces the notion that improvisation is to be understood as a private exploration in the double sense of unobserved and self-expressive,[23] making demands on 'each person's own resources without the complex necessity of interpreting an author's intentions as well'. In other words improvisation for Way is 'quite simply a play without script' and without an audience.

Newton's was gradually becoming a minority voice, at least within the pages of published texts. A popular handbook of the 1960s emerged, for instance, from Loughborough Training College where the influence of Slade and Way inspired a tutor, Robin Pemberton-Billing and a student, David Clegg, to collaborate in the writing of *Teaching Drama*, the introduction of which describes 'a typical lesson' as follows:

'It is early on a summer's morning. Outside the sun is shining. We are asleep in bed; very soon the alarm clock will sound...' The children seem asleep – some restlessly, some deeply. The teacher meanwhile has moved imperceptibly over to the stage, and suddenly he rattles a side-drum, and the class reacts – some quite violently. They seem absorbed in the real process of getting out of bed....'Go into the bathroom and have a good wash. Don't forget behind your ears! Clean your teeth and get dressed.'...The narration continues, and the children cut sandwiches and pack things to take for a day in the country.

They set off to catch a bus in a happy mood, whistling, running and skipping. To help them music blares through the loudspeaker: a 'pop' record from the past – *Jumping Bean* – just the thing to convey the spirit of setting off, and the children respond well to it. They meet friends and begin the bus journey, amid much slapstick comedy with imaginary bus conductors....

Now they are searching for wild flowers and listening for bird songs. '*Morning*' from *Peer Gynt*, sets the quiet atmosphere. They cross a farmyard and feed ducks....

The lesson proceeds with playing a ball game, fishing, swimming, getting caught in a shower of rain, packing up and returning home to bed. This was a 'first year class' (11-12 years). The authors explain that with a second year class: 'we might see a market in full swing – suddenly an old lady faints or a messenger arrives to announce that the king is on the way.' Making up their own plays from a given idea in small groups or a whole class Dance-Drama might typically make up a third year lesson. The authors then explain: 'Whatever the activity the first thing that they would strike the outside observer would be the atmosphere of sincere absorption.'

In contrast to this advocacy of teacher-narration and much nearer to Newton's conception of Improvisation, John Hodgson and Ernest Richards,[24] bestriding the education/ theatre divide, published an authoritative manual on how actors and adolescents might train in what they saw as a distinctive performance oriented activity. In describing the early stages of the work, the authors advise: 'At times, after discussion, groups can be asked to work on the same scenes, trying this time to correct the main faults or improve generally the clarity of expression and interest.'. Their perception of the aims of Improvisation, 'Growth of the individual as a person', nevertheless clearly echoed Brian Way's person-centred philosophy. Those teachers brought up on amateur drama or Speech and Drama no doubt at this time found Hodgson's and Richards' assumptions about Improvisation more palatable than the more confusing 'private' notion of Brian Way's theory, for it was the very discipline of improvising a scene for public performance that was seen by many teachers as contributing to that 'individual growth'.

This was the period, the mid-60s, when exciting experiments were being conducted by Keith Johnstone and others in Professional theatre. In his early appointment to work at the Royal Court Theatre under George Devine and before he emigrated to Canada (University of Calgary), Johnstone devised '*Theatre Machine*', a semi-rehearsed programme which was liable to change in public performance,[25] the first presentation of its kind in the UK. Hodgson and Richards' (1966) publication, *Improvisation*,[26] successfully attempts to embrace contemporary knowledge of professional actor-training and a rich resource of theatre tradition in the service of education. They relate improvisation to textual study and performance and introduce a new form of theatre education, the 'documentary', developed more fully as a genre by Albert Hunt.[27] Obviously confining their attention to Senior pupils and Youth Theatre, their voices may not have been so influential at a time when the Slade/Way/Heathcote philosophy appeared to be steering drama educational interests towards the younger pupil and away from performance art.

If Brian Way's special brand of Improvisation set him apart from some of his contemporaries in classroom and theatre, his introduction of a mode of dramatic exercise that went beyond, say speech-training or acting exercises, opened the door for further classroom experimentation in the name of drama. Dramatic exercise, in one form or another, was here to stay for the rest of the century.

'Dramatic Exercise form' developed by others

Role-Play

The earliest texts on 'Role-Play' as a genre emerged from America,[28] following experiments conducted at Harvard University on its use for Management Training. Most early writers on the subject claim that their work derives from the Psychodramatic techniques of Moreno (1946)[29] whose methodology dealt with personal trauma which the sufferer was invited to re-enact before an audience. The 'protagonist', using others from the audience as fellow actors, would display some aspect of his/her past life drawn from a social, often family, context. Enlightened Business Management translated these methods for commerce, recognising their capacity for training and even changing behaviour in agent/client, salesman/customer, employer/employee, employee/employee pairings. Role-Play became a means of putting relevant social behaviours under a microscope – and short-term exercises were invented as vehicles for this scrutiny by the rest of the class. Brian Way's concentration on the development of personal skills and his exercise format created a natural opening through which life-skill training could appear in school classrooms. Morry van Ments,[30] who became an authority figure in this field describes Role-Play as 'practising a set of behaviours which is considered appropriate to a particular role.' Notice this 'practising'. The idea that one can improve one's life skills by practising them in a safe environment was legitimised by Way and today is regarded as a critical teacher-strategy in a school's Personal Development Programme.[31] At first, of course, it was thought to be the proper province of the Drama teacher, who, as we have seen, welcomed it as a manageable classroom practice. It did not even require any kind of special space – just asking for two volunteers to enact an employee asking an employer for a pay rise was even possible in a room full of desks. Today it is part of the repertoire of the Secondary class teacher who, perhaps for an hour a week, is required to deal with interpersonal relationships.

Thus, in some hands, Way's notion of a dramatic exercise as a vehicle for the private practising of life skills such as concentration, sensitivity, imagination, speech and movement, became transformed into public scrutiny of contextualised functional skills. Others, however, saw dramatic exercise as an opportunity for relating to knowledge.

Dramatic exercise for knowledge

Whereas the Pemberton-Billing/Clegg publication of 1965 referred to above closely follows the philosophy and methodology of Brian Way, in Chris Day's *Drama for Middle and Upper Schools* a new emphasis emerges that introduces a 'subject-matter' component into the dramatic exercises making up the many examples of lessons included in his book. This text may be regarded as a good example of a writer at the 'cross-roads' of Drama Education. Day's theoretical rhetoric appears to echo Slade/Way aims when he writes of 'Drama as Doing', involving 'the whole self', but when he later affirms that 'it should not be surprising to find pupils writing, painting, reading, researching, tape-recording, filming or involved in thoughtful discussion during what is time-tabled as Drama, he is reflecting a Heathcotean influence.' Some items in this list, such as researching, discussion and writing take the horizons beyond self-expression and personal development to concern about content. In contradistinction to Way's position, Day values the intellect as well as the intuition and imagination. His work is un-mistakably child-centred, but not merely in style. Day pursues child-centredness beyond Way's limited conception by investigating[32] what topics interest children most, planning a whole range of lessons with various ages based on the results of his questionnaires, indicating the plan and outcome of each lesson, and showing how the pupils' responses affected new directions with further indications of how a topic might be extended. The notion of a lesson becoming a series of exercises all linked with a *theme* seems a significant advance on dramatic action dependent on a teacher narration of rather mundane actions.

Exercise structured for theatre form

The above has been an example of the dramatic 'exercise' mode being used to shape a particular kind of insightful experience related to knowledge. Later in the century it became not uncommon for a teacher to use the exercise form as an aesthetic or theatrical experience.

An example taken from my 1992 publication is of an exercise based on a very precise understanding of dramatic tension, intended to operate as a microcosm of a well-structured play. The exercise was part of a sequence, based on a Bible story, dealing with the attempt by Joseph's brothers to be rid of their father's favourite. In order to help the class feel what it might have been like to have to tolerate their brother's unfair treatment and to contain their jealousy, I set up the following 'pairs' exercise – in a sequence of 3 steps:

1. One of each pair was the boy Joseph, the other was an elder brother. 'For this first practice stand side by side, each hammering a stake in the ground. These will be used for a sheep-pen.' I discussed the length of the stake and the differences of strength of a man and a boy. 'In this first step of the exercise do not interact; simply show the differences between a mannish and a boyish way of knocking in a stake – pure miming.'

2. 'Now, still out of the biblical context, for the next step. Be any two brothers. The elder is going to teach the younger how to knock in a stake. What kind of thing will the older one feel he has to draw his younger brother's attention to?'

3. 'Now you will be in role again as young Joseph and the elder brother. The latter is determined to teach this idle lad how to drive in a stake. Joseph, however, is equally determined to use this as an opportunity to tell his brother about one of his wonderful dreams... in which all his elder brothers... bowed down to him!!!...

This is a dense exercise loaded, through language, through the symbolism of difference in size, through the opposition of boasting and teaching, with many levels of meaning. Effective, but like most exercises, of limited scope and duration.

Brian Way brought exercise into our drama repertoire. His intention was for his pupils privately to practise personal skills such as concentration, imagination, intuition, language and movement. Some educationists saw its potential for close investigation of interactional skills within typical family and business contexts. Others enlarged its scope to embrace the acquisition of knowledge. A further opportunity was seen, from the 1980s onwards, in its potential as a tightly controlled dramatic structure, a play in miniature.

Acting in Brian Way's classroom

Brian Way took the risk out of classroom acting. At a time when his fellow pioneer, Peter Slade, was urging a 'playful' release of fantasy, Way was circumscribing acting behaviour into prosaic exercise. At a time when some professional theatre was taking risks, when professional actors were engaged in their own exploratory workshops led by people like Keith Johnstone and Joan Littlewood, Way was consolidating the idea (started by Slade but without the 'exercise' orientation) of a dictated sequence of actions. When rehearsal rooms became hothouses for ensemble playing, Way kept his young actors working 'in a space on their own'. What was it then about Way's pioneering work that made it attractive to teachers in countries all over the world?

The key to understanding his approach lies, I believe, in his determination to sustain the notion of acting as a private activity. This was in keeping with the British obsession with child-centred education and the general interest of the wider, humanist movement in 'self-actualisation'. Without an audience the only standards were one's own. The drama teacher was not to impose some external notion of what acting should be nor offer any criticism of any kind. The young actor may have felt freed from criticism, but certainly could not escape from teacher instruction on what to do – and, usually, from the pace at which to do it. In most of Way's exercises, 'Acting' is reduced to reacting mimetically. He has virtually taken the word 'acting' out of the educationist's vocabulary, so that teachers are left with the impression that whatever goes on in the classroom in the name of drama has nothing to do with what people do in a theatre.

If drama is to be defined merely as 'practising living', then it would seem, at first sight, to be inappropriate to give attention to acting itself. It is the practice of social or personal skill that warrants attention, to the exclusion, it seems, of artistic endeavour. Such a conception no doubt made Way's approach accessible to all kinds of humanist teachers and therapists who would not have been interested in traditional performance.[33]

I think it can be claimed that Brian Way in his time had a broader influence on classroom drama than any other British exponent and yet his theory and practice will be given but a token place in my attempt to reformulate a conceptual framework for acting behaviours that could be useful to teachers today. It is as if we now have to outgrow his influence. The reader will judge whether I am doing a disservice to the considerable accomplishments of this man from whom I have learnt so much.

Notes

1 Towards the end of the war (1943) Brian Way was co-founder of The West Country Children's Theatre Company. He was later to found (1953) Theatre Centre Ltd, in London, from which he developed the largest school touring system in the country. Along with Peter Slade, he became an acknowledged authority on playing 'in-the-round' and audience participation. In addition to his authorship of 65 plays, he published *Audience Participation; Theatre for Children and Young People* Baker's Plays, Boston, in 1981. As early as 1949, when he was 26, he became Founder-Director of the first Drama Advisory Service and, subsequently (1950-51), editor of the magazine, *Theatre in Education.*

2 It is astonishing that these two men, untrained in the classroom, were both such able teachers of children. I had the privilege of watching Brian Way teach many times. Young people and adults alike responded to his generous, gifted, and inspired teaching. His particular strength was in freeing teachers themselves to be expressive and confident in his many workshops held throughout the country. As a Preston teacher, I was indebted to him for the regular visits he made to our north Lancashire town to oversee our training.

3 Hornbrook, D. (1989) *Education and Dramatic Art* Basil Blackwell Oxford p.12

4 Wootton in writing of Way's work comments: 'The link which Slade bears constantly in mind between what he calls 'the personal play of children'... and drama, has somewhere been lost'. Wootton, M. (1984) MA thesis (unpublished) *'An investigation into the determining influences on Drama in Education, 1947-77'*, Institute of Education, University of London p.45

5 Robinson, Kenneth (1982) *A Revaluation of the Roles and Functions of Drama in Secondary Education with reference to a survey of Curricular Drama in 259 Secondary Schools* Ph.D. thesis (unpublished) University of London Institute of Education, p.496 [pp.42-3 of Way's (1967) text]

6 This latter, intuition, was left out of his circular diagram on Page 13 by mistake, Way explained to Gavin Bolton and Mike Fleming in an interview on 1st November, 1993. In fact Way tended to emphasise education of the intuition at the expense of education of the intellect. Perhaps he is the kind of romantic Jerome Bruner, who was also interested in intuition, had in mind in commenting [Bruner, J. S (1974) *The Relevance of Education* Penguin London , p.99] that 'Only a romantic pedagogue would say that the main object of schooling is to preserve the child's intuitive gift.'

7 Fleming, M. (1982) *op cit* p.90

8 See Viola, Wilhelm (1936) *Child Art and Franz Cizek* Vienna

9 It should be pointed out that Way's influence spread through Local Education Authorities and Teacher-Training Institutions long before his 1967 book was published. In many ways Brian Way's book marks the climax of his years of freelance teaching in England. Ten years later, he left for Canada.

10 The seminal texts by Carl Rogers and Abraham Maslow, so prominent in the 'Human Development' Movement, were published in 1954. [Rogers, Carl R.

(1954) *Becoming a Person* Oberlin Ohio and Maslow, Abraham H. (1954) *Motivation and Personality* Harper New York]

11 The history of drama teaching in this second half of the century seems to have had a pronounced 'avoidance' streak', for following the 'direct' experiences of Brian Way and the 'movement as preparation for drama' of HMI favouring a Laban approach, the 1970s saw the growth in popularity of 'games' as principal ingredients of a Drama lesson. A typical publication of the period was Donna Brandes' and Howard Phillips' *Gamesters' Handbook: 140 Games for Teachers and Group Leaders* (1977) The Growth Centre, Newcastle-upon-Tyne.

12 Gorchakov, Nikolai (1954 translated by Miriam Goldina) *Stanislavski Directs* N.Y. p.38

13 Barker, Clive (1977) *Theatre Games* Eyre Methuen London pp.57-61

14 Way, B. (1965) *ibid* pp.78-81. Richard Courtney (1965) and Robin Pemberton-Billing and David Clegg (1965) were also strong advocates of 'relaxation' in the Drama classroom.

15 Way, B. (1967) *ibid* p.160

16 Way, B. (1967) *ibid* p.116

17 My attempt here to present a critical analysis should not allow the persistent overall sense of enjoyment emanating from Way's classrooms to be overlooked – nor must I forget that I myself taught this way in the late '50s and early '60s.

18 Grotowski writes that rehearsals should 'stimulate self-revelation'. [Grotowski, Jerzy (1969) *Towards a Poor Theatre* Eyre Methuen London, p 21]

19 Such 'crowd scenes', unstructured or loosely structured, appear in most of the 1960 publications, for instance Alington (1961), Courtney (1965), Pemberton-Billing and Clegg (1965). Even the Staff Inspector with special responsibility for Drama, A.F. Alington, [Alington, A.F. (1961) *Drama and Education* Basil Blackwell Oxford, p.49] wrote in 1961, following his retirement: 'The first purely group improvisations might centre round what may be called sensational subjects – headline stuff. 'Street Accident', 'Mine Disaster', 'Shipwreck'. ('Mine Disaster is usually a winner). Presumably, teachers felt that such 'man-as-a-victim-of-his-environment' incidents gave their pupils insight into limits of endurance.'

20 Alington, A.F. (1961) *ibid* p.48

21 For an extensive and thorough account of the development of Improvisation in Western Theatre and Education see O'Neill, Cecily, C. (1991) *Structure and Spontaneity: Improvisation in Theatre and Education* [unpublished thesis], University of Exeter and the book for which it became a basis, *Drama Worlds: a framework for process drama* Heinemann Portsmouth NH (1995).

22 Alington, A.F. (1961) *op cit* pp.29-63. Richard Courtney (1965) followed a similar line, giving the definition of improvisation as 'the impromptu creation of plays' [p.12]. E.J. Burton (1955) identified stages of sophistication in improvisation, from 'charades' to an advanced form of 'play-making' requiring attention to 'plot', 'characterisation' and 'speech'. Perhaps the broadest interpretation comes from Robin Pemberton-Billing and David Clegg (1965) who see the outcome of

any Speech or Movement (or Speech *and* Movement) exercise as Improvisation, a position which Way adopts.

23 Some of the work of Stanislavski and Copeau is associated with pre-performance improvised exercises, but such devices were seen as preparing the actors mentally and emotionally for a more truthful performance with a script and before an audience.

24 Hodgson, John and Richards, Ernest (1966) *Improvisation* Eyre Methuen London. John Hodgson came from professional theatre [but he was also trained as a teacher] and was Deputy Principal of the Old Vic theatre School, Bristol at the time of writing, later becoming Head of Drama Studies at Bretton Hall College of Education. Ernest Richards was Head of English and Drama at the I.M. Marsh College of Physical Education, Liverpool and was founder of the Liverpool Youth Theatre.

25 Johnstone's London work is described in *Impro: Improvisation and the Theatre* (1981) Methuen London. Frost and Yarrow (1990) include an excerpt from a programme note of a 'Theatre Machine' performance:

'THEATRE MACHINE is improvised performance. If you don't know the show is improvised, or don't believe it can be, then the bits that work well seem obviously rehearsed. The bits that flop you will think 'obviously not rehearsed' – you'll think those are the 'improvised' bits and you'll wonder why they improvise, if it doesn't work.' (p.57-58 of Frost and Yarrow).

26 A few weeks before he died [June, 1997], John told me he was part way through updating *Improvisation* for republication.

27 Albert Hunt [*Hopes for Great Happenings: Alternatives in Education and Theatre* (1976) Methuen London] further developed the 'documentary' style of theatre in a College of Higher Education in Bradford, moving into professional work when he became somewhat disenchanted with educational circles.

28 One of the first to reach England was *The Role-Play Technique: A Handbook for Management and Leadership Practice* by Norman R.F. Maier, Allen R. Solem and Ayesha A Maier (First published 1956; revised 1975) University Associates San Diego.

29 Moreno J.L. (1946) *op cit*

30 van Ments, Morry (1983) *The Effective Use of Role-Play: A Handbook for Teachers and Trainers* Kogan Page London, p.19

31 Government sponsored documents such as the Manpower Services Commission's (1982) *A New Training Initiative – A Consultative Document* while lending support to this kind of activity, also reinforced its limited scope. David Davis saw sinister political intentions behind such practice. See 'Drama for Deference or Drama for Defiance?' (1983) in *2D* Vol 3 No 1 pp.29-37.

32 This 'Project' may well be the first example of research into drama education. (Day, Chapter 2 and Appendix). It is curious that other exponents of drama education (including those well-placed for such research in Universities) failed to follow Day's example. The status of Drama in Schools today might have been considerably enhanced had serious research been sustained.

33 Within the therapeutic tradition 'Psychodrama', a system of therapy evolved by J.L. Moreno [Moreno, Jacob Levy. (1946) *Psychodrama* Vol 1 Beacon House New York], stood alone in its dependence upon a stage setting for its proper functioning. I can recall an uncomfortable moment when I first visited the Moreno centre in New York, unintentionally shocking fellow spectators by squatting at the side of the stage to watch – instead of taking my 'proper' place – in the auditorium beyond the footlights! Moreno's philosophy seemed to rely on a 'protagonist' (patient) gaining personal release from the opportunity spontaneously to reenact a past painful incident *within the formal conditions of a stage performance.*

SECTION FOUR
HEATHCOTE

CHAPTER NINE

DOROTHY HEATHCOTE 'LIVING THROUGH' DRAMA AND 'DEPICTION'

Introduction to Dorothy Heathcote

Dorothy Heathcote was appointed to the University of Durham Institute of Education[1] in 1950 at the age of 24,[2] four years, it is worth noting, before Slade's *Child Drama* appeared. It was not until the 1960s that leaders in the field became aware of her and her work. Perhaps the first time she was referred to in print was in the mid-sixties after her teaching came under observation of Her Majesty's Inspector for Drama, who described her work as follows:

Some teachers make a distinction between improvisation and improvised play-making. The latter has led to some of the most interesting work that we have seen. Close questioning of the pupils by the teacher has led to deep involvement or sense of relevance so that a new dimension has been added to apparently threadbare scenes. 'All right you are on an island,' says a teacher in the north, 'how did you get there? Who are you? Are you alone or with anyone?' This teacher and her students from an institute have conducted projects lasting a whole week in which the boys and girls in the school have investigated with great profundity such subjects as birth, marriage, death, in all their personal, social, anthropological, and artistic aspects.

The writer of the above is John Allen, HMI and the teacher he refers to is Dorothy Heathcote. The date of publication is 1967,[3] coinciding with the publication of Brian Way's *Development Through Drama* and the Government's report on Primary Education, known as *The Plowden Report*.[4] The two latter publications appeared to epitomise the spirit of child-centred education overtaking schools, but John Allen warned against paedeocentric zeal that absolved the teacher from clarifying thoughts and defining intentions. Of all the influential people in drama education [or drama in education[5] as once again it became known in official documents[6]], John Allen stood out as the one person having an overview of what was going on. His appointment as an Inspector strengthened a broad perspective he had been acquiring over a number of years. He had been a prominent member of the 1948 Ministry of Education Working Party on Drama in Schools, and, while pursuing his own eclectic interests in directing, broadcasting and writing about theoretical and practical aspects of theatre, he became an acute observer, from the sidelines, as it were, of how others who had a more direct influence on what might go on in the drama classroom, set about promoting their interests.

In the second section of this book, we attempted to analyse a wide range of 'trends' which sprang from or competed with the pioneer work of Harriet Finlay-Johnson and Henry Caldwell Cook, trends which, perhaps starting in the 1920s, still persist to the end of this century. The Drama teaching profession in this country has a history of 'taking sides', sometimes reaching a point where one set of exponents would not talk to its 'rivals'. John Allen, by the 1960s, was seen as a neutral and benign, but nevertheless shrewd, onlooker, who personally knew most of the leaders in the various branches of drama and worked hard at keeping communications open between them.[7] He was the right man in the right place when Jenny Lee, as Minister of Education, sought a report on drama in schools.

I have chosen to introduce this section on Dorothy Heathcote through this DES publication because John Allen's unbiased reporting provides a picture of drama practice in the 1960s. He reports broadly, showing respect for all kinds of dramatic representation from the nursery play-corner to Shakespearean performance, including accounts of improvisation, movement, mime, speech-training, language-development and the study of texts, relaxation and limbering exercises. He is not without criticism; he is aware of poor standards to be found in each branch of these activities, for instance the impoverishment of the literary side of drama and the reduction of movement to 'reeling and writhing', but, without a vested interest in a particular approach, he seeks high standards in all approaches and favours a balance between them.

Dorothy Heathcote too, from her position in the University, is also fully aware of these competing trends which she finds exemplified in the work of her own students,[8] who are all experienced teachers, but her innovatory work does not appear to build on any particular aspect of current practice. Her purpose seems to be to *dis*connect with even the best of that practice, choosing to alienate herself from the very vocabulary of her contemporaries and predecessors. To categorise dramatic activities as most people did, and as John Allen has done above, as 'speech' or 'movement' 'mime' or 'play' or 'improvisation'[9] or 'limbering' or 'textual study' or even 'child drama' makes communication about drama education seem possible, but Dorothy Heathcote worked outside these categories. Her work was not identifiable as any of them, for although speaking, miming, moving, improvising, studying texts etc featured in her work, they were not in themselves indicative of its essential nature.

John Allen, in the above quotation, gives Heathcote's work a label, improvised 'play-making', a term which appears to meet Heathcote's own occasional usage,[10] but, again, this is to attempt to describe the *activity*, not the central assumption behind the activity. In 1976 she said 'I don't have a name for what I do'[11] but she is not unwilling to show what she does through film and video tape and through her many articles in a wide range of journals all over the world. She is good at showing but not at explaining, for just as a painting is not finally explainable in terms other than itself, so Heathcote resists articulating her practice, only reluctantly struggling for the sake of her students to find the 'right' words, painfully aware of their reductive, distorting effect. Others, including myself, have sought to capture her philosophy and methodology. It seems that now, towards the end of the century, no article or book may be written about classroom drama without explicit or implicit reference to her practice,[12] although Hornbrook, as early as 1986, expressed surprise that her work was still being studied.

The essential nature of Heathcote's drama teaching

It is my purpose here to summarise her work sufficiently to look at implications of her approach for classroom acting. Such a summary is retrospective. By this I mean that I shall not attempt to show how explanations of Heathcote's work, her own accounts[13] and those of her interpreters, have evolved over the years, interesting as that would be.[14]

With such hindsight, I am in a position, therefore, to suggest that the essential nature of her work is bound up with her assumption that dramatic action, by its nature, is subordinated to meaning. Such a notion goes back to 1933 when Vygotski first made the following comment about child make-believe play.[15] He writes: 'In play a child deals with things as having meaning'. He suggests that whereas in 'real life' action is prioritised over meaning, the opposite occurs in make-believe. It seems to me that everything Dorothy Heathcote said about her work in those early attempts at explanation stemmed from this assumption, (not, as far as I am aware, ever stated explicitly by her)[16] that dramatic action was to do with attending to meaning, or, rather, meanings, to be negotiated with her class and leading to action. We have seen that as early as 1930 in this country, Susan Isaacs drew attention to a cognitive and hypothesising function of child make-believe play, but Heathcote, more than a generation later, seems to have been the first to take up this theoretical position. That drama education in Heathcote's hands harnesses make-believe's natural capacity for meaning-indicating, fundamentally contrasts[17] her methodology with that of Slade and Way for whom the 'doing' of drama was to be all-absorbing. In their work, as in child play, the potential for meaning-indicating was always there, but it was generally assumed that it was bound up with the personal and private, subjective engagement of each individual. For Heathcote it was the teacher's responsibility to make the most ordinary action seem extraordinary.[18] As she expressed it in an interview with me, a single, ordinary action, must appear THUS!

The possibility of a class proceeding to 'making-meaning' resided in her understanding of the nature of drama itself. In 1973 she used Kenneth Tynan's definition of drama ('Good drama...is made up of the thoughts, the words and the gestures that are wrung from human beings on their way to, or in, or emerging from a state of desperation'[19]) which, applied to her work, eventually became dubbed as 'Man in a

Mess'. Thus, if the purpose of Drama in Schools was to be understood as 'meaning-making', its substance was to be drawn from the frailty of humanity. Heathcote continues with the quotation from Tynan in which he defines a play as being 'an ordered sequence of events that brings one or more of the people in it to a desperate condition which it must always explain and should, if possible, resolve.' Heathcote affirms: 'In these two sentences lies the key to the essential nature of drama.' It is, of course, the two sentences *together* that formulate a principle for Heathcote: it is not enough to give children a taste of 'a state of desperation' through drama, for inherent in that dramatic experience must lie the potential for explication. Drama is to be about meaning-indicating, meaning-seeking, meaning-making and meaning-finding, always keyed in to her pupils' readiness to work in depth.

But such a perspective takes Drama *outside* curriculum norms. The meanings sought or indicated do not fit comfortably into identifiable disciplines.[20] As David Davis put it

> She (Heathcote) sees drama as the means of rooting all the school curriculum back in a human context where it sprang from, so that knowledge is not an abstract, isolated subject-based discipline, but is based in human action, interaction, commitment and responsibility.

Davis' observation places Heathcote's work beyond dramatisation as a method to teach curriculum subjects, valuable as that might be. She sees Drama as the very foundation of human knowledge at once personal, cultural and universal, pointing to a new conception of the curriculum and *overriding* the prevailing 'disciplines'[22] view of knowledge. Some critics of Heathcote have thought that she reduced drama to a methodology. I believe it to be nearer the case that she *raised* the level of school learning from subject-bound parameters to 'a study of Mankind'. The art form of Drama was to be a 'crucible' for knowledge.

I think it is fair to say that Heathcote was pioneering a view of education the implications of which she herself did not fully grasp. Attempting to revise our view of knowledge led at times to ambiguity. In Heathcote's efforts to describe her position, there appeared a constant slippage between the art of drama and learning outcomes, as though she was not always sure where she wanted to place the emphasis. Indeed, in the final paragraph of her perhaps most famous piece of writing, 'Signs and portents',[23] in which she discusses a teacher's need for skilful 'signing'[24] in working in role, she concludes:

> Finally, having spent a long time wondering why I have for years been irritated by the cry of 'let's have more drama in our schools', I now realise why I have always wanted to say, don't lobby for dramatics, lobby for better learning! It is, of course, because the heart of communication in social situations is the sign. All teachers need to study how to exploit it as the first basis of their work.

Heathcote's two basic, related assumptions underlying her drama praxis were, as I have argued above, that its participants engage with making meanings and those meanings relate to a human struggle.[25] Her remarkable methodology which we will now examine followed from this as night the day. Every aspect of her complex and (sometimes) obscure way of working stemmed logically from these two assumptions.[26]

Dorothy Heathcote's Drama Practice

'Living through' Drama

'What shall we make a play about?' seemed, in the earlier days of her teaching, to be Heathcote's most common starting point in getting down to drama with a fresh class.[27] [Many people assumed that such an opening *defined* 'living through' drama. We shall see that this is far from the case.] As she asked this question, her intention was to mould answers into a theme, context and particularity of action, operating jointly with the class as fellow dramatists to bring about a coherent text.[28] This combination of 'theme', 'context' and 'action' represents the principal strands of any play, along with 'plot' which latter Heathcote seemed in the eyes of many teachers to neglect, it being the one strand of play-making with which traditional teachers felt most comfortable. We have seen that Slade and Way stressed the importance of one action following another in story form; indeed, many of Slade's lessons were based on this kind of stimulus. For Heathcote, 'plot', the least important play component, was something to be appreciated by the pupils in retrospect, *after* the play-making. Her focus was always on one 'internal' situation breeding or foreshadowing the next 'internal' situation, rather than 'plot', for whereas the latter prompts a 'what-happens-next' mental set,[29] the former is more conducive to 'living through',[30] operating at seeming life rate, a modus vivendi that lent itself to staying with a situation sufficiently long to explore it and understand it more. Small group play-making, so popular in schools at this time[31] (and indeed for the rest of the century), often found pupils 'condensing' time, quickening up rather than slowing down. We shall see that Heathcote became dissatisfied with her early version of the 'living through' approach as sufficiently snail-like for the purposes of penetrating reflection,

The three strands of theme, context and particularity of action are not by themselves dramatic. They need the cementation of 'tension',[32] which in Heathcote's 'Living through' approach to play-making is injected by the teacher. As in all make-believe Play, the 'living through' of the participants is characterised by freedom from the consequences and arbitrary occurrences of real life, but while Heathcote harnessed this particular brand of 'freedom', she also insisted on a 'double burden': – both a selected dramatic tension and the need to understand its implications. The tension may take the form of a problem, a threat, suspicion, wonder, curiosity, resignation and so on – all the tension ingredients of theatre are available to 'Living through' drama. She does not, however, want the pupils to be so absorbed by the tension that they are caught in its grip. She wants the pupils to recognise the tension *as* tension and to understand something of its effect, a cognitive response as well as an affective one.

Nor does she want the pupils to be caught up in wondering how a dramatic episode is going to end. The pupils themselves must choose the outcome they will be most satisfied by or with which they can cope. In 'Making Magic' the first class of 5-6 year olds are searching for a lost baby. When one or two children suggest that the baby be found dead, Heathcote checks this out, to discover, not surprisingly, that their collective preference was for a live baby (one child later suggests a 'tied-up' baby, but that is ignored by the rest of the class) who would successfully be found. The details of how this success is to come about always remains an unknown factor, but a 'what happens next' drama, with its 'temporal bias' is avoided, but surprising things can still happen.

The existential potential[33] of Heathcote's work seems to be more of a promise than a practice. This may appear to contradict what I have claimed above to be an essential feature of her 'Living through' drama. While it is certainly true that Heathcote uses the power inherent in the present tense of spontaneous acting behaviour, she, paradoxically perhaps, distrusts abandonment to it. There are very few moments[34] in her videoed lessons when her pupils sustain their improvisational play-making beyond five minutes. More typically, hardly a minute goes by without Heathcote intervening with new input, checking, challenging, suggesting, protecting or high-lighting.

It is sometimes assumed that improvisational work by definition implies a flow of uninterrupted creativity. Indeed much 1960s drama suffered from this ideology.[35] In Heathcote's hands the 'being there' of the present and presence is a temporary luxury too valuable to be lost in existential indulgence. Rather it is a luxury to be examined and deconstructed to shape the next 'dip' into the present.[36] A number of writers[37] have seen parallels in this with the Bertolt Brecht's approach to Theatre.

With these continual teacher interruptions, the ensuing drama can at best be episodic, but this is to be one of its strengths, not a shortcoming to be regretted. Heathcote's aim is to construct a series of 'episodes', not a 'through-line' of the Naturalistic dramatist but the episodic presentation of Epic Theatre. Whereas Stanislavski appeared to aim at a seamless flow of events, Brecht writes as follows[38]:

> ...the individual episodes have to be knotted together in such a way that the knots are easily noticed. The episodes must not succeed one another indistinguishably but must give us a chance to interpose our judgement.

It may be misleading to make comparison with the presented work of leading practitioners in the theatre, for *'living through' drama is by definition a managed event, a different order of experience from stage drama*. It is not merely unrehearsed, but *unrehearsable*. Stanislavski's 'seamless flow of events' is the result of intensive rehearsal as is Brecht's Epic theatre. 'Living through' may parallel the stage play in terms of theme, context and action, but the procedure adopted is not that of the dramatist who remains outside his/her creation, but as participants reflexively negotiating from within the event the meaning of that event. The participants in 'living through' drama behave as we all behave when we make an effort to present a social event to each other in 'real life'. We *make* a party, a church service, a professional meeting and just as one cannot say: 'Oh, that was an enjoyable party, let's go through it again, so one cannot re-experience what one has just created in 'living through' drama. The party, the church service, the professional meeting and the 'living through drama *occur* and the experiences are what the participants *make* or *affirm*. The difference is that in 'living through' drama those participants have the fun of knowing that they are 'making it up' and of manipulating time and space without inhibition.

Although 'Man in a Mess'[39] is a convenient label for Heathcote's kind of work, it is misleading to the extent that she gradually drops this 'traumatic' aspect of her methodology during the late 1970s and 80s, while other drama exponents, myself included, retain and develop it. It is true that Heathcote's conception caused the work to veer towards those very dark themes prominent in any drama repertoire, but she often demonstrated that drama did not have to imply large-scale tragedy. Indeed, part of her purpose, as we have seen, was to 'make the ordinary extraordinary', as Schlovski expressed it, 'to *defamiliarise*'[40] There is a Brechtian flavour in this, but whereas Heathcote's purpose was to invite the participants to 'see afresh', Brecht's purpose in defamiliarising was unremittingly social criticism. Heathcote, I believe, wanted her pupils continually to make judgements but not necessarily political ones.[41]

As we turn now to examine Dorothy Heathcote's methodology, let us remind ourselves that much of the charm and whimsicality of Slade's story-building, the sheer delight of dancing freely to a gramophone record, the fun and speed of response to E.J. Burton's 'Abandon Ship!', the security of miming Courtney's cup of tea, the exuberance and wit of comic improvisations, and melting like snow in Brian Way's sunshine gradually disappeared from the repertoire of teachers coming under her influence.

'Living Through Drama' – Teacher-in-Role

That Heathcote nearly always plays a role herself to start, sustain and/or further the drama, has excited attention from both admirers and critics. In the early days of her career, the idea that the teacher should 'join in' was mystifying to most teachers.[42] To some such a ploy has remained indulgent and idiosyncratic.[43] For others, it is the principal strategy in classroom drama.[44] As we proceed with this analysis of her work, we shall see that 'teacher-in-role' falls into place as *the* defining characteristic of 'Living through' drama, for without 'teacher in role' the pupils' activity would be akin to child play, to 'dramatic playing', as I call it or 'symbolic play' to use a Piagetian term.

'Teacher in Role' – 'now time' and 'vulnerable space': the 'present' and the 'presence'

It is the aspect, 'now time', that is probably related most obviously to 'teacher-in-role'. Heathcote writes:

> I am constantly amazed by the miracle of how thinking about a dramatic idea can in an instant become that of carrying it into action. There is a world of difference between someone in class saying, 'Well, they would take all their belongings with them' and saying, 'Let's pack up and leave'.

A teacher saying 'Let's pack up and leave' *is there*, inside the make-believe. A fictitious world has been entered and the class are invited to join her. '*They would* take all their belongings with them' is hypothetical, impersonal, and safe in a well-tried 'teachers having a discussion' context. 'Let's pack up and leave' is 'now-time', personal, and unsafe – and the surrounding space threatens. Any gesture, remark or step, not only occurs in fictitious time; it is made visible in fictitious space – to be accounted for.

Let us for a moment compare with the security of space in Slade's and Way's 'Find a space on your own' Drama. Dressed in PE kit, spread evenly throughout the school hall, each child could hide safely in his 'cell' of exercise space. In Heathcote's class, the security during the pre-discussion of a whole class huddled *together* (probably sitting on the floor en masse) suddenly evaporates with 'Let's pack up...'or even with just 'Let's...........', for not only is it present tense, it is inclusive. The cluster of pupil bodies on the hall floor and the teacher are now together in a fictitious space- which can no longer be relied on to behave as school space should! An uneasy hiatus, astride two 'worlds', demands the pupils' collective, tacit agreement to enter the fiction. And any slight remark, gesture or even silence may be read by the teacher as belonging to that world. The pupils are caught in a new reality which can only persist if they are prepared to take a risk and join the teacher.

This 'teacher-in-role' strategy clearly invests the teacher with considerable power. When she starts her role, she is, at it were, 'holding all the cards'. One is reminded of Grotowski's retrospective thoughts on the time when his actors sought 'audience participation' from unprepared spectators. He wrote[45]:

> Years ago we tried to secure a direct participation of spectators. We wanted to have it at any price... We compelled spectators to 'perform' with us... We reached a point where we rejected these kinds of proceedings, since it was clear that were exerting pressure, tyranny of sorts. After all, we were putting the people who came to us in a false position, it was disloyal of us: we were prepared for this sort of encounter, while they were not.

Clearly, if the pupils are anticipating the 'teacher-in-role game', it becomes a different order of experience, but if seen as unexpected behaviour of a teacher, it increases the teacher's power potential. As we proceed with this study we shall come across some of the many ways Heathcote used to *qualify* the impact of teacher's role, while retaining something of its punch. The comparison with Grotowski cannot be sustained, of course, when it is realised that Heathcote selected her cards according to her reading of the needs of the class and with a view to giving the pupils the confidence to play their own cards. Growtowski's actors compelled the spectators to join in the actors' play.

'Teacher-in-Role' – Interpretation

In using 'teacher-in-role' the teacher is providing a 'script'[46] or 'text'[47] to be 'read'[48] by the pupils. This is, of course, a script[49] in the making, never written down. When, for example, in a lesson with 5 year olds (subsequently given the title of 'Making Magic'[50]) Heathcote takes on a series of roles of different women who open their doors to a group of children who are enquiring about an abandoned baby, she is demanding of those children that they 'read' each context and respond accordingly. To their horror, the sixth51 'woman' grabs the 'baby', saying 'No, I haven't lost a baby, but I've always wanted one!' Suddenly their role of smug achievers is capsized and they temporarily flounder in astonishment and guilt, eventually, drawing on a degree of collective persistence they did not know they had, winning the baby back again. This new 'page of the script' in 'Making Magic' required a high degree of adaptation from the 'readers', and, correspondingly, the teacher is 'reading' the 'script' of the pupils, which is being 'written' at two levels. She is following and adapting to their input within the fiction and their input as themselves, for as they 'write' their responses to the new crisis in the drama, they are also variously displaying signs of over-excitement, loss of attention, competition for attention, thoughtfulness, more courage, less courage, more inventiveness and fidgeting. The teacher in turn attempts to pitch *her* response to this mixture of signals, trying to find just the measure that will accommodate the whole class.[52] Taking up the accusation from one child that she was 'a witch', she briefly came out of role[53] (as a way of giving them all metaphorical 'space' in which to regain control as 'children doing drama', so that, in turn, they might gain control as 'victims of a witch') ostensibly because she needed their advice on how she should 'play' a witch. She then resumed that role (that is, *the role endowed by the children*) presenting a 'witch script' to be 'read' by a newly energised class.

The teacher-in-role's function is that of a dramatist, a dramatist who not only is supplying the words but also the accompanying non-verbal signals, so that the 'reading' required of the pupils is multi-dimensional. And as for any script, it is loaded with 'givens'. As *dramatist* the teacher is dictating at both structural and thematic levels. But there is a world of difference between a dramatist's 'givens' and those 'givens' emerging from a dramatist *function*. The ideas, words, characters and tensions within a dramatist's script are givens *outside* the actor, words on paper awaiting the the actor's gradual internalisation or 'ownership'.[54] In 'living through' drama [and this is a key feature], **the givens exist in the very medium, within the very form, in which the pupils are going to work.** Richard Schechner[55] likens the givens of life to 'raw food', waiting to be cooked by art. If we extend this metaphor, we can say that in 'living through' drama the givens *are* *already partially cooked*, and therefore more easily digestible by the teacher's class. **The direct accessibility of such 'partially cooked' elements of dramatic art as manipulation of time and space, tension, surprise and style used consciously by the teacher enhance the participants' chances of ultimately grasping how drama works,** as well as challenging their understanding of the theme or issue in hand.

There is no doubt that teacher's initial interpretation controls the pupils'. In Heathcote's own words, a teacher is 'using the art form in order to help them take a look at *this*' and the 'this' is the 'script' predecided or thought up on the spur of the moment by the teacher. Even when the teacher appears to be letting the children choose the topic,[56] her way in to that selected topic represents an initial interpretation by the teacher to be 'read' by the pupils.[57] Not until the children make their own interpretation can the Heathcote method be said to be working, for her aim is to pass over the dramatist's responsibility to the pupils, an aim that Heathcote is prepared to wait a long time for – two, three or four lessons on, depending, not on age, but on their maturity in drama-making.

One of the principles of art-making Heathcote understood from the beginning was that you cannot give children power, blithely saying 'Over to you to do what you like with'. Certainly she generated excitement and at times her 'performance' in role seemed awesome, but its effect often beguiled the onlooker who, caught up in that excitement, missed the double signal from Heathcote, saying 'Take over when you are ready'. That moment of taking over from the teacher-dramatist can only occur when the pupils are ready to interpret commitedly, imaginatively and rationally in the light of what has gone on before.

Rationality looms large in Heathcote's work. Her classes are always being invited to 'look for implications', 'check the motivation', 'assess the consequences', 'make decisions', but this is the rationality that springs from a 'feeling context' spontaneously created, drawing on 'common knowledge'[58] or, as Jerome Bruner[59] puts it, 'Folk Psychology'. Heathcote appears to be handling the everyday coinage of schooling in her regular use of terms such as 'learning', 'meaning' and 'knowledge', but these concepts in Heathcote's hands are not propositionally based,[60] even though, written down, they could be mistakenly read that way. Let us consider Heathcote's summary, spoken towards the end of the Video Tape called 'Making History' in which she worked with top juniors in Tom Stabler's[61] School. She is near the end of a two-week project on Saxon history and comments:

> I think the children realised the sharing of the amber was sharing of trust and the acceptance of the stranger into the household. The monks I think recognised something of the responsibility of the book as well as the glory of the book [*the whole project had been based on the making of a Saxon book which, in their drama, suffered many adventures through history. The 'book', an elaborate artefact based on authentic sources, was made by the pupils themselves before the drama with Heathcote began*], and all the class realised: 'How strange that you cannot choose what you do; that you are expected to do what tradition says'.

Such comments on 'the meaning' of the experience or on what the pupils have 'learnt' from the experience, or on what now counts as 'knowledge' are not based on logic but on interpretation. Heathcote's statements are more emblematic[62] than propositional; they are resonant, context-bound and value-laden.[63] Above all they are interpretative, saying no more than that if the drama experience has had significance for all or any of the children that significance might be described as 'such and such', just as one might pick out the possible themes of a play.

'Teacher-in-role' – A Cultural Perspective

That Heathcote almost always worked with the whole class together in the initial stages of a new piece of work was more than an organisational preference. Her whole approach is based on a communal perspective, so that the pupils take on their roles primarily as 'we', the people of 'this culture', and not as 'I', an interesting individual interacting with other individualistic characters. It is the collective motivations of the group rather than idiosyncratic psychological[64] desires that give the drama its dynamic. '*Man*' in a Mess is rarely about a particular personality; it is about the problem we have to face.

To say that Heathcote was influenced by authoritative writing in other fields is to overstate her position. She may at times have adopted 'fashionable' terminology from other fields but in a somewhat superficial way, managing to preserve (the mark, perhaps, of a 'true pioneer') a unique degree of insulation from external input, but there was one writer, the anthropologist Edward T. Hall[65] of Chicago, whom she had the pleasure of meeting and who helped her to find a language for what she had intuitively understood. Hall had become interested in how the deepest values of a society or cultural group are those acknowledged only when threatened. He called these a society's 'formal laws', unspoken rules governing people's lives at a deep level, and absolutely non-negotiable.[66]

In Drama the tacit rule is often made explicit. When Dorothy Heathcote, through her choice of role, endows a group with their roles, she operates on the assumption (and wishes them to do likewise) that they are controlled by unchangeable laws. Indeed these laws are what gives the group its identity. Thus, in the classic example of the BBC's (1972) 'Three Looms Waiting', when she was working with the young adolescents from Axwell Park Community Home, the non-negotiable element at the start of the drama was that they were British soldiers submitting to a German officer. 'Throw your guns through that window' from Heathcote was not a matter of choice; the action symbolised their submission, without which the drama could not progress or even start. Only when the pupils accept this 'rule' can they know who they are. When, in the 'Making of History' the 'Saxon villagers' hear that there might be surplus corn at the Monastery, the pupils' hasty 'Let's go to the Monastery' is thwarted temporarily by Heathcote who recognises that the pupils designated as 'monks' cannot be so unless they have some inherent *value* to cling to, some *law* that will give them an identity and a way of proceeding. When the Saxons eventually *do* arrive at the Monastery, it is as a meeting of two cultures: guardians of a precious book with total faith in God's providence meeting villeins who want food, not words in their bellies. The 'Abbot's (a ten year old boy): 'You do not understand why this book is so important. It's part of our life. We need it so much. It's what our Lord said.' conveys something of the embedded values of a distinct culture. Had Heathcote not intervened and delayed that meeting, the boys would simply have accommodated to the scene's confrontational but not its cultural implications. Later in this series of lessons, 'Vikings' are required and, reluctantly, Heathcote, because of shortage of time, gives up the idea of preparing the ground for yet another culture and a pretty empty scene ensues.[67]

Teacher-in-Role – a 'teacher' perspective

Overriding the 'teacher-in-role' function as a 'dramatist' or as a 'character' is the teacher as inspirer, carer, challenger, protector of children – and of the individual child. No drama can be promoted if the teacher is not sensitive to both the collective mood and the individual's needs. A unique feature of 'teacher-in-role' is that its functioning potentially and *simultaneously* embraces the requirements of both the art and the artists. When Heathcote shouts: 'Throw your rifles through the window, now!', she is not merely symbolising the authority of the German Officer over the British captives, she is insisting on submission by the pupils to the teacher's authority, (a state of affairs she knows will not last long). When in 'Making History', 'as if' in a state of frustration and resignation she says: 'I've had enough...it's up to the rest of you now', she is *literally* as well as *figuratively* urging towns-folk/pupils to take more responsibility. These are obvious, perhaps crude examples to do with who should have the power, but almost every requirement of the 'play' and need of the 'players' can be fed through 'teacher-in-role'. In 'Making History', when the two 'cultures' meet, her choice of language in role is a deliberate attempt to bestride both cultures: 'A book doesn't fill empty bellies', she yells at the 'Abbot', thus providing the 'fellow villagers' with a model of style and a sense of 'oneness' but, more importantly, feeding the pupils' imaginations with pictures from both cultures within one pithy rebuke. In 'Making Magic', she can in her role say in awed tones to the 'King and Queen', 'Do you know where the Robbers' Castle is...? (and, apprehensively)......can you take us there...?' A teacher setting up drama, in a traditional way, and not using 'teacher-in-role' would find herself saying to the five year old boy and girl playing the king and queen, 'Now, can you lead the rest of the children round the hall as though you're going to the Robbers' Castle?' The '*as though*' is a *teacher* planning a fiction from outside it [Schechner's raw food!]. With '....and can you take us there?' we are *in* the fiction [partially cooked food!].[68]

Perhaps, more significantly, 'Teacher-in-role' can raise the potential level of the content. The teacher's dialogue always seeks to take the pupils beyond their current level of discourse,[69] whether it is to challenge the reasonableness of the pupils' (characters') contribution or to bring a formality to the proceedings or to give a particular child a status the class were failing to provide or to broaden or narrow the choices or to give a glimpse of a level of generality or universality presently out of reach of the children. What is said by the teacher *coming out of role*, a comment perhaps casually 'dropped', while appearing to get on with something else, may supplement any of the 'teacher-in-role' ploys. For instance, when in 'Making History', the 'villagers' appeal to their pagan gods, they are challenged by the furious 'monks' – 'a new religion talking to the old one' is the passing gloss offered by Heathcote. She does this, not with any expectation that they are even listening, let alone understanding. Nevertheless she holds a conviction that contextualised language however obscure or unfamiliar may be accessible when pupils and teachers share that context as fellow artists and not as 'teacher teaching pupils'

Critics of Heathcote's teaching would not be prepared to accept that Heathcote treated her pupils as artists, or indeed that her work had anything to do with the aesthetic.[70] Malcolm Ross, for example would see the aesthetic in drama education as of 'over-riding obligation' and argues that Heathcote's concern to teach about content diminished the art of Drama. His arguments are to a large extent countered by Mike Fleming[71] who suggests that the aesthetic should not be seen in drama education as having primacy over understanding something, or the other way around, but rather that 'aesthetic meaning' represents an integration of many factors including artistic *and* pedagogical elements: 'The increase in understanding which gives content to the teacher's teaching remains part of the aesthetic dimension.' 'Content' cannot be detached from 'form', nor 'form' from 'content'.

Cecily O'Neill was perhaps the first to identify the dimensions of theatre form within improvised teacher-led class playmaking and to articulate a theory of form for drama in education exponents. In her *'Drama and the Web of Form'*,[72] she identifies 'time' as the key dimension of dramatic art, for both scripted or improvised 'texts'. In her doctoral thesis,[73] she extends her argument to include continuity, repetition, variation and contrast as part of 'the broader principle of rhythm' to be found in all art and theatre in particular. It is out of this theory of art that she developed her conception of 'Process Drama', which we shall be looking at further in the next chapter.

Heathcote's traditional strategies

Heathcote's 'traditional' strategies – Ritual, Movement and Depiction

There were times in the classroom during the first half of her career when Dorothy Heathcote looked like any other drama teacher. So much attention is given by writers to her innovatory ploys, especially 'teacher-in-role', that those occasions in her teaching when she stays *outside* the pupils' drama are sometimes overlooked by writers. I have put 'traditional' in commas, for all the strategies Heathcote employed in that period need to be seen in the context of her own overall conception about drama education which was startlingly inventive, with the result that the most ordinary teaching strategy could become transformed both by her overall intentions and her particular usage.

In the use of ritual, movement and depiction, however, Heathcote appeared to inherit the practice and philosophy of Emile Jacques-Dalcroze and Rudolf Laban. The latter trained her at Bradford Theatre School, giving her a strong sense of the quality of movement in space and awakening her understanding of the basic elements of theatre. From Jacques-Dalcroze she seems to have acquired a sensitivity to the relationship in visual presentation between the 'specific' (to use Jacques-Dalcroze's term) and the abstract. Both Jacques-Dalcroze and Heathcote were excited by the significance (or *signi*ficance, as Heathcote puts it) of an object in theatrical space. Heathcote may be at her most imaginative when she is selecting the visual image, making decisions about: – two or three dimensional?, size? kind of material?, positioning?, authenticity?, accuracy?, resonance?, how framed (*literally*)?, how framed (*metaphorically*)? movable? accessibility to spectators?, can they touch it? walk round it? *who* are the spectators?, when to appear?, combined with which other objects or people? how many clues? are the clues to be obvious or subtle? what kind of gestures, if any, will match the object's degree of particularity/ abstraction? will 'sound' or the 'human voice' enhance the presentation? will the written word enhance? etc. etc. Dorothy Heathcote outside the drama displays her theatrical touch just as surely as when she is playing a role *within* it. Although it is the latter she knows has the greater potential for subtlety, ambiguity and complexity, it is from *within* it that she feels most at home in working with children.

In setting up rituals such as processions (evident in both 'Making Magic' and 'Making History') her work resembled that of Slade and Way. She even followed, very occasionally, their tradition[74] of using background music. Her theatrical artistry was again revealed in her use of 'depiction',[75] a term she used broadly to cover both still and moving 'pictures' and the use of another person 'in role'.[76] However 'still' in reality, there must be for Heathcote a metaphorical movement to the depiction, always going beyond itself, 'a memory activated, or future indicated, or circumstances reflected upon, considered and *interrogated*'.This kind of strategy, which depended so much on clarity of 'signing', was not available to Slade and Way, who would have dismissed it as theatrical. Dorothy Heathcote saw it, as she saw ritual and movement as public expression in space and in arrested time. Laban helped her always to see 'the act of do', so that any action or gesture in drama always carried its dance connotation. She further explains Laban's influence[77]: '...you thought MOVE and could see MOVE in everything to do with drama without you having to be called a dancer or an actor'[78] For Heathcote it was not a break in methodology to move from 'living through' drama' to 'depiction' or 'ritual'. She perceived the underlying 'dance' in each of these,[79] always setting her sights on what Emile Jacques-Dalcroze regarded as 'musical gesture'. Writing in 1967 about Improvisation she indicates how her mind works[80] (and here she is sharing common ground with Peter Slade who might well have written what follows):

> Let us take a situation often used by teachers in Primary Schools – the capture of Persephone and the ultimate agreement between the earth mother and Pluto. Persephone is often playing with her friends when the God of the underworld takes her to his kingdom. Here we may have the *sounds* of children's voices at play, their *movements* at play. Suddenly this may be frozen into *silence* and *stillness* as the God emerges with *sounds* unlike those previously heard and the *movements* unlike those previously seen... The friends may then depart in *movement* totally unlike their first play and the place be left in complete *emptiness* and *silence* or there may be the *sound* of Persephone's weeping. Likewise all these situations will be richer if *light changes* occur as well, and *musical sounds* may be used effectively too.

The three basic elements in theatre of sound/silence; light/darkness and movement/stillness[81] combined with the elements of Laban's efforts, space, energy, pace and level, are always there in her perception of classroom drama. In depiction, these elements are overlaid by, as we have seen above, the further consideration of the abstractness or specificity of an object in space. Jacques-Dalcroze was faced with the inappropriateness of a dancer picking up real or artificial flowers from the stage, for to him the specificity of the flowers aesthetically diminished and offended the abstractness of the dancer's space. In turn Heathcote was sensitive to a comparable dilemma of, say, an inter-action between two such incompatible planes of experience as pupils relating to an effigy. Although Heathcote draws on Goffman,[82] particularly his *Frame Analysis*, to explain her notion of 'framing', I believe it is primarily her intuitive *aesthetic* sense rather than her *social* perception that guided her to recognise appropriateness. As modern-day trainee doctors about to sit an examination, the junior school children can legitimately scrutinise the 'portrait' [another teacher posing 'in role'] of Dr. Lister and then, later, 'step into' his period and his place by the convention of a 'knock on the door'. What the pupils cannot do is talk, as pupils, directly to Lister. Here we have another example of the 'non-negotiable' – the trainee doctors only exist in so far as they are serious thinkers about discoveries in medicine. It is that highly selective, 'classic',[83] strand alone that can carry them over the threshold of time and place.

A major strategy, for which it is difficult to find a name, could be described as distinctly 'Heathcotian'. It involved elaborately planned, carefully sequenced experiences, usually involving pupils in 'reading' others' presentations, writing and discussing. In carrying out such a sophisticated project or programme she is dependent on neither her 'living through' drama with which her early work is associated nor its revised form she calls 'Mantle of the Expert'. She has used such projects more and more in recent years, especially with groups not primarily interested in doing drama or as a framework for a professional week-end conference.[84]

Often the project requires the participants to observe or create un-dramatic, brief episodes, illustrating something from 'life'. Of interest to this study is whether such bland demonstrations could be said to be drama at all. In *IDEA 95: Selected Readings in Drama and Theatre Education*[85] I suggested that the most low-key demonstration might qualify as 'theatre' in that, just as the Lady of Shalott imprisoned in her tower overlooking the river flowing down to Camelot sees in her mirror life passing below as events, so pupils or any of us looking at a demonstration of some aspect of life are invited to see it as life, a conscious act of abstraction by a spectator. I wrote:

> That mirror frame, for the Lady of Shalott, is a kind of theatre: it is a peep-show; what is happening there is not real life; she can treat the images as fiction. The furniture of her room is real life. As she follows the shadows appearing from one side of the mirror to the other, she does not know what will happen, but, whatever it is, she is safe from it, beguiled by it, but safe, protected. Even in quiet times when nothing could be said to be happening, the frame is filled with her anticipation, just as an empty stage[86] is 'filled with waiting' Like the Lady of Shalott's mirror a theatre is a defined space 'filled with its own future', its own future, it can only be treated as a fiction – by whoever chooses to spectate, chooses to see it 'as', chooses to interpret.

This quotation, I believe, captures the defining elements of theatre. There must be a spectator *attending* to it and that spectator must *intend* to perceive the event 'as meaningful'[87] Lars Kleberg[88] puts it that the mere presence of a spectator is not in itself enough to make theatre: 'To be theatrical, an event must also point to something beyond itself, represent something, in a way that a boxing match or lecture on anatomy does not.'

It may be useful, therefore, to regard the use of demonstration scenes as occasions of 'theatre'. Indeed some would argue that they carry the same purpose as Brecht's *Lehrstuck*, his 'Learning-plays' in which audiences are treated as a collection of *individuals* ready to learn. Theatre, according to Brecht, 'becomes a place for philosophers'[90] Wilshire argues that Brecht's notion of 'involved detachment' applies to any good theatre, but it may be that in his 'Learning-plays' Brecht intends to give more emphasis to the 'detachment' aspect of this dialectic, as indeed is the intention behind Dorothy Heathcote's scripted scenes.

It seems to me that such scenes, with the intention of having spectators 'read' them 'as meaningful', are, at least minimally, an example of theatre.[91] In case this is thought to be a self-evident conclusion, a reminder that Peter Abbs sees Dorothy Heathcote's work as 'Devoid of art, devoid of the practices of theatre...'[92] may be timely.

Acting behaviour in Dorothy Heathcote's classrooms
Acting behaviour in 'Living through' Drama

The choice of terminology

I have been careful to slip in the word 'behaviour' after 'acting' in the above title, for when I interviewed Dorothy Heathcote and posed the question about classroom acting, her immediate, unqualified response was to say 'Oh, I wouldn't call it *acting*! When I directed plays with amateurs I don't think I even then used the word *acting*! I would ask them to find out why they were doing a particular action, what their motives were.' She and I laughed and shared the idea that a director was more likely to say to an actor 'Stop *acting*!' She added 'I think behaving is the word I use in my mind.' It would be fair, I think, to add that she sees children in drama behaving 'significantly'.

It seems reasonable to assume too that for Heathcote 'acting', put at its lowest, is indeed associated with something false, deceiving by trickery, artifice, pretending or perhaps working purely technically, giving a faultless performance while mentally making a shopping-list, a form of behaviour not to be found either in the classroom or the amateur stage. At its best, however, she would see the art of acting as 'the highly controlled and perfect selection of behaviour to interpret a playwright to an audience'. We can recall that Frances Mackenzie (1930), director of training for the British Drama League, eschewed the use of the term in respect of children and non-professionals, not because it was pejorative but too sophisticated. Finlay-Johnson, Caldwell Cook, E.M. Langdon and Marjorie Hourd had no such inhibitions about its usage. Slade and Way avoided the term with children because of its theatrical overtones. They saw acting as something pupils would grow into when they were ready. Heathcote seems to be denying even this, not, however, because of some level of immaturity she sees in the children, but because classroom drama, in her view, requires a different mind set of the participants, one that is not framed by the need to behave like an actor – or, as we shall see, even like a pupil!

Whatever usage of the term 'acting' her predecessors adopted, they would no doubt have agreed, in true Western theatre tradition, about its defining feature: that is, that 'real acting' was to do with developing a 'character'.[93] Indeed the reluctance of those who chose not to apply the term to children's make-believe behaviour appeared to stem from the assumption that 'characterisation' was beyond the immature. Whereas Peter Slade excludes the term 'characterisation' in relation to children completely from his most recent (1995) publication, Brian Way saw it as part of the natural development of the child, becoming more discriminating as the child gets older.[94] The Schools Council team (1979), on the other hand, drew a distinction between playing a role and playing a character[95]:

> In taking up a role...the individual is basically representing an attitude or set of attitudes. The role they are identifying with may be a pure stereotype – a charity worker, a company director. If the child begins to identify more completely behind the role, he begins to move into characterisation.[96]

To both role-play and characterisation the authors apply their new term 'acting-out',[97] which they see as 'the distinctive feature of drama'. Their whole book is devoted to the examination of an activity in which pupils temporarily adopt attitudes in order to explore ideas. Ken Robinson,[98] one of its authors, later puts the distinction between 'acting-out' and 'acting' slightly differently,[99] the former, in his view, applying to 'exploratory activities of classroom drama', the latter exclusively to 'the activities of those who act a part to an audience.', – thus investigation of a 'character' does not in itself qualify as 'acting', unless it is to occur on stage,[100] a view which coincided with my own at the time, reflecting, it seems, my 1979 continuum referred to in the introduction to this book. At that time I saw 'performing' and 'playing' polarised on a public/private basis, but I also made the mistake which Robinson avoids of seeing what the pupils do as 'dramatic playing' and what the actors do as 'theatre'. Robinson corrects this by defining 'theatre' as the *encounter* between actors and audience, and not what actors do.[101] My original idea for a continuum of contrasted *activities* of make-believe play and theatre, I later amended to contrasted *dis-*

positions or *intentions* either to be *in* a make-believe event or to *communicate* a make-believe event. This revised version will itself be subjected to challenge in the final chapter of this study.

The Schools Council team in using terms such as 'role-play', 'attitudes' etc. are adopting the language of sociology, the newly popular science of the 1970s, in order to convey a progressive kind of Secondary Drama practice to do with negotiating meaningful social situations. Dorothy Heathcote herself appeared to adopt this kind of language, especially when she wrote[102]:

> I define educational drama as being 'anything which involves persons in active role-taking situations in which attitudes, not characters are the chief concern, lived at life-rate (i.e. discovery *at this moment*, not memory based) and obeying the natural laws of the medium.'... I maintain that problem-solving is the basis of learning and maturation.

McGregor *et al* hoped (reasonably, enough from Heathcote's[103] above remarks) that the attempt to create a new way of talking about drama would embrace all modern practice, both the fairly safe 'make up a play about privilege and deprivation'[104] kind of drama and the more risky 'living through' approach of Dorothy Heathcote. If in writing about characterisation Brian Way, following the Naturalistic theatre tradition, could be said to have *psychologised* the character-building process, now all forward looking drama could be described as *socialising* it. As we have seen, however, the common ground shared by a group in Heathcote's classes tended to be *culturally* rather than *socially* bound. To describe 'preserving the word of God for posterity by hiding the book from the marauders' (as in the 'Making History' video) merely as an adopted social 'attitude' seems reductive and appears to miss the kind of fundamental level of understanding sought by Heathcote. It seems to me that Heathcote's own usage of sociological terminology served her inadequately – but it was fashionable at that time![105]

Some features of acting behaviour in 'Living through' Drama
In Heathcote's 'Living through' drama, more usefully described perhaps as anthropological than sociological, acting behaviour, at its best, involved a group identification (conscious or unconscious) with a

set of values implicit in whatever culture or sub-culture was being created. The fictitious identity of the group was sustained by the collective enterprise and the extent to which individuals submitted to that enterprise. This is what places Heathcote's drama in a different order of experience from both Child Drama and from a traditional view of improvisational work in which individual characterisation formed the starting point.[106] This is also why Robert Witkin's (1974)[107] elegantly articulated theory of personal expression in the arts can have little bearing on Heathcote's practice, for in 'living through' drama the initial behaviours are nearer to a group contracting to feel their way into a value system, rather than, as Witkin would have it, a 'subject response' to an impulse. In Heathcote's classroom there is a task for the group to carry out or a problem for them to solve. At its most unsophisticated level of practice their actions may not look any different from a group of pupils carrying out a 'real' task; at its best the pupils will effectively and economically use the basic dimensions of theatre: darkness/light, stillness/movement; and sound/silence. In this respect, Heathcote has claimed, the pupils are 'following the same rules' as actors[108] who are also bound by these elements of the theatre art form.[109] One could add that *outside* dramatic acts we continually attempt to sign significantly within those same 'theatre' dimensions.[110]

What is of supreme interest here are the parameters of behaviour emanating from the implicit values of the fictitious sub-culture that control how those tasks may be tackled. Choices may be made by the pupils only within those constraints, which may affect *style* (even the hungry Saxons in 'Making History' may approach the Abbot only with some measure of restraint), *knowledge* (the pupils have to remember that as Saxons they cannot read the words in the precious book), and *understanding* (they have to have some sense of what it is to have the crops fail and be hungry). Outside these cultural constraints there are *organisational* (a whole class cannot effectively stand in front of the Abbot without blocking views or crushing, so the pupil playing the Abbot must use his role to instruct them to sit on the floor as soon a possible), *aesthetic* (the 'book' will only become important if it is well placed) and *reflective* (the pupils are 'makers' and 'spectators' of their own 'Saxon' actions, judging their effect and their effectiveness) imperatives. Thus at its most sophisticated all six dimensions may impinge on that basic engagement with the task.

And that basic engagement is an act of *building* a culture, rather than *representing* a role or attitude. This concept of acting behaviour as collectively *'making'* and *'affirming'* I believe to be critical to our understanding of 'Living through' drama. It falls outside the usual contrasted assumptions about child acting, that either children *'become'* or they *'impersonate'* their roles. It lies in marked contrast to the traditional expectations of 'Improvisation' which, for example, John Hodgson and Ernie Richards outline. Nor does it fit the Brecht's concept of 'gestus', requiring the actor to both represent and comment. It is nearer to what we do in everyday life when we present ourselves as belonging to a group, say, of teachers, or shoppers or students, and as such it is set apart from stage acting while sharing similar dimensions. Its significance, of course, lies in the children's submission to the disciplines required of that culture. When its inner laws are expressed the pupils have, to use Heathcote's well-known phrase, 'stumbled on authenticity'.

Although it may seem inappropriate to apply the word 'sincere' to the work of Heathcote's pupils in 'Living through' drama, Dorothy Heathcote favours the term 'authentic' as not inappropriate for some moments of acting, when, (she is here speaking from a pupil's point of view)[111]:

> ...you know what you are doing is right. You know how soldiers are... but it's your idea of how soldiers are and you've taken it as far as you can within the context, but because you know that's what you've done, you've widened your experience of soldiers, because *this* context and *this* teacher have challenged you to take it a bit further than you ever could have done by yourself. But also it adds to your understanding of being a person. There's more people inside you because you've done this.

I think Heathcote is assuming here that if it 'feels right' for the participant it will ring true for others, that authenticity in acting behaviour is a unity of 'process/product' and of private/public. It is again significant, however, that Heathcote says '...you know how soldiers are...you've widened your experience of soldiers...'. She cannot bring herself, as others might, to say 'You know how *a soldier* is...' The pupil acting authentically in Heathcote's eyes is presenting soldiers.

Spectatorship in 'Living Through' Drama

The boy referred to above is also presenting soldiers in his own eyes, a spectator, as it were, along with the other participant/spectators of the presentation. There are at least three levels of spectatorship involved here: an awareness of what is happening to himself, an awareness of what is being 'made', in this case, a presentation of 'soldiers', and an awareness of what could happen or needs to happen to further the drama. Mike Fleming uses the term 'percipient' to embrace both participant and the dramatist functions. The pupil's natural feeling response to the immediacy and particularity of the dramatic moment is qualified by the spectator/dramatist overview – and further qualified by knowledge of the safety net, as in all make-believe play, of another world (a 'real' one?) in which to take refuge. And, most importantly, is the underlying pleasure of creating something which may serve to override all other feelings.

Enhancing the acting in 'Living Through' Drama

Heathcote exploits two 'lures',[113] to promote the image of the work itself. At some point early in the work, she will insist that 'someone else somewhere in the world is doing this', implying that we're not just playing games – this is a real problem for someone. A further 'bait' to the pupils is the promise of an audience, not, of course, the audience one rehearses for but the audience to whom the pupils will be able to teach something. As Heathcote put it in the interview: 'They won't come to see our performance but to understand something.' Thus the pupils are persuaded, should they need it, that what they are doing is important in two ways, 'that it is actually happening to others as well as us', and that 'others, even people like headmasters, can learn from what we do'.

Emotion and acting behaviour in 'Living through' Drama

We have seen that raw emotion has no place in 'Living through' drama. The content may well be about a 'Man in a Mess', but the spectator/audience function combined with the pleasure in creating function is so strong that painful experience is filtered through that distanced perspective. Thus as Fleming says[114]: 'The feeling of anger in drama is real but it would be misleading to actually say the participant is angry.' Heathcote herself would prefer to put it as 'the feeling of anger is *explored* in drama'.[115]

As we have seen, in Heathcote's approach a further distancing is guaranteed by her continual intervention and demand for further reflection. One can see, however, that in less experienced hands the pupils could become over manipulated either by the teacher or by powerful pupils in the class who exploit the drama for ends related to the 'real world'.[116]

However, the more common problem, it seems to me, is not in the drama becoming 'too raw' but in its failing to be credible enough. At its worst, the pupils are simply left outside the teacher's play[117] or they resort to 'pretending' feelings, as though they were in a traditional drama where characters are required to show their feelings of 'surprise' or 'hate' or 'jealousy' or 'amusement' to an audience. If the pupils fall into the latter trap, the teacher has misunderstood the basic task driven structure of 'living-through' drama.

Although Heathcote herself has written (perhaps on only one occasion) of the importance children feeling 'real' emotion 'in the heat of the moment', when one examines how she illustrates such a moment, her explications are wrapped up with 'thought and planning'. She admits that 'emotion is at the heart of the drama experience', but in her dramatic work emotional experience invariably turns out be the kind that a community can share: the participants *collectively* suffer fear, anxiety, sadness, disappointment, hope, or relief etc. about, or as a result of, a planned enterprise, such as guiding Macbeth safely through the jungle after battle – and such feelings, as we have seen, are further modified by the 'percipient/pleasure' function. For Heathcote the principal component of all acting behaviour is the 'self-spectator', which protects the participants into a level of emotion from which they may remain safely detached, both *engaged* and *detached*.

In the next chapter we shall see that interest by some of Heathcote's followers in giving participants an exciting 'theatrical' experience through the use of 'Living through' drama has led to a dramatic 'genre' in the classroom whose objectives in some respect are no longer consistent with Heathcote's intentions.

Acting in Depiction
'Man in a Mess' or 'living through' implies, as we have seen, 'being there': 'Let's pack up and go!' demands instant response. Dorothy

Heathcote sought other methods belonging to a straight theatrical context; one was 'depiction'. The use of 'tableau' or 'still picture' is probably one of the most popular drama ploys in the Western world and appears at first sight to be what Heathcote means when she uses 'depiction'. However, it soon becomes clear in discussion, that she sees 'tableau' as a superficial form of presentation that confines the participants to the external features of an action or feeling.[118] 'Depiction' for Heathcote is an arrested movement, a form that penetrates.

There appear to be two root sources for this depth of demonstration. Heathcote believes that the body can draw on 'deep wells it already knows', that somatically it has the capacity for capturing long-held modes of expression.[119] The second source is the personal value system. There is a fascinating difference here with the 'living through' drama which puts the group in touch with the formal, informal and technical laws of a sub-culture. In 'depiction' it is the personal values of:

'I do this.........................an action

Because...,,....... ....,,,,,,,of a motive

Therefore................,,.........my investment is in

My models that bred this investment

Because this is how my life should be – my stance or values[120]

Each of us carries this hierarchy of values and each action we make is susceptible to this kind of analysis. Heathcote sees depiction as an action (usually stilled)[121] portrayed by a pupil in a way that gives a glimmer of a character's belief system. This is perhaps nearer to Brecht's 'gestus', for the pupil is not the 'character', but demonstrates the character and at the same time provides a kind of commentary on what the action 'means'.[122]

The 'demonstrating' is bound up with active spectatorship from the rest of the class.[123] Of prime importance is the 'reading' by the audience. Depiction is nothing without a 'reader'. The spectators provide the raison d'etre of the depiction. Indeed, if the 'actors' are inexperienced in drama, Heathcote will make sure from the beginning that somehow or other it will be the *non*-actors, the audience, who will be put on the spot.[124] Active spectatorship may go from mimimal involvement (discussing what they see) to placing something within the 'picture' or giving each actor a line of dialogue, redirecting the scene or even[125] replacing the actor.

'Depiction' appears to be in marked contrast to 'living through' drama. Whereas the mode of acting in the latter may described as existential, not easily repeatable and audience-independent, the former could be said to be illustrative, repeatable and audience-dependent. It seems to me that contrast between the two modes inevitably centres on the difference required in acting skills and structure. As such the issue will be central to the final chapter of this book.

In the meantime, we need to complete this account of Dorothy Heathcote's work. As others were seeking an alternative version of her methodology that found its most profound expression in teacher workshops, Heathcote was experimenting with a world of enterprise culture, finding there a new educational vista that could revolutionise teaching and that, in a curious way, harks back to the vision Sir Percy Nunn (1920) had of how education might be. In the next chapter, wI shall suggest that my own work, along with that of Cecil O'Neill and Peter Millward represent a reinterpretation of 'living through', as indeed does Heathcote's own 'Mantle of the Expert', which will also be examined.

Notes

1   Institutes of Education were formed at this time by Universities to promote in-service training for experienced teachers. Until the 1980s they were separate from Departments of Education which concentrated on inital training of teachers. The Durham Institute (located in Newcastle) became part of Newcastle University in 1954.

2   For a full biographical account see Sandra Hesten's unpublished Ph.d thesis, entitled 'The Construction of an Archive and the Presentation of Philosophical, Epistemological and Methodological Issues relating to Dorothy Heathcote's Drama in Education Approach'. Dr. Hesten was responsible for building a 'Dorothy Heathcote archives', at Lancaster University, which comprehensively houses an extensive collection of published and unpublished material by Heathcote, her past students and colleagues in the field. Hesten's detailed and scholarly analysis of Heathcote's work, written in 1995, makes interesting comparison with Betty Jane Wagner's more vivid attempt, 19 years earlier, to captivate her readers with the possibility of 'dancing with a whirlwind' [Wagner,

B.J. (1976 (1979, this edition)) *Dorothy Heathcote: Drama as a Learning Medium* Hutchinson London p.231]. Betty Jane Wagner is currently (1997) revising this publication.

3   DES (1967) *Drama: Education Survey 2* HMSO, p.38

4   DES (1967) *Children and their Primary Schools (The Plowden Report)* HMSO

5   The first use of the term 'drama *in* education' appeared, as we have seen, in the Ministry of Education publication, *The Teaching of English in England* (1921) HMSO. It is significant, I believe, that the Inspectorate did not want to adopt Slade's 'Child Drama' terminology.

6   Dorothy Heathcote used the term 'drama in education' in relation to her own work, so that it gathered both a broad and a narrow meaning. Sometimes it meant 'non-performance'; at others it referred more particularly to the kind of classroom drama emerging from the North-East.

7   After serving as HMI with special responsibility for Drama, John Allen became Principal of The Central School of Speech and Drama. Throughout his career he was seen as a prestigious figure, serving all aspects of professional, amateur and pedagogical drama and dance education. Now, long retired, I believe people still regard him as that 'wise onlooker', and, as I do, still seek his advice.

8   A book that seems to embrace all the 'trends' is *Creative Drama in Schools* by a York teacher, Brother Barnfield, in 1968 [Barnfield, Gabriel (1968) Creative Drama in Schools Macmillan London]. His chapter headings [including 'Rhythm'; 'Movement'; 'Dance'; 'Improvisation'; 'Mime'; Character and Plots'; 'Dance-Drama'; 'Speech'; 'Play-reading'; 'Production'; 'Lighting' and so on] seem to embrace all the trends of the previous 30 years.

9   Heathcote did once write at the editors' request an article entitled 'Improvisation' in a pamphlet, *'Drama in Education'*, by the National Association for the Teaching of English and published by Bodley Head [Heathcote, D. (1967) 'Improvisation' in *Dorothy Heathcote: collected writings on education and drama* (Eds: Johnson, Liz and O'Neill, Cecily) Hutchinson London, pp.44-48, but its content bears little relationship to contemporary practice in Improvisation – and she tended subsequently to avoid using the term.

10 One example is in *The Uses of Drama* by John Hodgson [Heathcote, D. (1972) 'Drama as Challenge' in The Uses of Drama by John Hodgson (Ed) Eyre Methuen London pp.156-165] in which she refers to the children 'making knowledge clear to themselves' in a 'play-making situation' [p.160]

11 Wagner B.J. (1979) *ibid* p.13

12 In the last decade a handful of writers have been critical of her work. One of her first critics was John Crompton (1978), who facetiously entitled Chapter 17 of his thesis: *'Drama as Dorothy Heathcote'*. For a well-reasoned account of the early stages of the ensuing debate see Ken Byron's two articles, 'Drama at the Crossroads', Part One and Two in *2D* Vols. 6 and 7, Autumn 1986 and 7 respectively.

13 Like many leaders in the field of Drama education Dorothy Heathcote tended to employ terminology from other disciplines according to what was in fashion. For

instance, in the early '70s it would surprise no-one that she adopted Liam Hudson's notion of 'convergent and divergent thinking' [Hudson, Liam (1966) *Contrary Imaginations* Methuen London] in 'Subject or System' (1971) in Nigel Dodd and Winifred Hickson's *Drama and Theatre in Education* Heinemann London, whereas by 1989 she is using a term like 'blurred genre' from Clifford Geertz's (1983) *Local Knowledge* pp.19-36 Basic Books, in her address to the NATD Conference October 1989

14   It is curious that the only publication devoted entirely to an account of her work came from America: Wagner, B.J. (1976) *op cit.* It is not surprising that some attempts, in the earlier days, to describe her approach should misconstrue [John Hodgson, for instance, writing in 1972, described her active participation as like 'a Moreno-style Director' (Hodgson, John (1972) *op cit* p.156)], but, sadly, much later writers also misinterpret, for instance, Hornbrook's charge that Heathcote's approach reveals 'a commitment to naturalism' could not be more misleading (Hornbrook, D. (1989) *op cit* p.76). It is relatively easy for me to spot stark errors such as these in other people's writing; I may well be blind to my own misinterpretations of Heathcote's work. My understanding has evolved over 30 years of contact. The *way* in which I have chosen to describe her approach through *these* chapters differs markedly from my earlier accounts [see, for example, *Drama as Education* (1984)] but I hope that each occasion for writing takes me nearer the essential characteristics of her complex practice. Let us hope that I am not guilty along with others cited here of misrepresentation.

15   Vygotski, L.S. (1933 [trans. 1976]) 'Play and its Role in the Mental Development of the Child' in *Play: Its Role in Development and Evolution* by Bruner, J.S. et al (eds) Penguin Harmondsworth, pp.537-554

16   Perhaps the nearest she gets to explicitness is in the middle of her lesson with a group of adolescents at the Royal Court Theatre Conference [Robinson, Ken (Ed) (1980) *Exploring Theatre and Education* Heinemann London p.29] when she remarks to her class 'We only have to find a meaning'.

17   It seems extraordinary to me that John Crompton, in his M.Ed thesis on *A Critical Evaluation of the Aims and Purposes of Drama in Education* (1978) unpublished, University of Nottingham, concludes of Dorothy Heathcote: 'What she does differs little from Slade's practice...' p.344

18   Sandra Hesten, (1995) *op cit* p.97 links this ordinary/extraordinary aspect of Heathcote's purpose with Meyerhold's 'Theatre of the Grotesque'

19   Heathcote uses this quotation from Tynan in Heathcote D. (1973) *op cit* p.157. She abstracted it from Tynan, Kenneth (1957) *Declarations* McGibbon and Kee London

20   The recognition that Drama was something more than a school 'subject', was voiced as early as 1920 by E.M.Gilpin (1920 *op cit*, p.178) who suggested: 'It [Drama] seldom, or never, has the status of a school 'Subject', and yet may it not be more than any one subject – a synthesis of many?'

21 Focus paper delivered to NADIE conference in Sydney entitled 'In Defence of Drama in Education' subsequently published in *The NADIE Journal* Vol 15, No1 Summer 1990.

22 Fleming (1982) *op cit* p.141 has pointed out that educational theorists such as p. Hirst and R.S. Peters reacted against the excesses of Progressivism, epitomised for them in the *Plowden Report*, by reaffirming the 'public modes of experience', as reflected by the 'disciplines'. Fleming quotes from *The Logic of Education* [Hirst, P. and Peters R.S. (1970) Routledge, p.ix] which its authors saw as providing 'a much needed reconciliation between subject-centred and child-centred approaches to education.' Dorothy Heathcote, I believe, does not 'centre' her work in either direction.

23 Heathcote, Dorothy (1980) 'Signs and portents' in *Dorothy Heathcote: collected writings on education and drama* (Eds. O'Neill and Johnson 1984) *op cit* p.169

24 From 1980 Heathcote started to adopt the language of Semiotics which no doubt fitted her campaign to persuade people, particularly teachers, to see non-verbal or extra-verbal communicating as basic to all teaching and not just a prerogative of theatre. Typically of Heathcote, she draws from an idea behind a new movement in scientific, sociological, theatrical or anthropological thought and adapts it, indeed reshapes it, to her own needs. She sees no need, thereafter, always to draw attention to her original source which sometimes would not be recognisable. In this particular instance of Semiotics, Heathcote invents her own very useful terms: significant and significantly.

25 Heathcote herself puts it less grandly in the video tape of 'Making History', dated 1971. She says: 'There's the drama of big 'uns telling little 'uns what to do...there's the drama of ordinary people just being plain awful to each other and having to learn how to get on. I suppose this is our social drama, our 'kitchen sink', drama if you like, and there's this other drama of large events over which we have no control, the great catastrophes, the great miracles, where all you do is struggle through.' [Video Tape 1. No: 0.03.48, 'Making History' Newcastle University Library]. Sometimes when Dorothy Heathcote wanted to give a class she had not met before a choice of topic, she would offer that choice by asking the class which of these three kinds of drama they preferred – See, for example 'Evoking Gut-Level Drama' by Betty Jane Wagner in *Learning: The Magazine for Creative Teaching* (US) March, 1974, p.18.

26 I think it is fair to say that because these two assumptions were so obvious to her, she did not always see the need to spell them out to her readers.

27 Dorothy Heathcote taught classes of all ages regularly as her most effective way of training her students. These sessions became known as 'demonstration lessons'. It was fairly common, as part of a summer school abroad for her to teach a volunteer class every day for one or two weeks for a couple of hours, so that continuity with a theme could be demonstrated.

28 Using the term 'text' here in its broadest sense, as does Hornbrook in *Education in Drama* Falmer London (1991) p.49.

29   See Britton, James (1970) *Language and Learning* Penguin Harmondsworth

30   'Living through' became a favourite way of identifiying Heathcote's approach which I have retained in this book as a suitable title for what is a major dramatic genre, which adopts a 'teacher-in-role approach. She uses it herself, for instance in 'Drama as Challenge' [in Johnson and O'Neill (1984) pp.80-89].

31   Many observations of this kind of drama making are to be found in the Schools Council's *Learning Through Drama: Schools Council Drama Teaching Project* (10-16) [McGregor, Lynn, Tate, Maggie and Robinson, Ken (1978) Heinemann London.

32   One of the confusions evident among drama teachers at this time was that 'Drama was '*Conflict*', rather than 'tension', so that teachers and pupils alike assumed that drama could not occur unless people were put in opposition to each other – schools halls and drama studios became very noisy places! It was regarded as normal for improvisational work to be based on family confrontation. (There are many examples in the work observed by the Schools Council Drama Teaching Project (10-16)

33   I have applied the term 'existential' in most of my publications to a dramatic mode of 'being in the present'; of 'something occurring now'. Children's uninterrupted play is of this ilk. I have sometimes called it a 'dramatic playing mode'.[See, for instance, Towards a Theory of Drama in Education (1979) Longman London]

34   'Mantle of the Expert' responsibilities excepted, as we shall see in the next chapter.

35   David Self has a telling personal anecdote relating to a comment from one of his teacher-trainees following Self's struggle to get good discipline from a comprehensive school class: 'On the bus back to college, one student was worried. 'With all respect' he asked, 'aren't you afraid you might have repressed their natural spontaneity?' [Self, D. (1975) *A Practical Guide to Drama in the Secondary School* Ward Lock London p.7] This matches my own experience in the 1970s. I recall working with a group of teachers on a week-end in-service course who complained bitterly that when I interrupted their play-making I was 'ruining their creativity'.

36   It is this continual interruption by Heathcote of her pupils' work that has gained her the reputation in some quarters, of 'Fascist' interventionist.

37   One of the first admirer's of Heathcote's work to draw attention to similarities between Brechtian theatre and Heathcote drama was Oliver Fiala in 1972. Dorothy Heathcote herself showed interest in parallels being drawn in 'From the Particular to the Universal' in *Exploring Theatre and Education* by Ken Robinson (Ed) Heinemann London (1980) in which she takes a poem by Brecht and, line by line, 'translates' its meaning into a teacher in the classroom orientation, not, it should be said, to everyone's satisfaction. As Nicholas Wright, writing in the same publication puts it: 'Heathcote's reading of the poem represents another point of view'. (p.101).

38 Brecht, Bertolt, (1984) *Brecht on Theatre* [Edited and translated by John Willett] Hill and Wang New York p.78

39 Another popular term used to describe Heathcote's work was 'gut-level drama'. It appeared in the title of an article by B.J. Wagner [Wagner, B.J. (March,1974) 'Evoking Gut-Level Drama' in *Learning: the Magazine for Creative Teaching*. In a private letter B.J. Wagner explained to me that she was persuaded by the journal editors against her better judgement to use this phrase in the title. However, the term seemed to 'catch-on'. This was perhaps unfortunate, for Heathcote sought to balance emotional engagement with 'a cool strip' of reflection.

40 Shklovski, Victor, 'Art as Technique' in *Russian Formalist Criticism: Four Essays* trans. by Lemon, L.T. and Reis, M.J. (1965) pp.3-57. Heathcote herself quotes from Shlovski [Heathcote, D. 'Material for Significance' in *Dorothy Heathcote: Collected Writings on Education* (1984) *op cit* p.127] when she says: We very readily ccase to 'see' the world we live in and become anaesthetized to its distinctive features. The art permits us 'to reverse that process and to creatively deform the usual, the normal, and so to inculcate a new, childlike, non-jaded vision in us'.'

41 It is possible that Chris Lawrence [See his review for *National Drama* Volume 4 No.2 (1996) of *Drama for Learning* by Heathcote, D. and Bolton G. (1995) Heinemann New Jersey] would not agree with this point, for he seems to be arguing that Brecht and Heathcote share reconstitution of society as an all-embracing moral purpose behind their work.

42 John Fines and Ray Verrier, two most distinguished practitioners in the teaching of History and Drama, were so stimulated by Dorothy Heathcote's example, that they became a team to try out her methods with the teaching of History – and seemed to take 'teacher-in-role' in their stride, as though they had known no other method. Their very readable book explains it all! [*The Drama of History: an experiment in co-operative teaching* (1974) New University Education London].

43 Malcolm Ross was probably the most vehement opponent of 'teacher-in-role'. Although he advocated the forming of a '...special relationship – that allows teacher and pupil *to play together*' (Ross' italics) [Ross, Malcolm (1978) *The Creative Arts* Heinemann London, p.24], he saw 'teacher-in-role' as of a more manipulative order than a playful sharing: 'Every such manipulative act takes away something of the child's freedom and responsibility for his own actions: too many drama teachers I feel are ready to jump into role to heighten the tension, thereby running the same risk as the art teacher who takes his brush to the child's painting.' [Ross, M. 'Postscript to Gavin Bolton' in *The Development of Aesthetic Experience* by Malcolm Ross (Ed) (1982) Pergamon Oxford p.149]. See also Hornbrook, D. (1989) *op cit* p.15.

44 Cecily O'Neill's publication [O'Neill, C. (1995) *op cit*] *Drama Worlds* virtually opens with a leader's 'in-role' dialogue: 'I hope no one saw you come here. I sent for you because...' and play-making begins.

45 Grotowski, Jerzy (March 1973) 'Holiday' in *The Drama Review* No. 17, p.129

46   It is noted that recent writers on child make-believe play are adopting the term 'script' to describe a canonical repertoire of actions and words a child invents in relation to familiar events. See, for instance, 'Playing with Scripts' by Katherine Nelson and Susan Seidman (1984) in *Symbolic Play* by Inge Bretherton (Ed) Academic Press Orlando

47   Cecily O'Neill, in her doctoral thesis (1991) writes: 'The word 'text', before it referred to a written or spoken, printed or manuscript text, meant a 'weaving together'. In this sense it is clear that there can be no performance without 'text', but while there is always a text there may not always be a script. To conceive of the text, whether written, improvised, or transcribed as the weave for the event is useful....we can perceive of the text as a kind of design for action, a kind of net or web, woven tightly or loosely, and organising the materials of which it is made.' p.140. Of the two words I have used here, it is probably 'text' that is more generally useful, although in this instance I am using 'script' to convey a parallel with a traditionally accepted view of giving pupils a written script to which they are expected to respond.

48   Beatriz Cabral has made a penetrating study of a postmodern conception of 'readership' in relation to pupils and teacher-in-role. [Cabral, Beatrice, Angela, Vieira (1994) '*Toward a Reader-oriented assessment in drama in education*' Ph.D thesis (unpublished) University of Central England]

49   Peter Slade also provided a 'script', but his was a story-building shared with the children before they got on their feet in action. It nevertheless had to be 'read' and later 'interpreted' by his pupils.

50   'Making Magic' was made into a video tape in 1971. It is housed in Newcastle University library.

51   Previous roles included 'a deaf lady', 'an obsessive polisher', 'a sly lady, suggesting hidden motives', 'a lady who put the baby in a kennel', a lady who tried to feed the baby with a bacon sandwich'.

52   Teachers constantly find themselves in this position of attempting to contain or embrace a large group, but it is not surprising that many drama teachers feel it too crude a ploy for artistic work. Malcolm Ross puts the point forcibly: ' large group work (the normal school drama set-up) seems to me to be virtually impossible in most school situations – except at the most superficial and so educationally pointless level.' [Ross, M. (1982) *ibid* p.149] In this instance, however, it should be noted that Dorothy Heathcote, having 'shocked' the class' knows how to 'cool' it, an aspect of her work which Ross seems to miss when he urges that drama lessons are too 'extravagent and excitable, often on account of some commitment by the drama teacher to giving the children a good (i.e. a 'hot') time in every single lesson.' (*ibid* p.149). There may be some justice in Ross' comment here. It may be that lessons he has observed simply represented a misreading of Heathcote's approach, for it was never her intention to wind children up into a state of excitement. On the other hand, Ross may have suffered from having observed only examples of bad teaching. It is a curious coincidence that his colleague Robert Witkin in his illuminative theoretical text [Witkin, Robert W.

(1974) *The Intelligence of Feeling* Heinemann London, p.81] includes but one detailed description of a drama lesson with a view to demonstrating drama education's excesses – and this, too, appears to be a singularly inadequate example of teaching. Both men seem inclined to make a law out of 'bad cases'. Nevertheless their criticisms were reflecting some apprehension about the emotional and interpretive elements of Dorothy Heathcote's method.

53 A constituent skill of teacher-in-role is the ability to know when and how to come out of it.

54 In the chapter on Finlay-Johnson, I use the term 'ownership' in respect of 'ownership of knowledge'.

55 Schechner, R. (1977) *op cit* p.38

56 In the first of the two lessons on the 'Making Magic' tape, the children instruct the teacher that a queen has lost her baby, but in the second lesson, with a different class, the 'abandoned baby' idea is the teacher's.

57 Heathcote sees this initial interpetation by the teacher as 'making a channel for their [the pupils'] thinking'. See Video (1971) 'Making History' Part One 0.15.02.

58 Mike Fleming draws attention to the usefulness of seeing the knowledge base of drama, not in terms of a 'discipline', but rather as 'common understanding' an expression derived from R.K.Elliott. Fleming writes: 'What he (Eliott) has in mind seems exactly the sort of understanding of human situations which the teacher of drama is likely to promote.' [Fleming M. (1982) *ibid* p.161]

59 Bruner, Jerome (1990) *Acts of Meaning* Harvard University Press Cambridge, Mass

60 I now believe my attempt in *Towards a Theory of Drama in Education* to couch learning through drama in propositional terms was misplaced. [Bolton, G. (1979) *op cit* p.60]

61 Tom Stabler [Stabler, T. (1978) *Drama in Primary Schools: Schools Council Drama 5-11 Project* Macmillan London] headmaster of Ward Jackson School, Hartlepool, an ex-student of Dorothy Heathcote's, was responsible for the Schools Council Primary School project which ran concurrently with the Secondary investigation.

62 Using a term adopted by Bruner (1990) *op cit* p.60

63 See Fleming, M. (1982) for a thorough discussion of the place of concepts such as 'learning', 'meaning' and 'knowledge' in drama education.

64 It is to be regretted that David Hornbrook cannot see this key characteristic of Heathcote's work. He complains [Hornbrook, D. (1989) *op cit* p.126] that groups are seen 'as simply an aggregation of individuals relating to each other'.

65 Hall, Edward T. (1959) *The Silent Language* Doubleday Chicago

66 Hall gives an instance of the non-negotiable and formal in respect of a visit to an Arab country earlier this century by a group of American scientists who advised a village suffering from typhoid that one of their water holes needed cleaning up

and a pump installed. Their advice was ignored because that water was sacred, a source of virility.

67 Heathcote comments in the subsequent interview: 'This isn't good drama at all. For the moment they were just simply the means by which we could bring about the destruction of the monastery. But lots of people mistake what those Vikings were doing for real drama. That's just empty 'doing things' with no real motivation at all. And it isn't any good the teacher having the motivation; the kids have to have it – and this is where it takes time.' [Video Tape (1971) No. 1.19.38]

68 For a thorough discussion of the wide variety of 'registers' Heathcote employs both in and out of role see Wagner, B.J. (1976 in USA, 1979 in UK) *op cit* pp.38-47).

69 This is an obvious link with Vygotski's 'zone of proximal development'. [Vygotski, Lev (1938) *Mind in Society* Cambridge, Massachusetts

70 Malcolm Ross and Peter Abbs created a strong anti-Heathcote camp. I have already (See Page 301 above) quoted Ross' resistence to 'Teacher-in-role'; Abbs (See Abbs, Peter (1992) 'Abbs Replies to Bolton' in *Drama* Vol 1 No 1 Summer) writes of the above kind of work as 'subvert(ing) the place of drama as an arts discipline'. Abbs does not disapprove of the method as legitimate pedagogy, but he feels it does a disservice to Drama itself. Likewise Malcolm Ross forcibly expresses his concern about what he sees as an abuse of Drama. He is in particular, in this quotation, complaining about the position I have adopted [Ross, M. (1982) *op cit* p.148]: 'The issue revolves about the centrality, in drama in education, of the related ideas of drama as expression and art-form, Gavin is proposing a much wider range of functions for drama in education than I would wish to endorse. Indeed he seems ready to settle for any learning, any educational outcome that genuinely benefits the pupil – rather than the concentration upon, and (in his estimation) likely failure of purely aesthetic outcomes...I would wish to see an exclusive commitment to the aesthetic...if drama has, traditionally been unable or unwilling to admit this over-riding obligation, then that might be one reason behind the persistent problems of drama education.'

71 Fleming, M. (1982) '*A philosophical Investigation into Drama in Education*' (unpublished, Ph.D thesis, Durham University)

72 O'Neill, Cecily '*Drama and the Web of Form*' (1978) unpublished MA Dissertation, University of Durham

73 O'Neill, Cecilia Clare (1991) '*Structure and Spontaneity: Improvisation in Theatre and Education*' (unpublished doctoral thesis), University of Exeter, p.168

74 In the 1960s the use of 'background music' became the norm for many teachers. For instance, Pemberton-Billing's and Clegg's Teaching Drama is filled with lesson examples relying heavily on percussion instruments and records, with a lengthy appendage giving precise record numbers. [Pemberton-Billing R.N. and Clegg J.D. (1965) *Teaching Drama* ULP]. Dorothy Heathcote used records sparingly, sometimes to create atmosphere, sometimes to stimulate, and sometimes, as in 'Making Progress, a series of lessons preparing 'A' level students to

take an examination on Pilgrim's Progress, to 'hide behind'. With young or vulnerable adult classes she often favoured choral singing by the whole group, usually using whatever song or hymn the class cared to choose, as they 'journeyed'.

75 It is interesting that a somewhat reduced version of Heathcote's 'depiction', often referred to as 'tableau', (a term we saw first used by Finlay-Johnson) has now become the most popular form of dramatic activity in our schools towards the end of the century, to a point of being overused. [See Fleming, Michael (1994) *Starting Drama Teaching* Fulton London p.93].

76 In 'The Treatment of Dr. Lister', for example, Heathcote uses an adult in role as Dr. Lister [a penetrating analysis is given of this series of lessons by John Carroll (Carroll, John (1980) *The Treatment of Dr. Lister* Mitchell College of Advanced Education Bathurst Australia). It contains the video transcript in Appendix A. [The reference number is VT 1047, University of Newcastle]. A further account is given within Heathcote's 'Material for Significance' See: Johnson and O'Neill. (1984) *ibid* pp.126-137. Early in the series, the junior age pupils first see 'Lister' within a picture frame, to be viewed minutely but from a distance. Later, they communicate with him, entering 'his' time from 'their' time by the convention of knocking on an imaginary door to enter 'his office'.

77 Heathcote also had considerable respect for Veronica Sherborne [Sherborne, Veronica (1990) *Developmental Movement for Children* Cambridge UP] a leading figure in the Physical Education field who adapted Laban methodology for the benefit of, particularly, physically challenged children.

78 Sound Tape (24.2.96) No 160-180

79 It is worth noting that Heathcote's use of language, often poetic or archaic, at moments of true creativity attempts to capture the *abstract*, as she comments, or asks a question.

80 Heathcote, D. (1967) 'Improvisation' *op cit* p.47 of Dorothy Heathcote

81 It is these same elements that Heathcote turns to as late as 1995 [Heathcote and Bolton (1995) *op cit* p.195 when she is pressed to describe what basically theatre means to her.

82 Goffman, Erving (1974) *Frame Analysis* Penguin Harmondsworth

83 'Classic' is Heathcote's choice of word, meaning 'highly selective as to position, language, tone and pace of communication.' [Heathcote, D. (1984) 'Drama as Context for Talking and Writing' *ibid* p.145 (footnote)]

84 Among her most recent projects is the preparation she did for an international week-end's study of her work in June, 1996 at the International Centre for Studies in Drama in Education at the University of Central England. The publication from that conference: Davis, David (Ed 1997) *Interactice Research in Drama – Education* Trentham Stoke on Trent

85 Bolton, Gavin (1995) 'DRAMA/drama and Cultural Values' in *IDEA 95· Selected Readings in Drama and Theatre Education* NADIE Publications pp.29-33

86   Bruce Wilshire [(1982) *op cit* p.x] tells of an amusing event when the theatregoers attended a makeshift theatre in a warehouse. As they waited for the 'play' to start the 'main door of the warehouse in the middle of the wall rolled up and opened' – and the events of the street outside became 'theatre'.

87   Langer, Suzanne (1953) *Feeling and Form: A theory of Art* Routledge and Kegan Paul New York

88   Wilshire, Bruce (1982) *op cit* p.39

89   Kleberg, Lars (1993 [in English]) *Theatre As Action* Macmillan London, pp.42-3

90   Brecht, Bertolt (1936) *Left Review* translated by J. Willett

91   It is perhaps worth noting at this point that Wilshire [Wilshire, Bruce (1982) *ibid* p.89] adds another dimension to a definition of 'theatre', repeatability, a requirement fulfilled by this 'project' method, for, indeed the scenes are often repeated over and over again for more searching observation, but of course such a definition would appear to preclude improvisational drama.

92   Page ix of the Preface to David Hornbrook's (1991) *Education in Drama* Falmer London

93   Andy Kempe, in his *The GCSE DRAMA Coursebook* (1990) Blackwell Oxford, p.178, gives a Glossary definition of acting as 'This involves not only adopting someone else's attitudes and beliefs as in role play, but developing a sense of their character by altering the way you speak and move.

94   See Way, B. (1967) *op cit* p.174-5. The child, according to Way, begins his early characterisation with 'intuitive and unconscious exploration of characters of the inner world of fantasy and imagination' and then moves to unconscious exploration of characters in 'the real world'. [In this distinction between 'fantasy' and 'real' he is following E.M. Langdon]. He includes two further stages: conscious attention to cause and effects in character building and, finally, the exploration of 'inner factors (motivations)' (p.175).

95   McGregor, Lynn, Tate, Maggie and Robinson Ken (1977) *op cit* pp.11-12

96   This hierarchical perspective on acting behaviour is adopted by many writers, including Norah Morgan and Juliana Saxton (1987) whose 'Categories of Identification' will be referred to again in the concluding chapter of this book. Morgan, N. and Saxton, J. (1987) *Teaching Drama: a mind of many wonders* Hutchinson London, pp.30-37

97   The term 'acting out' did not appear to be readily accepted among subsequent drama education writers. Chris Day ['Teaching Styles in Drama' in *Issues in Educational Drama* (Eds: Day, Christopher and Norman, John) Falmer London, p.81] is one of the few who adopted the expression as a useful way of specifiying an 'enactive mode of learning'. It is interesting that when Hilton Francis undertook the publication of a Vocabulary of Educational Drama in 1973 and 1979 (revised) she did not include either 'acting' or 'acting out' in her glossary of terms. [published by Kemble, Banbury]

98   Ken Robinson is currently Professor of Arts Education, University of Warwick. A copy of his Ph.D thesis (1981) is housed in the Drama archives of Durham University.

99 Robinson, Ken (1981) *op cit* p.145. See also 'Drama, Theatre and Social Reality' in *Exploring Theatre and Education* (1980) by Ken Robinson [Ed] Heinemann London pp.149-150.

100 During the mid and late '70s 'exploring a character' became a legitimate drama workshop practice. By this was meant, not a character necessarily related to a play, but one invented by the workshop participant. I can recall one week-end workshop for teachers in which the participants arriving on the Friday evening would give themselves a character which they were require to sustain in all the public rooms throughout the week-end!

101 Robinson makes a further comparison: 'In comparing drama and theatre then, I am comparing two types of social encounter which use elements of make-believe and forms of role-play. I am not comparing the professional super-structures which have grown up around them.' [Robinson, K. (1980) *ibid* p.150]

102 Heathcote, Dorothy (1971) 'Drama and Education: Subject or System?' in *Drama and Theatre Education* Heinemann London, p.43

103 It should be made clear at this point that what might be described as individual characterisation did sometimes emerge from Heathcote's 'living through' drama. A classic example is the 'stool pigeon' [For an interesting analysis of this piece of characterisation, see 'Experiencing Drama: what's happening when children are doing drama at depth?' in *Schooling and Culture* (Spring 1979) Issue 4 by Geoff Gillham] in 'Three Looms Waiting', a role that becomes isolated from the rest of the other roles. One should, however, still be cautious in applying the term 'character' to such a role, for the part only existed in so far as the boy adopted a 'stool-pigeon' function; other possible dimensions of his character as a person did not become relevant – although they *could* have done. 'Living through' drama may potentially, however rarely, centre on the development of a three dimensional character in the Naturalistic theatre sense, providing such an exploration emerged naturally from the dramatic context as an evolutionary process.

104 This is an example from Page 11 of their text, in which pupils typically work on some 'underdog' issue. Ken Robinson later describes this kind of activity as follows: 'Most classroom drama intends to put children in the role of initiator. The general function of these activities is heuristic: they are to do with discovery. In this way they are *explorative* – of issues, themes, events – and *expressive* – of attitudes, ideas and feelings about the issues at hand.' [Robinson, K. (1980) *ibid* p.168]

105 A close examination of the kinds of lesson examples included in the Schools Council publication reveals that the authors have not actually included the kind of 'teacher-in-role' controlled, 'living through' experiences to be found in Heathcote's classrooms. It may be, therefore, that the application of sociological terminology best fitted the kind of Secondary Drama that was actually going on in most teachers' classrooms at the time; Heathcote's kind of teaching was taking a long time to filter through.

106 This point may account for some of the difficulties Americans have with understanding Heathcote's approach while admiring its outcome. Their tradition is singularly related to 'developing one's character' as a starting point to

improvisatory work. See my key-note address, entitled 'Out of Character' to the Columbus, Ohio 1995 conference. [Bolton, G. (1996) 'Out of Character' in *Drama Matters* Vol 1 No 1 Spring]

107 Witkin, Robert, (1974) *op cit*

108 Heathcote, Dorothy (1975) 'Drama and Learning' in McCaslin, Nellie *Children and Drama* David McKay New York p.85 of 2nd (1981) edition

109 Although, for Heathcote, children in the classroom are not called upon to be 'actors acting', they nevertheless avail themselves of the basic theatre elements. It is in this respect that Heathcote changed from playing down the need for knowledge of theatre when talking to teachers to recognising that there were certain theatre basics that were essential for all teachers. [Personal correspondence, May, 1996]

110 In 'Signs and Portents' (1980 *op cit*, p.160 of Dorothy Heathcote: *Collected Writings on education and drama*) Heathcote herself broadens the common rules between actors and children to embrace all living: 'Actual living and theatre, which is a depiction of living conditions, both use the same network of signs, as their medium of communication; namely the human being signalling across space, in immediate time, to others and with others...'

111 Interview Tape 2 Side A No 340

112 Cecily O'Neill (1995 *op cit* p.125) improves on my (Bolton 1979) version of 'this is happening to me and I am making it happen' by introducing an explicit 'spectator' dimension: 'I am watching this happening to me, and I am making it happen.'

113 'Lure' is a word Heathcote has used regularly in recent years to mean 'the bait with which to catch interest'. She carefully grades that level of interest into 'attention first, then interest, then all the others thro' to involvement and commitment.' [Notes in response to manuscript, May, 1996)

114 Fleming, Mike (1982) *ibid* p.259. Fleming is here defining R.K. Elliott's [Elliot, R.K. (1966-7) 'Aesthetic Theory and the Experience of Art' in *Proceedings of the Aristotelian Society* Vol. LXVII use of 'predicable' i.e. that the emotion is present in the participants but not 'predicable by them'.

115 Notes in response to manuscript (May, 1996)

116 David Davis cites the example in 'What is Depth in Educational Drama?' [Davis, D. (1976) *Young Drama* Vol 4, No 3, October pp.89-94] of a girl with some kind of physical deformity being chosen by the rest of the class to play a witch, so that the 'real life' isolation and victimisation continues within the drama. John O'Toole (1992 *op cit* Chapter 3) also gives an alarming, but intriguing, portrayal of 'Mary' in a drama on the theme of madness in which the participant overcomes the destructive gibes of her fellow 'patients'.

117 Geoff Gillhan discusses this point in his (1974) unpublished *Condercum Report* for Newcastle upon Tyne LEA under his catchphrase 'play for the teacher' and 'play for the child'.

118 I suspect that she has not had the chance to see the remarkable achievements of some drama classes using this form. It is a dramatic tool carried to perfection, I believe, by Carole Tarlington's Vancouver Youth Theatre up to 1995.

119 To illustrate this difficult point, Heathcote gave me an example of a photographer, before and after World-War 2 taking a photograph of old people in the streets, the same streets, of Warsaw, their shoulders, in the second set of photographs bearing their years of oppression.

120 This table of values is adapted from Heathcote D. and Bolton G. (1995) *op cit* p.19.

121 In the interview dated 26.02.96 Tape 1 Side B No. 820, Heathcote offers a vivid image for depiction: 'Depiction is like a humming bird that is still but still flying.'

122 By 'gestus' I understand Brecht intended the actor to evaluate the action. According to Shomit Mitter [Mitter, S. (1992 *op cit* p.48], in Helen Weigel's portrayal of Mother Courage, 'we have simultaneously both the character's dogmatic blindness, and the actress' exasperation that it should be so.' Heathcote demands of depiction that the participant simultaneously demonstrates the action while offering a kind of personal sub-text for the audience (the rest of the class) to inspect and perhaps make judgements about.

123 This concept of 'active spectatorship' began with Harriet Finlay-Johnson and seems to have been neglected by exponents until Dorothy Heathcote reintroduced it. It is Harriet Finlay-Johnson of course to whom Dorothy Heathcote has always felt most close.

124 Even as I write this in April, 1996, Dorothy Heathcote is preparing a course for senior doctors from other cultures on doctor/patient signalling. It can be fairly guaranteed that there will be no 'living through' drama and that where 'depiction' is needed from members of the class, they will be heavily protected by the spectators appearing to carry the greater responsibility.

125 The Forum Theatre of Augusto Boal [Boal, Augusto (1979) *Theatre of the Oppressed* Pluto London] independently of Dorothy Heathcote, used this extreme version of active spectatorship, but confined the content to society's victims. What began as an urgent, honest use of theatre in a political crisis has now become, if the demonstration of 'Forum Theatre' at the second IDEA conference in Brisbane (1995) is anything to go by, a commercial, and rather cynical, enterprise. Examples of his original conception of Forum Theatre included in his publications [see for example, his account of using Forum Theatre in a Psychiatric hospital in which the patients in the audience demonstrate how a patient in the enacted scene should have been handled (Boal, A. (1995) *The Rainbow of Desire* Routledge London pp.53-56)] show how its successful application is dependent on the audience having a vested interest in the problem enacted on stage.

CHAPTER TEN

RE-INTEPRETATIONS OF DOROTHY HEATHCOTE'S 'LIVING THROUGH' DRAMA

This chapter will be divided as follows:

'Living through' Drama as a complex programme of dramatic experience

'Living through' Drama in its most unsophisticated form

'Living through' Drama as 'Mantle of the Expert'

'Living through Drama' as a complex programme of dramatic experience, extending 'Man in a Mess'

The first section of this chapter will present a more personal account of my own work than I intended to include. It was never within my plan to cast myself as a pioneer in drama education, on the grounds that whereas I may have made some original theoretical contribution to the field I have always felt that my work was largely derivative, indebted as I am to Peter Slade, Brian Way, Dorothy Heathcote and to others in amateur and professional theatre, but it has become pressingly obvious now to me that I have to a large extent been responsible for a re-interpretation of Heathcote's methodology that has taken 'Living through' Drama in a direction never intended by her and perhaps, from her point of view, off-target, if not misguided.

217

A new direction for 'Living through'

The point has already been made in the previous chapter that emotional engagement and detachment characterised all Heathcote's work. The evident modification of emotional engagement did not always protect her from misinterpretation – by her followers as well as her critics.[1] That emotions could arise naturally and sometimes powerfully from an agreed make-believe context appealed to the imaginations of some of her admirers who saw new possibilities in drama workshops. Just as leading directors in theatre were beginning to experiment in rehearsals with somatic means of generating feeling, some leaders in the classroom were setting up intensely emotional dramatic contexts. 'Living through' became associated with 'deep' emotional experiences.[2]

Imperceptibly, in the hands of some of Heathcote's emulators (I include myself here), the target group for 'Living through' drama changed from Heathcote's 'pupil-centred' work to 'adult-centred' (usually teachers) refreshment. In-service training was in vogue and almost every local education authority in this country committed itself to running week-end drama courses for its teachers.[3]

My own contribution to such courses set a pattern of almost total workshop participation. Thus 'Living through' drama became accepted by some as something *adults* successfully did together and there is little doubt that these groups of highly committed teachers gradually transformed the potential of this way of dramatising. It became a carefully crafted and deeply felt theatre experience – important in itself and only incidentally committed to learning something. Typically, as 'the experience' came to a close, the questions immediately pursued would relate to 'how was it for you?' and/or 'how did you feel?', *questions Dorothy Heathcote would never find herself asking.* Only after this personal debriefing would the week-end course or the Summer School get round to asking: 'How might we apply this experience to the pupils we teach?', an example, to Dorothy Heathcote, of 'putting the cart before the horse', although she 'has no quarrel' in principle with the idea of adults 'exploring what it's like to participate in drama work'.

This reversal of teacher priorities (not, I may say, recognised at the time – during the 1970s) had fairly considerable repercussions which are summarised below:

1. The beginnings of a new form of adult workshops were being tested. Previous workshop experience in drama had taken the form either of investigative work on playscripts or Brian Way type exercises related to concentration, sensitivity, intuition and relaxation etc., or Laban Dance. Dorothy Heathcote rarely (almost never) gave her own adult students a sustained 'living through' experience – whatever practice they tried out was always with 'teacher hats' firmly on. At the beginning of a week-end course I would say 'Take off your 'teacher hats' for the time being so that you can have a 'dramatic *experience*'.'

2. Because neither the leaders nor the participants fully understood that they were creating a new genre, any attempt at explication continued to be couched in 'learning objectives' associated with Heathcote's original version of 'living through'.

3. Writers such as myself unnecessarily *struggled* to demonstrate the aesthetic or artistic dimensions of the work when, had it been understood as dramatic art in its own right[4] rather than as a 'learning area', its artistic intent would have seemed self-evident. The 'struggle' lay in trying to accommodate a language of learning within the language of theatre.

4. Whereas Heathcote's approach had always been 'child-centred' in the sense that she based all her practice on her observation of what children were capable of (and beyond!), the alternative yardstick for thinking about drama in education (especially the Secondary age group) became the potential in the material for exploitation by skilled adults. Thus I was able to give an account in my 1992 publication of a drama sequence on Robin Hood with 9/10 years old pupils, which translated with facility to a powerful theatre experience with adults.

5. I strayed from the Heathcote tradition while believing I was following it. The new genre required a different language which it has taken twenty years to find. The confusion caused by this drama-centred work masquerading as learning-centred led to difficulties in communication, in spite of such concepts as 'process', 'pupil choice', 'negotiation', 'problem-solving', and, above all, 'living through' appearing to supply common ground. At an adult

level, the existential quality of 'living through', uninterrupted by a teacher, but based on that teacher's careful structuring, was often sustained, in time and depth, well beyond what most classes of children would be capable of. Some teachers felt they had a new vision of what their pupils might emulate. Such teachers and Dorothy Heathcote were looking in different directions – while sounding as though they were facing the same way!

One of the dangers of this 'experiential' approach was that some who had found the kind of workshops described above as personally satisfying, mistakenly associated the new genre with therapy, a view far from my own and sickeningly offensive to Dorothy Heathcote. There is little doubt that all the arts and any other satisfying experience (like, for some, 'gardening') may be therapeutic, but that cannot be and must not be a goal in an educational setting.[5] Another danger in this approach was that its exponents, at least in the 1970s, zealously confined the dramatic form to an improvisational mode, eschewing alternative forms such as script, exercises and depiction. Preliminary tasks might be necessary to set up the theme, but, once launched, it was thought that sustained, whole class improvisation offered the most potent experience. Its 'success' often depended on the intensity of the theme, providing a dynamic sustainable through a whole workshop. Given skilled leadership and commitment by the participants this sustained approach often worked, participants claiming they had had a worthwhile experience. In our enthusiasm for engaging with significant themes, we failed to notice that Dorothy Heathcote was gradually turning away from drama as 'A Man in a Mess'.

David Davis is an example of a leader in the field who experimented with breaking away from whole group 'Living through' experience, finding an alternative form in the use of a carefully structured, sustained exercise in pairs that, because of its structure and retention of a sense of 'living in the present' as opposed to the more typical 'practising' or 'investigating' goals, had greater potential than the traditional exercise form. For Davis,[6] a criterion of good work was the extent to which the participants in an improvisation actually suffered the relevant emotions. According to his paper 'What Is 'Depth' in Educational Drama?' 'real' feeling is to be generated: 'If the improvisation is carefully built up, it may be possible that the woman gets a real feeling of fear.' He would sometimes adopt Stanislavski's 'objectives', giving separate instructions to each actor before an improvisation, deliberately giving them (unknown to each other) conflicting objectives' so that irritation, or hurt or confrontation was guaranteed. Of course, he knew too that the eagerness of his classes to play such an exercise always qualified the rawness of the emotional engagement. Nevertheless the intensity of the exercise combined with its psychological focus, was a departure from Heathcote's combination of detachment with a cultural, rather than psychological, bias.

A word should be said here about the BBC films that have given Dorothy Heathcote's work such prominence. Because the cameras did their work well the acting behaviour of individual children in 'the Stool Pigeon' and 'Death of a President' scenes, may have become inflated in the minds of spectators. When, for instance the 'Stool Pigeon' breaks down and weeps, this appears to be a remarkable moment of natural, spontaneous expression of emotion (some might be led to think, epitomising Heathcote's work at its best). It was, however, a piece of effective contrivance between an astute film director and the boy actor who had previously raised the question with Heathcote and the class whether it would appropriate for his character to cry.' Likewise the deft hiding of the keys when the guards suddenly arrive, had been worked out technically ready for the camera to 'make authentic'. More importantly from Heathcote's point of view, much of the preparation for the scene was taken up with building 'self-spectatorship' in all the boys and a rational examination of how people like guards signal power. By the time they 'performed' for the cameras, their engagement was as much an intellectual understanding as a 'feeling' experience. Reading Davis' 'What is 'depth' in educational drama?', one is left with the impression that he, like many of us, saw it as a camera fortuitously picking up on a child's moment of shock at having betrayed his friends. Of course, in some sense, this was the case, but Heathcote knows the emotion of the incident was properly backed with intelligent calculation, understanding and self-awareness.

An example of my own teaching
I have elected to describe below a sequence from my own teaching that I believe typifies the attempt to discover an elaborate, sophisticated

sequence of dramatic experiences (using a variety of dramatic forms, but having, at some point, a 'significant' existential, 'living through', element) that aimed to build some kind of satisfying theatrical experience.

A lesson devised originally for adolescents preparing to study 'The Crucible' by Arthur Miller

This is an elaborate form of 'living though' drama, a dramatic sequence sustaining a single thematic cycle of experience, depending, as we shall see, on many dramatic forms. A version of the plan was first used with adolescents in the late 1980s, and later in adult workshops.[8] The description below was written as part of a 'teaching' document for students of drama education.

One of the difficulties for young pupils engaging with a dramatic text based on historical material is that their grasp on the hidden values of a 'strange' culture such as Puritan Massachusetts in the 17th century is too slender for them to make connections with their own lives. They may be inclined to regard people who were prepared to burn witches as quaint or mad or too childish to be worth bothering with. My purpose therefore in setting up a drama experience about the play before they read the script was to whet their appetites and to make the circumstances of the play seem more familiar.

In Miller's text he introduces the idea (based on historical fact) that a group of young girls gained so much power over the community that by merely pointing an accusing finger at any adult in the community, that victim would be sent to the stake.

My initial task towards preparing this lesson was to find a *pivotal* scene which would portray the period while at the same time capturing the sense of potential power over parents lying within the hands of their off-spring (I did not make a distinction, as Miller did, between boys and girls). The picture in my head, drawn from Miller's play, was of a community of families torn by rumour that some of their adolescent children might have been dancing naked in the nearby woods and engaging in black magic. I knew that, unless the class I was going to work with were very experienced, a confrontation between parents and children or any attempt at giving them the experience of 'dancing in the woods' would deteriorate into embarrassed flippancy or empty technique, for they would simply be engaged in presenting the surface of incidents rather than grappling with the implicit values underlying the incidents.

This is undoubtedly the drama teacher's continual dilemma – how may a class of pupils begin to engage with a culture's deepest values before they have any real grasp of either those values or the contexts in which those values might be expressed? In the early days of drama teaching, we used to rely on 'characterisation' as providing a base from which to begin, which we now realise is a dramatic cul de sac, for it too hastily sketches psychological differences at the expense of cultural sharing. It is of little educational and dramatic use to give the young actors a chance to enjoy defying their 'parents' if they have no shared understanding of a cultural system that is based on *respect* – for parents and the authority of the church and *fear of* God. To engage in an act of deceiving and lying to 'parents', however lively the improvisation may seem, actually takes the pupils *away from* the Puritan period and Arthur Miller's play – unless their act of deception can be carried out in the knowledge of the full horror of the cultural and religious rules they are choosing to break. *This* has to be the pivot of the scene.

With this in mind, I see a scene taking place in the town's meeting-house or chapel, with me in role as the 'Minister' or 'Pastor', shocked at the rumours I have heard of dancing and witchcraft, inviting the families I have sent for whose houses border onto the woods, to send their off-spring to the altar rail to swear on the Bible that they are innocent. This act of deception will be an isolated action, carefully timed, public and formal. Pupils may begin to engage dramatically with an unfamiliar context if the structure of a scene draws on that context's *formal* rules.

This picture I have of a pivotal scene represents the beginning of my planning, but, typically of this kind of programme,[9] it cannot necessarily be the beginning of the lesson itself. There are usually a number of steps emerging as preparation for such a scene. I will attempt to give an explanation of each step.

1. I talk briefly about Miller's play, mentioning that Puritans of the period feared many things, including the supernatural – rather like our superstitions today. I then laid out on the ground, far apart, five or more big sheets of blank paper around which pupils could group to make a rapid list of all the superstitions they could think of.

This is a useful releaser of class energy. Informally squatting on the floor they could just instruct their appointed 'scribe' to write whatever came into their heads, while they hear me, their teacher, half seriously, urge them to make a longer list than the next group. All light-hearted and fun – deliberately *not* striking a tone appropriate to the play.

2. I then ask them to walk round all the sheets, putting their initials by all the superstitions that they personally are sometimes affected by.

This 'signing one's name' is an act of commitment and also has bearing on Miller's play, when John Proctor, in the last Act, cannot give the authorities his *name!* As they sign, I ask them, casually and light-heartedly, to count the number of superstitions they identify with. We then do a count, laughingly starting with the highest number (I think 25 was the most!) and then going down to 3 or 2 or even 1 – and 'there may even be someone here who denies being affected by any of our list....' A chill creeps into my voice...notice this '*our*' list, an *exclusive* and *excluding* touch. The one or two who have not signed anything are suddenly isolated... not belonging to the rest of us... different...'Come into the middle of the room and let the rest of us form a circle round you' ... 'We don't like people who are different...' I then invite the others to harass the isolates. (It only lasts a minute or so – I'm not a sadist!) I stop it, put my around the 'victims' and thank them for showing us what 'The Crucible' is about: 'This play is about gaining power by accusing people who seem to be different...'

3. All sitting in a circle now, I suddenly mime picking up a doll 'a poppet, as they called it in Salem...' I slowly lifted the doll's petticoats, narrating as I carried out the actions, and thrust a long needle deep into the doll's belly...'for I have the power to curse as the children of Salem did, and if I wanted to curse someone I sent them this impaled poppet.' Again suddenly, I turned to my neighbour in the circle, thrust the 'doll' into his hands and instructed 'pass it on' – and when, eventually it came round to me again – I refused to take it.

Each child has a momentary public attention, as everyone watches how s/he receives and how s/he gives. A curse has descended on us! – and we have a feeling that 'theatre' has started.

4. Breaking the threatening mood, I invite the pupils to divide into 'family' groups, limiting each family to two or three adolescent children. They are invited to think of themselves as a family portrait, a still picture which will not only convey the 'purity' of the off-springs and the father as 'head of family', but also, if they wish, the less than passive role of the mother, who, I suggested, might have more authority at home than the public image of the 'head of the household' embraces. Any such authority in a female member of the family must just be hinted at in this 'portrait'. The final responsibility for the portrait lies with the 'parents', who are to try to make their children look like the most respectable and god-fearing children in Salem! I then, with each family formally facing inwards to the rest of the group, address each 'head of family' in turn, asking him to introduce each 'child' by name and to tell us whether each child has for example learnt to read the Bible aloud at meal-times.

This exercise is an example of a complex form of depiction, in which the participants prepare a still tableau for inspection which becomes elevated into a 'staged' performance of formalised, improvised, questions and answers *as though we are in the existential present*. This is, of course, a very stiff interchange, anticipating the rigidity of address needed for the 'chapel' scene and giving the class chance to test whether they are capable of treating such formalities with due seriousness. It also accustoms the pupils to the strategy of 'teacher-in-role'. [Notice this chance I give the girls playing 'mothers' to take on a more forceful role, albeit subtly, for when I first tried this sequence, I realised that it virtually leaves these girls out as 'passive onlookers', unless I give them a chance to find an important niche. Preparation for creating the portraits included a brief discussion about clothes – greys and blacks – hidden ankles and wrists and necks; daughters could use head-scarves so that 'not a thread of hair could be seen'.]

5. 'Parents, you may think, that your children are as innocent as you have made them look in this portraiture, but I have to tell you that, last night, round abour midnight, some of your children were seen dancing naked in Salem woods – near your houses'. Having announced this, I then invite them to split up, inviting the 'parents' to leave the room while their 'children' write down, each on a slip of paper, the word GUILTY or INNOCENT. Then they show what they have written to each other and we have within this 'children' group a number who took part in last night's dancing and those who did not. I invite them to memorise which is which – and then I hint darkly that those who are guilty, who will be denying that guilt in the next scene, 'playing a part of the innocent', might like, at some point when it seems most favourable, to drop hints that bring the accusation of guilt on the wrong children, on the innocent! – just as in Miller's play.

Notice this 'last night' – we are now into 'drama time'. Allowing the pupils to choose whether they want to be guilty or innocent is a very important part of the proceedings. It gives them a feeling of being in charge of themselves and it creates a 'real' secret from the actors playing the 'parents' who, in actuality, do not know which are the offending offsprings.

6. The chapel scene begins with the families entering and the 'minister' giving them permisssion to take their usual family seats in the 'House of God'. In my role I then give them the news of sacriligeous behaviour in the woods. I warn them of the wrath of God and speak of dire punishment. I then invite each 'child' in turn to come forward, place a hand on the Bible (it has obviously to be not a Bible, of course – this is Drama) and say after me: 'My soul is pure'.

Thus they can 'be' those citizens of Salem, because the context is so tightly structured that at every moment behaviour is regulated by the cultural laws of the context and of the occasion. The actors have no room for manoeuvre within the the imposed strictures, but of course the greater the limitations the more subtle can be the creativity – and individual input was sometimes astonishingly inventive – within the 'rules of the Puritan game'. The restrictions are both safe and constructive. It is the deep values of the culture that are dictating behaviour not 'personality'. The 'plot' for the scene was that the pastor had sent for the families – even though it was week-day and harvesting time – and they had had to change into their stiff 'chapel best'.

7. The 'minister' now instructs each family to seek privacy in one of the many chapel vestries in order to interrogate the children and 'get them to confess' so that they may be publicly admonished.

This is the most testing part of the whole session. If the previous steps have not been handled well, this scene, which requires small family groups to operate separately with the 'parents' taking charge (replacing the 'teacher-in-role' function of the teacher, as it were) will collapse. The security of the previous scene is replaced with *too much* room for manoevring in this one. Only if the pupils are by now committed and if the 'parents' take on their responsibility is it going to work. My role is, of course, still available to intervene as the 'Minister just going round the vestries to see if anyone has confessed', should it be necessary. If all goes well, one or two innocent people will be 'named'!

8. Final scene, back in the chapel, in which the Minister invites confessions, and, just as in 'The Crucible', accusations. This scene may go in any direction. At its best, the class take over and the 'Minister' plays a minor role in the ways things are handled.

This handing over of power to the class is of course very important and cannot always be achieved within one session. In this particular lesson, such class autonomy is built into the plan. If it works well, the pupils will not only be trying to think inside the Puritan situation, but also trying to adopt a kind of stylised language to accompany their posturing.

9. Outside the drama, the 'children' reveal the truth! – and there is much laughter for many of the 'parents' were genuinely deceived.

A sign of a worthwhile drama experience at this point is whether the pupils, out of role, feel an urge to talk about it to each other. If your class remains respectfully silent, waiting for you to tell them what to do next, something has gone very wrong! – and this happened to me on one occasion. Mostly however, this sequence seems to have all the ingredients that make for good 'theatre' -and creates an eagerness to turn to Miller's text.

I showed the full plan of this 'Crucible' lesson to Dorothy Heathcote whose reaction was to applaud its intention but to express doubt about the viability of using direct improvisation [that is, an improvisation where the pupils attempt to become characters from a text] in relation to a text about to be studied. She saw a danger of such a 'dramatic experience' becoming so attractive in itself without any guarantee that it be true to the text. In thinking about what *she* would do, her mind immediately turned to the question of how the pupils should be *framed*. We shall see that *framing* and *task selection* become the pivotal structures of Mantle of the Expert.

Cecily O'Neill's approach to Process Drama

Cecily O'Neill[10] who introduced the term 'process drama' into our drama education vocabulary has long been associated with the work of Dorothy Heathcote, notably since her collaboration with Liz Johnson in collecting within one volume the writings of Dorothy Heathcote published in international Journals over a period of 20 years. Two years before *Dorothy Heathcote*, appeared *Drama Structures: A practical Handbook for Teachers*,[11] written by O'Neill in collaboration with an ex-student of Heathcote's, Alan Lambert.

This latter text begins unambiguously with 'Drama in education is a mode of learning.' By this date, 1982, although the general public might have needed some persuasion about the validity of this statement, there was a fair guarantee that most of the people likely to read such a book would perceive the assertion by O'Neill and Lambert as familiar rhetoric.[12] Nor would their readers be surprised that the lessons described in the book included the use of 'teacher-in-role', teacher narration,[13] whole group decision-making, small group tasks, interaction in pairs, the use of depiction, enquiry into issues related to curriculum subjects, moral dilemmas, related written work and art work. What was new for readers was the authors' attempt to show, in considerable detail, patterns of carefully structured dramatic sequences based on Heathcote's methodology and philosophy. Sample examples of 'Living through' drama already available in print were to be found in: Heathcote's various journal articles in which she would refer to key moments of a lesson; in Betty Jane Wagner's (1976) analyis, which tended to abstract vivid incidents from lessons to illustrate Heathcote's pedagogy; and in my own 1979 publication which tended to use actual classroom practice as illustrative of some theoretical point. O'Neill and Lambert's purpose was rather different. By giving *detailed* reports on lessons they had taught in schools, they sought to help readers identify, not a formula, but guidelines for developing a cumulative process of learning when planning to engage a group of pupils with a topic of interest. Each sequence had been tested with more than one class, so that alternative routes are sometimes included in the account.

Before Heathcote's work became known the pattern most familiar to teachers was 'plot'. O'Neill and Lambert see 'structure' as overriding 'plot', even when the dramatisation is embedded in a time sequence such as their lesson based on '*The Way West*'. The authors warn:

Since this theme has a kind of narrative shape provided by the 'journey', it is important not to allow the linear development of story-line to take over. If it happens, the work may become merely a series of incidents – 'what happened next'. Instead, drama is likely to arise from moments of tension and decision, or when the settlers must face the consequence of their actions.

Following faithfully Heathcote's search for ways of opening up an understanding in her pupils that every person's action betrays deeper values, the teacher of 'The Way West', in using the device of 'family' photographs, demands of one or two pupils to answer the following kinds of questions from their picture frame: 'What are you looking forward to in your new life?'; 'What do you fear most in the months which lie ahead?' 'What do you miss?'; 'Any regrets?'

Above all, their work derived from a respect shared by Heathcote for how a dramatist works. These practitioners understood, for instance, how the deliberate manipulation of events *out* of their natural time sequence multiplies the perspectives from which they may be viewed. 'Looking back' or 'looking forward' to an event highlights and makes accessible hues of significance not available if one can only be *in* the event. The potential for 'Living through' Drama expands, making a cascade of possibilities if the present embraces the past and the future, if the pain of an event was 'yesterday' or the implication of an event is 'tomorrow'.

O'Neill and Lambert fed this 'expanded 'Living Through' into many of their lessons. The creative manipulation of time became part of their 'dramatist's' repertoire. An example from Drama Structures is entitled 'Disaster'. O'Neill begins the lesson with:

'Twenty-five years ago, in a certain community, a terrible disaster occurred. The way of life of that community was change forever. The young people of the community who had been born after the disaster decide to commemorate the twenty-fifth anniversary by presenting a play about the disaster. They hope this will remind the people of what happened, and will prevent such a disaster from ever happening again.'

This class of fourteen year pupils were then invited to select a disaster. They decided that a man-made, rather than a natural disaster, would be more interesting to explore and chose a nuclear explosion, not due to war, but to a result of a series of blunders on the part of the government.

O'Neill begins the work on this theme by inviting the class in small groups to show some background to the disaster, such as what errors of judgement were made and how communities were affected by it. These are played without comment, simply supplying images of an event. O'Neill now reverts to her original ploy – the idea of young people born after the event using an art form to commemorate it. Thus the 'Living through' mode, the sustained '*now*', as it were, of the drama is occurring *outside* the time of the incident and yet safely invites concentration on that incident.

However, and this is my reason for using this particular illustration, Cecily O'Neill drew from her dramatist's palate, a colour Dorothy Heathcote was by the mid-1970's deliberately avoiding. O'Neill describes the next step of her lesson:

> ...the teacher...takes on the role of a visitor from the State Council for the Arts, and tells them that she is very pleased that they are working so hard to commemorate this tragic incident in history. She admires their talent, as well as their effort and dedication. However [my italics], *she is slightly unhappy about the way they have chosen to approach their text. They seem to be taking a rather negative view of the whole incident. They also seem to have got their facts wrong. She tells them that it is now known that the disaster was due to the sabotage of one employee, who had become unbalanced due to overwork...*

Gradually, the pupils begin to recognise they are being subjected to an act of deception which becomes clearer when 'this nice lady from the State Council for the Arts' further suggests that should they consider changing the form of the commemoration, a great deal of financial support from the Government might be forthcoming. Suddenly, as a direct result of teacher intervention, the pupils find themselves in a play about State repression for which the 'Disaster' was but a pretext – and O'Neill has in this one strategy moved her work in a direction with which Heathcote has less sympathy.

This injection by the dramatist/teacher of dramatic irony into the structure of the sequence is an example of moving the experience towards the new genre for which I may initially have been responsible and to which Cecily O'Neill eventually applied the name 'Process Drama'. It is a sequential programme, derived from Heathcote but crucially independent of her in respect of its theatricality and made up of a wide range of *dramatic* forms, from 'living through'. to work on scripts. Within three introductory pages of her later publication, O'Neill (1995) is able to claim both that *'Process Drama* is almost synonymous with the term *drama in education'* **and** that it is a 'theatre event'. Significantly, there is no reinforcement in *Process Drama* of 'Drama in Education is a mode of learning'. It is not that O'Neill is now denying learning outcomes, but that by seeing her brand of drama education as a genre of theatre, the term 'learning' appears too narrow, too limiting, too reminiscent of teaching objectives. In *Drama Structures* (1982) the authors, while struggling towards a new form of 'Living through' Drama, nevertheless cling to specified learning categories.[14] In *Process Drama* (1995) the participants are not treated explicitly as 'learners', but as active agents making theatre happen. O'Neill explains[15]:

> When drama techniques are valued only for their capacity to promote specific competencies and achieve precise ends, and remain brief, fragmented, and tightly controlled by the teacher or director, the work is likely to fall far short of the kind of generative dramatic encounter available in process drama.

It is the language of theatre that Cecily O'Neill now applies to her study of how Process Drama works. This is not the traditional language of climax, shape plots and sub-plots but contemporary theatre language of episodes, transformation, ritual, spectatorship, alienation and fragmentation. She is intent, by references to dramatists and theatre theorists, on drawing parallels between the components of a play performance and those of a drama sequence. It is *improvisation*, however that she sees at the centre of Process drama, even though she may employ depiction and scripts as part of the sequence.[16]

O'Neill's interpretation of 'Living Through' Drama is sophisticated in its conception and multiformal in its methodology. The impression should not be made however that all interpreters of Heathcote moved towards complexity. We will now examine an example of teaching that occurred in a Primary School in 1987 which qualifies as 'Living through' drama in that 'teacher-in-role' is used continually to sustain a sense of 'being there', but its lack of planning, lack of opportunity for pupil reflection and undeviating use of a 'dramatic playing' mode, move it into a version of Heathcote's approach that Dorothy Heathcote herself would not employ. At the same time, its contrast with Process Drama could not be more marked, and yet we shall see that it is equally dependent on elements of theatre.

Research[17] into 'Living through' Drama by Peter Millward

I have suggested that the above accounts of practice by Bolton and O'Neill, respectively, represent a re-interpretation of 'Living through' practice, but in attempting to give instances from Heathcote's practice in the previous chapter, I may have lost sight of its definitive character. One of the confusions is that although the words 'living through' imply that important sense of 'being there in the present and presence', Heathcote's methodology also builds in its opposite of 'being outside it'. There is a mercurial inside-outside dialectic that heightens awareness. Thus 'Living through' implies continually arresting the process of living to take a look at it, and it is the *'spectator'* as much as the *'participant'* that re-engages with that 'living'.

We will now look at Peter Millward's account of his own unique experimentation in 'Living through'. It is unique in a number of respects, one being that he did not intend, when he set up the experiment, that it should turn into drama. His initial interest was in how eight-year old children contribute to a discussion and for this purpose arranged to have a teacher colleague take a mixed ability group of six children to an empty staffroom so that Millward could sound record the proceedings. What started as a discussion on volcanoes Millward suddenly took over simply because '...it felt right'.[18] Even when the recording of this tentative venture into drama was over, Millward did not immediately see it as a basis for his research. However, *three months later*, he invites the same six children to continue the drama from where they had left off, which they do with only a modicum of prompting from Millward. For the first recording, the children and the the original teacher (who took no part in the drama) continued to sit round a staffroom table as they 'slipped into' drama. For the second recording, they moved around in a chosen space in the hall. Throughout both recordings Millward was in role. Thus the data for this research is uniquely a record of the dialogue that emerged from the interactions of a teacher and just six pupils in a fiction-making context, the topic of which was ostensibly 'living under a volcano', an extension of what they had been discussing. The teacher had no preconceptions of where it was going and certainly no notion of teaching the six something about volcanoes.

We have a complete recording, then, of an unassuming, unsophisticated version of 'Living through' Drama. In addition, we have Millward's penetrating analysis from an ethnomethodological perspective. Millward gives us both an unpretentious, 'pure' example of 'Living through' drama and a way of talking about it that is of critical interest to this study.

The Drama

Having asked permission to interrupt the discussion Millward finds himself saying:

Teacher   Can you imagine that each of you... are a person who lives in a little village by a volcano, all right? And I'm a stranger and I'm coming to talk to you. All right?

All   Mmm

Teacher   Can you do that from this moment? Stop being yourselves for a moment, well, be yourselves... but [laughter] be yourselves in this village.

Ian   Mmm

Teacher   All right?

All   Mmm

Deceptively fumbling, Millward invites his group of six to stumble with him into living beneath a volcano, interrupting a discussion on what it must be like for people living in such circumstances. The 'fumbling' of course is this teacher's way of ensuring that what ensues is 'Living through'. He could have said, 'This has been a very interesting discussion; shall we turn it into a play?' Millward believes there are two traps in such a question. Firstly, the 'we' ['shall we turn it into a play] reinforces the framework of 'a teacher and six pupils' for in that staffroom that is who they are. Having engaged in discussion they (the said 'teacher and pupils') would have then switched to a different 'teacher and pupils' task, that is, – making up a drama. According to Millward, 'Pupils doing drama' about volcano living is of a different order from 'living under a volcano'. Hence Millward's deliberate 'Stop being yourselves...well, be yourselves in this village' muddle. It is his way of saying '*Be here now*'. They are not to '*do drama*' but to 'present experience dramatically'. Of course they will continue to be pupils with a teacher and the school staffroom will remain as a stubborn reminder of who they are and where they are, but in the 'dramatic presentation of experience' such a school framework may fade (but never entirely disappear) in favour of the new framework of people living here, at the foot of a dangerous a mountain.

Secondly, making a play about people who live beneath a volcano traps the class into an unhelpful assumption about the nature of drama. It is one (Peter Millward has pointed out) that writers on drama education misleadingly convey when they imply that the meaning of drama lies in its faithful representation of a 'real' world. Such writers do not always take care to distinguish between drama as an experience in its own right and drama as a duplication. 'Shall we turn our discussion into a play?' appears to be inviting a class to consider people who live beneath volcanoes and *represent* their lives by imitating them as best we can. This would, in Millward's terms, be '*doing drama*', drawing on an imitative talent that does not belong to 'Living through'. Thus the two traps within the question, 'Shall we do a play about people living beneath a volcano?' relate to *who* (teacher and pupils) and *what* (representation of those volcano people).

Millward could, of course, have chosen to invite the six children to 'just play' at living underneath a volcano, clearing a space in the staffroom for them to do so. Assuming they were capable or motivated to be so engaged, this would have amounted to what I have defined above as 'dramatic playing'. For Millward, however, this was not an alternative choice. Straightaway he brings in teacher-in-role, a dimension, as we have seen, critical to 'Living through'. His choice of role ('And I'll be a stranger and I'm coming to talk to you') is highly significant at a number of levels affecting the ensuing drama. Three will be discussed below.

(1) 'And I'm coming to talk to you' deftly takes them into the drama without a break, for talking is what he is already doing, so that when he continues with:

Teacher   You know, what I can't understand...is, being a
           stranger and not living in a place like this little village
           which you live in with that great volcano smoking
           away all day... what I can't understand is why you still
           stay here... why do you keep your village down here
           below this great volcano?

they, the children, are able to continue sitting in their chairs[19] 'hearing' that they are somewhere else and no doubt 'seeing' the 'stranger's uplifted nod in the direction of something towering above them. Only in the second session of this drama, three months later, do the six 'get on their feet'. This sedentary acting behaviour represents a huge contrast with the Stone/Slade/Way 'physical education' starting-point for drama work. All that appears to be necessary, for drama of this kind is a token physicality (in this instance the upward movement of the stranger's eyes). Necessary, but obviously not always sufficient, that is, for we shall see actions later take on central importance.

(2) By taking on a role of someone who may ask questions Millward appears here to be perpetuating 'the power teachers have over children' and exercising his teacher 'rights' to ask questions. The diffident style of the teacher's language, however, is sufficient to signal that the social context has changed. Just as the *physical* change was virtually non-existent, so the structural aspect of 'teacher asking questions to which children answer' has not changed. What has changed is this teacher's whole demeanour including his choice of paralinguistic signals. The first two dimensions, the physical and the structural components, keep the children anchored in a school setting; it is the *style* of presentation, illuminating 'stranger' and 'village dwellers' that appears to be just sufficient, at this testing moment of opening up a 'Living through' drama, to help the children present their experience dramatically. Only just sufficient, for after a four second silence from the class, one boy risks 'You get plenty of water', an answer, as Millward points out, safely poised between two structures, for such an answer cleverly satisfies both 'pupil responding to teacher' and 'villager responding to stranger' contexts. The same boy's subsequent generalisation ('There's

water in the ground in some volcanoes') suggests a reversion to the former context, but the 'stranger's 'Do you all have hot water in your huts?' now throws out a challenge to establish a 'volcano' context in which they can no longer cling to being pupils in a staffroom..'Yes', they answer in turn – and when, to the teacher's follow up question, 'Has any of you [*and here the 'stranger' adopts a newly serious tone*] ever had a ... close friend... hurt... or even killed by the volcano?', one girl affirms that this is the case, they are suddenly people endowed with a past history – and there is no going back.

3. We have seen that an important part of Dorothy Heathcote's management of 'Living through' drama is her constant departure from role in order to get a class to reflect and dig deeper into what they are creating. Peter Millward has chosen one of the few roles open to a teacher that have their own built-in reflection device, for as a 'stranger' he can pose questions at an ever deepening level and, equally important to 'Living through' drama, his 'strangerness' inherently contributes to creating an image of the children as a community, for his role is a catalyst to their collective role. His 'strangerness' to a community provides the natural dynamic for giving it an identity, which the rest of the dialogue proceeds to do. From 'past injury', the questions and answers between stranger and villagers moved to 'thoughts of climbing the volcano', which the children turn into a taboo, for reasons to do with 'jewels at the top' ('*you can see 'em glittering at night'), which turn out to be a 'sign of the great god*'...who turns climbers into victims... kept '*in the heart, the heart of the volcano*'. To the teacher's question 'How do you know he (the great god) put them there?', one of the answers is '*We just believe in him*'. Others know he is there, '*cause you see him on a night... his... great crown in the sky... against the sky*'. All of which speedily, but with no prompting from the teacher, turns into a drama in which, before 'high priests' the 'stranger' is challenged with '*Have you learnt the great laws?*'

Thus in a response to a teacher whose mind was pursuing matters of practical significance to do with constant hot water and climbers getting hurt, the children take their play into mystical and canonical realms. They are penetrating into a community's values – and it is the teacher's choice of role that has created the opportunity to do so. Everything they do subsequently in their 'Living through' is sustained by this deeper commitment, which they have to work hard to maintain.

The ethnomethodological theory adopted by Millward [and by me in so far as it helps distinguish between 'living through' drama and 'doing a play'] is of social experience as a managed accomplishment, of social life existing 'in the manner through which we attend to it'. His purpose is to extend that theory to embrace drama. He argues that just as there is tacit agreement among those involved in a social situation to make that situation meaningful through their talk and actions, so people participating in presenting experience dramatically honour the same agreement and draw on the same kind of 'common knowledge' to make the dramatic situation meaningful. In the everyday presentation of experience,

> meaning is located in the work done by those involved to give their experience stability and character so that it may appear to themselves and others as real.

The above fits very well too as a description 'living through' drama. Only when something goes wrong in our everyday management of social experience are we made to be aware of this collaborative effort. In 'living through' drama, however, we are conscious of what we are doing; we know that it is make-believe and therefore without the consequences of everyday experience, but it is meaningful as everyday experience is meaningful, in that the way we work at it is, reflexively, a constituent part of its meaning. The dramatic context is not a 'given' to be enacted (as in 'doing drama'); it is a managed accomplishment to be treated, as for any social context, 'as real'. If social life can be described, as Rom Harré does, as 'a kind of conversation',[20] so can 'living through' drama, for they are both dependent on a shared frame of mind, generated from the same resources, composed of the same elements, and made effective through communication and inter-pretation. Both 'Living through drama' (along with the dramatic play-ing of children without a teacher) and everyday experience are wrought from the efforts of the participants. They may draw on familiar patterns of social codes, but each moment is newly forged. In the 'volcano drama' the children work at making sense of the contingency of their inventions – testing a stranger, guarding their treasures and beliefs etc. Because it is make-believe, their universe is hugely enlarged and they knowingly invent their 'new conversation'.

Just before the second phase of their drama (three months later), Millward injected a dramatic tension into the work. The children had already evolved a situation in which two of the children were in role as guides[21] to the 'stranger' encouraging and helping him to climb the mountain, whereas two others were disapproving of the 'stranger', and disapproving of his taking the test. Millward, outside the drama, encouraged the latter to behave, however, as if they had the stranger's 'best interests' at heart. With this ploy, of course, Millward is straying from Heathcote's refined version of 'Living through' to unashamed 'Man in a Mess' [in this instance it is the *stranger* in the Mess!], but one can sense the huge enjoyment and sense of power the children gained from the subtle deception. At one point in the sequence, it is thought necessary by the 'guardians' that the 'stranger' should meet their father, a 'blind man' whose disability, so it emerged, had been caused by doing the same 'test'.[22]

We have seen in previous chapters that teachers, workshop leaders and directors are fascinated by 'blindness'. We have had instances from Brian Way, who believed that moving with ones eyes shut gave one a sense of blindness, Stanislavski who tricked his actress, Maria, into terror of isolation, and Clive Barker, who worked technically with his actors on the difference between being blindfolded and 'pretending' to be. Cecily O'Neill also used sight deprivation when, in one of her published lessons, 'Frank Miller',[23] she created a game of finding each other through touch. Millward's class of six young children create blindness out of dialogue, as a playwright would. It is not the boy playing the 'blind father' who has to work to portray that role. He is not required as in Clive Barker's exercise to convey that his open eyes can't see. His blindness is established by the very way people tend to present disability in a social context:

Mark:	Ah, here he is now [said as though the man cannot present himself]. Come on... careful... over here... come on...
Julia:	Mind the steps.
Mark:	Careful...careful down.
Julia:	One more. There you are. We'll get you a seat.
Mark:	He's made it now, as you can see.
Julia:	There you are. Sit down on there.
Mark:	Sit down. Right... he made it here.

Here is a remarkable example of how a particular person's handicap[24] is not his alone, but also 'other people's perceptions' of a person with a handicap, as Millward puts it. The others speak of the blind man as though he were not there, quite incapable of speaking for himself. Thus they are meeting *two* objectives. Making blindness visible is part of presenting the social structure, but at the same time, they are conscious that by doing so they are moving their drama along, for that 'stranger' will be made more and more uncomfortable by the evidence of this blind man's failure to pass the test unscathed.

The 'teacher/pupil' structure has faded even more into the background, as they confidently make sense of what is going on and also see what is going on as a drama. Their drama-making has at least two aspects: their dialogue becomes more publicly viable as they acquire a stronger sense of spectatorship towards what they are creating; and the structure of what they are creating becomes closely allied to a well-made play. Peter Millward demonstrates how dramatist's skills of handling beginnings, endings, entrances, dramatic irony, symbolism and sub-texts[25] etc. are part and parcel of these eight year olds' dramatic repertoire. Millward warns us that we should not be beguiled into assuming that these beautifully managed constructions are stored up in their minds as calculated effects waiting to be expressed. They *discover* what they are doing as they do it. This is artistic spontaneity, grounded in understanding of what is needed, at it best. The meaningfulness of the event inheres in itself, without reference to some 'real' world out there or to some preconceived script or to some previous discussion. 'Living through' drama essentially operates from *inside* the event; there is no model of fact or form, nor is there any felt need to maintain the 'teacher and pupils' social structure. Its defining component, however, is 'teacher-in-role'. Peter Millward just followed the direction the children took; in doing so he *honoured*[26] their creativity. When it seemed appropriate, from outside the drama he guaranteed dramatic irony by encouraging a theatrical deception, and then he continued to follow.

Teacher-in-role continues, as we shall see, to be critical to Dorothy Heathcote's own reinterpretation of 'Living through' drama: 'Mantle of the Expert', however, depends on an even more sophisticated usage.

Mantle of the Expert

In Drama for Learning Dorothy Heathcote (1995) describes her first intimation, in the mid 1970s, of an alternative to 'Man in a Mess' drama. She and her students were conducting, at the request of a school, a project with all the classes on the theme of 'The Nativity', when she found herself landed with three 'naughty boys' who were thought too disruptive to stay with their classes. So Heathcote made the role of the 'Three Wise Men' their particular contribution to the project. Automatically she turns the work into 'Living through' drama by playing the role of servant to the 'Three Wise Men'. To understand Heathcote's approach one needs to understand that where the participants are themselves required to take on a role[27] in improvised as opposed to scripted work, she sees no alternative to helping them 'from the inside' by taking a role herself. Whatever similarities may be found between her and her predecessors, 'teacher-in-role' is distinctively Heathcotian.

In her earlier 'Man in a Mess' days, her planning for the three boys would have centred round the nature of the 'mess' – how to find the way; suppose one of the camels falls sick?; shortage of water across the desert etc, but on this occasion, conscious that she must get these lads doing something, in fact *anything but acting*, she let the tasks dictate the meaning of the experience. So, examining genuine maps of the night sky;[28] making wills, grooming camels, bartering for water; guarding the precious gifts became the dynamic of the work, which could still cater for the above named 'Man in a Mess' themes, but the boys were now in control as *'experts'* not in role as *'suffering a crisis'*. As Heathcote puts it: '...it was the *tasks* we did on our journey as Magi that created the power, curiosity and vulnerability of the three wise men.' She further writes:

> I began to realize that this 'expertise of viewpoint' could help teachers with little conscious understanding of theatre to get things started *under* the story line instead of merely replicating narrative. Also, because children enjoy playing at 'busy authority' (as younger children enjoy 'playing house'), the work could be launched via short, precise, honed-for-the-purpose tasks relevant to the theme.

'Busy authority' sums up the 'Mantle of the Expert' role. From this point in her teaching, Heathcote saw 'busy authority' as the fictional springboard from which all learning could be pursued. Rarely, from this point in her career, is 'what shall we make a play about?' to be heard in her classrooms, for such a question opens the wrong door – and suffering a crisis directly is to remain a firmly closed door. Like Harriet Finlay-Johnson before her, dramatic activity is to be explicitly tied to the curriculum. Of course if that curriculum were to include 'Drama' in some traditional sense, then Mantle of the Expert can accommodate it, for the method can be used to teach anything – including 'theatre history'.

Thus Heathcote unambiguously adopts the position of an *educationist* harnessing the potential of drama, setting herself apart from her contemporary drama specialists who see drama as an important area of a person's education[29] – in competition with other curriculum subjects. Whereas their attention necessarily is on drama, hers is on the curriculum and whatever is to be taught determines the kind of fiction that will be needed. However, and this is critical to the approach, the *fictional starting point will rarely be that of the matter being studied.* Thus, if we take examples from Heathcote (1995), the American students studying 'Watergate' were in role as 'people running a museum'; for the topic of 'an aircrash' the pupils were in role as 'radio engineers'; for a study of China, the roles were running a hotel management training school. The fiction, developed before the relevant aspects of the curriculum are directly engaged with, provides the continuous *'enterprise'* (*or, 'subculture'*[30]) *and dictates both the 'rules' of how things shall be conducted and the particular 'way in' to the curricular knowledge or skill.* In one 1995[31] example, the pupils learn about the Science of Light, but their entry into the topic is through the perspective of mediaeval monks needing to extend their scriptorium. In another example the class of nine year old pupils enjoy the excitement of capturing a tiger, but they are in role as 'experts' working for OXFAM, so that their 'tiger' experience is at one remove. It is 'Man in a Mess' conducted with a cool eye of 'this is how it was for *them*' or 'this is how it would be for *them*'; never 'this is happening to us now'.

This asymmetric correspondence between a sustained basic role and a temporarily evoked second or third role allows Heathcote to indulge in an infinite variety of techniques in the creation of the secondary roles. The pupils are released from being inside an event in their secondary role, but required to be inside the enterprise of their primary role, that is, they *actually* carry out tasks as experts, designing, tracing, writing formal reports and letters, measuring, looking things up in authentic adult texts, decoding, practising, visualising, hypothesising, demonstrating, rehearsing, devising regulations, instructing etc. The tiger hunt is not happening in the 'here and now' but OXFAM is established in the continuous present and presence of an OXFAM headquarters. It can be said, therefore, that OXFAM provides the context for the here and now of the 'living through'.

This interweaving of two levels of fiction demands a sophisticated 'dramatist's' touch from the teacher. She can never adopt a teacher position unless she comes out of role; she can only be a colleague to fellow experts or a visitor who needs advice (always on behalf of 'someone else who has sent her') from experts. It is the way she sets about endowing her pupils with 'expertise' that requires the dramatist's skill. Her dialogue must belong to an OXFAM *text*. Traditional teacher language of 'Would you like to make a project folder...?' is out of place and becomes: 'Does anyone have the West India file?' Thus a professional vocabulary and an implied history are woven into the dramatist's text in one short question.

In setting up the secondary roles, a whole range of theatrical devices are available. Perhaps the most formal of these is 'Chamber Theatre' which Heathcote favours as a theatre genre suitable for the classroom. We have already had a glimpse of the facility in Heathcote for the artistic manipulation of time and space in the description above of the pupils 'who crossed a time zone' in order to converse with Lister. Chamber Theatre represents a more formal convention[32] and can only be used where there is a 'given' script.

'Chamber Theatre' is a branch of the American 'Reader's Theatre' to which Heathcote has been attracted,[33] one suspects, because of its capacity for staying 'true' to the literary text. Chamber Theatre,[34] retaining the same degree of literary integrity but offering scope for greater flexibility,[35] seemed ripe for absorbing into the Heathcote system of teaching. Heathcote and Bolton (1995) write[36]:

> An interesting feature, especially relevant to an educational context, is that while leaving the responsibility of expressing the underlying motives and feelings to the narrator, in order to function the actor must nevertheless *understand* those motives and feelings. Thus, paradoxically, the students may feel strongly the tension of the event, picking up by osmosis the feelings of the characters as described by the narrator *because* the burden of having to express those emotions is removed. The narrator almost invokes the feeling and emotion in the student as they demonstrate the behavior that conveys the story.

Less formal devices for the secondary role take an infinite number of forms. For instance in a Mantle of the of Expert project on King Arthur of England the pupils' primary role is modern American bee-keepers, but one of their secondary roles is representing the discoverers of a mediaeval manuscript (one, which earlier in the project they had themselves made) hidden for centuries in a box in a tree trunk, split by the force of a bull's horn caught in it during a storm. The enactment of the part of this incident in which one boy climbs into the tree, lifts the box, unties the rope and opens the box proceeds as follows:

> Finally, a boy is chosen to climb into the tree trunk to retrieve the box. The class, with their 'binoculars' [hands curled round eyes] for seeing, instruct him where to put his feet, while he is actually sitting on the floor with eyes closed, matching his climbing actions [in his mind] to their guidance, until he tells them 'he is there'.
>
> Once there, *they* turn away so they can not see *him* as he unties the rope, giving an account (to which they can only listen) of what he is doing and of what the newly found box looks like. He draws out the length of rope, requiring his colleagues to haul him and the box out of the hole.

This highly disciplined, stylised presentation is then followed by the 'fun' of opening the box, 'discovering' the manuscript and trying to read it as though they had never seen it before! They are looking at some writing they prepared in their primary role through the eyes of their secondary role. Heathcote would claim that this degree of 'prismatic' sophistication takes these 12 year old pupils into dramatic realms opening up layers of meaning unattainable by straightforward enactment.

How shall we sum up this pioneer's approach? What is it that her followers must acquire or understand first and foremost? The answer, I believe, lies in 'authenticity'. There is an educational principle amounting to a moral imperative pervading Heathcote's Mantle of the Expert approach.[37] By authenticity she means rigorous attention to and respect for what is true, true for the scientist and scholar and for the artist and craftsman. A passionate interest in things, in how things are made and in who will be responsible for them underlies her emphasis on *tasks*, for tasks rely on that kind of knowledge. Thus the very foundation of Dorothy Heathcote's methodology is focused on the school curriculum at a level that demands the integrity of scholarship. It will be a long time before our leading educationists and politicians recognise the potential in her work, and yet in the following quotation from an educationist there is a kinship with Heathcotian philosophy:

> (The purpose of science is) to make our pupils feel, so far as they may, what it is to be, so to speak, inside the skin of a man of science, looking out through his eyes as well as using his tools, experiencing not only something of his labours, but also something of his sense of joyous intellectual adventure.

This advocacy of 'looking through an expert's eyes came from Sir Percy Nunn in 1920. In Chapter Three I was dismissive of Nunn's insistence that it should be the *power* of make-believe rather than make-believe itself that should harnessed. But Nunn sees the Scout Movement, as an example of the ideal in education in which the learner's role, with all the trappings required of the 'Scout' identity, inherently extends the boy's vision, motivation and capacity for learning. Dorothy Heathcote has found a way of bringing the power of make-believe into the classroom so that her pupils can be 'inside the skin of the expert' and achieve 'his sense of joyous intellectual adventure', using, not the identity of a Scout Movement culture, but that of an enterprise culture.

Notes

1   Her most articulate critic in this respect was Margaret Faulkes-Jendyk ['Creative Dramatics Leaders Face Objective Examination' in *Canadian Child and Youth Drama Association Bulletin* 1975].

2   Emotionalism was 'in the air'. In keeping with the progressive 'humanist' movement, such group interactions as 'T Groups' and 'Encounter Groups' validated the flow of uninhibited emotion. For some, and I include myself to some extent in this 1970s trend, Drama was another opportunity for releasing 'genuine' feeling. In the professional Theatre, Stanislavski, for example, went through a phase of manipulating his actors by deception. I have already given a brief account in which he puts an actress through a frightening experience, triumphantly exclaiming: 'Now you know what blindness is like.' [Gorchakov, Nikolai (1954) *Stanislavski Directs* translated by Miriam Goldina, New York pp.297-298]. David Selbourne [Selbourne, D. (1982) *The making of Midsummer Night's Dream* London p.51] describes how Peter Brook used 'noise and harassment to, and beyond, breaking point' in order to drive 'Hermia' to appeal for help from Lysander out of 'panic'.

3   These were paralleled abroad in countries such as Canada and USA by Summer School drama courses.

4   My sympathies are with David Hornbrook in this. He helped to shake us out of a confusion.

5   It is not the place here in this thesis to examine the differences between drama education and therapy. Historically, distinctions have been blurred, especially in the minds of teachers dealing with what used to be called 'remedial classes'. One of the British experts in the field of therapy entitled her first book 'Remedial Drama' [Jennings, Sue (1973) *Remedial Drama: A Handbook for Teachers and Therapists* Pitman London] – notice the sub-title. A much later publication by Robert Landy [Landy, Robert (1986) *op cit* pp.7-16] draws a distinction between 'Drama in Education', 'Drama in Recreation' and 'Drama in Therapy.

6   David Davis is currently teaching at the University of Central England and was responsible for setting up the Drama Education Archives which house many video tapes of Dorothy Heathcote teaching in Birmingham Schools.

7   See hand-written note by Heathcote, dated 16.05.96

8   This description of the 'Crucible lesson' was written in preparation for a forthcoming publication by Contemporary Theatre Review (Ed: Dan Urian, Haifa University) Harwood Zurich.

9   Professor Cecily O'Neill of Ohio University, in her book *Drama Worlds: a framework for process drama* Hutchinson New Jersey pp.34-5, also gives an account of this 'Crucible' sequence. A close analysis of my teaching has come from the pen of Margaret Burke of the University of Brock. See, for example, her account of a session with adults based on the Nursery Rhyme, 'Miss Muffet': 'Learning from a Master: Bolton at Ohio, 1995' by Margaret Burke (1996) in *The Journal of Ohio Drama Education Exchange* Vol 1, No 1. pp.51-66. For an

account of a session with High School students at the University of Victoria on a 'serious accident', see *Teaching Drama* by Norah Morgan and Juliana Saxton (1987) Hutchinson London pp.8-13.

10 Cecily O'Neill currently divides her time between her responsibilities as an Associate Professor of Drama Education in the School of Teaching and Learning, Ohio State University, Columbus and her free-lance work in England and other countries

11 O'Neill, Cecily and Lambert, Alan (1982) *Drama Structures: A Practical Handbook for Teachers* Stanley Thornes, Portsmouth New Jersey

12 By this time there were a growing number, if small minority of Arts education experts, such as Malcolm Ross, David Aspin and Peter Abbs whose theoretical position embracing the idea of a generic base for all the arts prevented them from accepting learning as of prior importance in drama education..

13 Narration by the teacher in Heathcote's and O'Neill's work had many different functions, but usually avoided dictating actions by the pupils of the kind described in the chapters on Slade and Way.

14 They are (1) Learning arising from content of the lesson; (2) Social learning; (3) Skills and (4) Intrinsic Learning – 'a growth or change in understanding' (pp.14-15).

15 O'Neill, C.C. (1995) *ibid* p.5

16 O'Neill uses the term 'improvisation' broadly to include many kinds of dramatic activities, but it is the 'living through' element, that is, the use of 'teacher-in-role' to set the scene, to clarify it or to move it on, that gives Process Drama its dominant (but not consistent) characteristic. She appreciates, of course, that 'improvisation' will be more readily understood by her readers who no doubt see the use of 'teacher-in-role' as but one of many kinds of 'impros' or 'improvs'.

17 Millward, Peter (1988) *The Language of Drama: A study of the way in which people accomplish the dramatic presentation of experience*, unpublished Ph.D thesis, University of Durham Vols 1 and 2

18 Millward, Peter (1988) *ibid* Vol 2 p.iv. Millward explains: 'There was no plan to move the discussion into drama and it is not easy to say why I decided to interrupt; it just seemed a good opportunity.'

19 This example has some similarity with what I have elsewhere [Bolton, G. (1992)...*op cit* pp.60-61] described as 'Sitting down' drama, an introduction to dramatic behaviour I have found very useful with classes unused to drama, but I have not come across any account of it other than my own.

20 Harré, Rom (1983) 'An analysis of social activity: a dialogue with Rom Harré' in *States of Mind: Conversations with Psychological Investigators* by Jonathon Miller [Ed] BBC London p.159

21 It is typical of 'Living through' drama that what starts as a collective role (in this instance, 'children who live beneath a mountain', gradually becomes individualised as it is required by the drama, so that now the children are adult 'guides', 'guardians' and 'priests', one of whom, on the spur of the moment, becomes a 'blind parent'.

22 Peter Millward has published this excerpt from his thesis in 'Drama as a Well-made Play' in *Language Arts* February, (1990) National Council of Teachers of English. References made above to this section of his thesis will also apply to this latter publication.

23 O,Neill, C.C. (1995) *op cit* p.ix

24 or 'challenge' as some politically correct pedants would have it, although it should be borne in mind that these children are set on making out their blind person as inadequate.

25 Millward illustrates [See pages 489- 492 of Vol 1] a vivid example of the working of a sub-text within the transcript. One of the pupils, Julia, uses the offering of tea to the 'stranger' as a subtle way of manipulating and revealing a complex relationship. On the surface, her 'tea' talk fits her 'hostess' role, but underneath it is about power.

26 To use a term Dorothy Heathcote often employed.

27 It should be noted that in the 'cultural' project' described in Chapter 9, she did not play a role at any point – because the participants were never in a fictional role; they were observers or directors or dramatists, but never actors.

28 One can assume that had Heathcote been working on Millward's 'Volcano' drama, her pupils would have early in the work been 'examining volcanoes' – a direction Millward would happily have followed if his class had not taken it into more mystical realms.

29 John Somers is an example of what I mean here. In outlining a contemporary perspective on *Drama in the Curriculum* [Somers, J. (1994) *op cit* p.55], 'Mantle of the Expert' does not warrant a mention even with 'curriculum' as the context for his writing, and in one of two references to Dorothy Heathcote he perpetuates the 'Man in a Mess' image, long dismissed by Heathcote as too blunt an instrument for sophisticated curriculum learning.

30 This concept will be discussed in the final chapter.

31 Heathcote, D. and Bolton, G. (1995) pp.48-81

32 Heathcote has led the way in experimenting with different kinds of imaginative conventions. A useful text by Jonathon Neelands [Neelands, Jonathon (1990) *Structuring Drama Work* Cambridge University Press] summarised many of them to help teachers in their practice. Subsequently, interesting material has been provided as a series of publications by Ray Mather. [See especially Mather, Ray (1996) 'Turning Drama Conventions into Images' in *Drama Vol* 4 No 3/Vol 5 No 1 Summer/Autumn 1996]

33 See video (A2 1991) of her session on 'Chamber Theatre', UCE archives.

34 The seminal text on the subject is *Chamber Theatre* by Robert S Breen (1986), William Caxton, Evanston Illinois. According to this author, Chamber Theatre was first demonstrated in 1947 at Northwester University (where, America's greatest pioneer of Creative Dramatics, Winifred Ward, was Head of Department of Speech [Ward, Winifred (1930) *Creative Dramatics* Appleton, New York].

35 Robert Breen writes: '...there is a technique for presenting narrative fiction on the stage in such a way as to take full advantage of all the theatrical devices of the stage without sacrificing the narrative elements of the literature.' [Breen, R. S.(1986) *ibid* p.4]

36 Heathcote, D. and Bolton, G. *ibid* p.213. This kind of classroom practice has connections with Marjorie Hourd's use of miming by the pupils while the teacher reads a poem – the pupils' understanding may well surpass their ability to express it.

37 Unable to recognise this moral imperative in Heathcote's work, David Holbrook [Holbrook, D. (1989) *op cit* p.126] appeals for a moral stance.

38 Even a leading figure in education such as Professor Ted Wragg of Exeter University, a man for whom I have a lot of respect, seems not to be interested in having a look at Heathcote's 'Mantle of the Expert' approach to Education. In a recent letter to me [June, 1997] he acknowledged having read of her work, but expressed no interest in finding out about 'M of E'.

SECTION FIVE
TOWARDS A CONCEPTUAL
FRAMEWORK FOR CLASSROOM
ACTING BEHAVIOUR

CHAPTER 11

This book has described a wide range of classroom drama practice. Any historical account may leave the reader with the impression that some activities, popular in their time are now too outdated to be useful today. I would like to suggest that the principles behind all the activities, if not their format, may still be applicable to some current teaching circumstances. The same applies, I believe to the kinds of acting required by the activities. None is so inappropriate that no place could be given to it today. The good teacher, recognising that any instance of acting is open to abuse and overuse, will tend to favour a wide range of acting behaviours.

What has changed over the years is the conceptual basis from which writers have argued for their particular methodology. This publication, and this final chapter in particular, is trying to outline a conceptual framework which could allow teachers adopting an eclectic approach to communicate with each other by sharing a common language. By common language, I do not mean common vocabulary or terminology. *My* choice of labels for categories is quite arbitrary. It matters not whether we choose to name, say, the acting required for a tableau as 'showing' or 'presenting' or 'demonstrating' or whatever – I have chosen, as it happens, to call it 'presenting'. What does matter is that teachers can *share the conception* of a mode of acting *as* a definable category and see such a classification as serving a useful purpose.

A central problem in attempting to categorise behaviours of any kind is to determine what *level* of categorisation would have the most practical use. The danger is that we fall in love with *differences* and indulgently spin out innumerable classifications – a good time could be had taking each illustration of practice of the previous chapters of this book and, slotting each into a category of its own, still have categories left over! At the other extreme is the temptation to ignore differences entirely and go for *samenesses* – and to ones delight one finds that there is only *one category. All acting is the same!*

It is this latter trap that David Hornbrook has fallen into when he writes, 'It is my contention that conceptually there is nothing which differentiates the child acting in the classroom from the actor on the stage of the theatre.' And, of course, *at the conceptual level he has chosen to operate he is right.* The first part of this chapter will appear to demonstrate just how right he is, for I shall begin by studying what acting behaviours share in common. Attractive as this may be, how *useful* is it? Is there, therefore, a *minimum* number of categories which could show essential differences at a fundamental level while retaining this important sense of *oneness*, for one can appreciate what persuaded Hornbrook to overstate similarities – much of the history outlined in this book has been about people failing to recognise common ground.

I have kept my classification to a minimum of three major categories, or rather, two major categories and a powerful sub category – after which confusing statement! – I can only hope that the basis for my divisions will become clear towards the end of this chapter!

Common ground of all classroom acting behaviours
The account of the work of five pioneers and other leading exponents of classroom drama has revealed many different kinds of activities executed in the name of drama, but 'entry into fiction' is what they (mostly)[1] share. I wish to argue that other common ground includes the mimetic, aesthetic, generalising, communicating and focusing features commonly associated with acting.

A psychological feature common to all acting behaviours: The tension between imitating and inventing

I began this study with John Allen's (1979) translation of Aristotle's 'Mimesis' as 'an act of recreation', a term suggesting invention as well as imitation. The story of this century's drama teaching reveals marked contrasts in the degree and kind of imitation involved. Irene Mawer's (1932) 'practice in walking like kings and queens', for instance, represents an extreme version of imitative behaviour required by a teacher of her pupils, as Peter Millward's (1988) deliberately ambiguous instruction to his class '...stop being yourselves for a moment, well be yourselves... but be yourselves in this village...' seemingly precludes imitation; 'seemingly', for, as we shall argue later in this chapter, any form of enactment requires a public medium sufficiently referential to be understood by others. I have earlier quoted from Ernst Cassirer who captures the tension between imitating and inventing. '...reproduction never consists in retracing, line for line, a specific content of reality; but in selecting a pregnant motif.'

However, there seems to be a cluster of terms used by writers to explain the two-pronged psychological relationship between the actor and the 'real' world and between the actor and the fiction. I want to suggest that **Identification** may be a useful umbrella term under which the imitative/inventive tension of 'Mimesis' could be subsumed along with other recurring characteristics. I have already favoured 'identification' over Peter Slade's and others' insistence on 'sincerity' as a prerequisite for Child Drama. Indeed I defined the process of identification in terms that simultaneously expand both on 'Sincerity' and 'Mimesis': 'The child abstracts a 'truth'[2] from the situation as s/he sees it for the purpose of representation. What is represented is the child's understanding of, not a fascimile of, a reality.' I have written 'child' here, as I am concentrating on classroom behaviour, but the same could be said of the actor on stage, or, indeed of one of Caldwell Cook's 'players' who offers, not Hamlet, but his understanding of Hamlet expressed through an act of *interpretation*.[3] It may be dualistic to suggest in this way that the player's 'interpretation' *reflects* his 'understanding', implying two discrete stages of a temporal sequence, as though, having (internally) 'understood' Hamlet, he *then* proceeds (externally) to 'interpret' him. Nevertheless, it seems important to the practice of drama to give a place to the notion that there may be a mismatch between understanding and interpretation, that, for instance, an act of interpretation may, through lack of skill or commitment, fall short of a person's understanding, or, conversely, that engagement in an act of interpretation may itself extend the understanding.

To link the *inventive* face of Mimesis solely with 'interpretation', however, is to concentrate on its intellectual aspect, whereas a central feature of acting behaviour is its potential for spontaneity, a quality the Psychodramatist, J.L. Moreno, experimented with in his patients as early as 1922 when he set up the first 'Therapeutic Theatre' in Vienna. Most of the educationists supporting the notion of improvised drama have valued it for its immediacy. There seems to have been an assumption that 'spontaneous' was synonymous with 'creative'. Brian Way built his whole theory of education on the importance of intuition as opposed to intellect. Even working on a Chamber Theatre script, Dorothy Heathcote insists that the players 'discover on their feet' the best way to convey the multiple meanings of the text. According to Shomit Mitter, Stanislavski, towards the end of his career, refound his faith in the somatic and advised his actors to 'start bravely, not to reason, but to act'. Perhaps the antithesis of imitation is best expressed in the term 'disponibilité', described by Frost and Yarrow as 'a kind of total awareness, a sense of being at one with the context: [with a] script, if such there be, actors, audience, theatre space, oneself and one's body.' Simon Callow captures its essence with[4]:

> You are the master of time and rhythm, and you play with them like a jazz musician. You create pleasurable tension and then relieve it pleasurably. You hear everything as if for the first time. The performance is not so much new as newly revealed.

Only if 'identification' can embrace the notion of spontaneity as an essential part of Mimesis is it useful to us as an umbrella term. Identification must imply a sufficient capacity for ownership of the fiction to allow free play within both the interpretation and 'the moment of it happening'.

Thus, in the context of acting behaviour, 'identification' stands for a many-stranded, radial connection between a person and the 'real world' *and* between that person and the fiction created, involving 'understanding', 'imitation', 'individual interpretation', 'group consensus', 'commitment', 'sincerity', and 'disponibilité'. John O'Toole (1992) writes of the *quality* and *degree* of identification, treating them almost synonymously, and suggesting they will vary according to commitment, maturity, and dramatic skill. An implication here is that quality of identification is objectively assessable. This may be so, but it seems also to be the case that even ill-informed identification may remain 'true' for the participant and, further, the *degree* or intensity of the identification may be relatively high in spite of inadequate information or knowledge. The possibility of a direct correspondence between degree and quality of identification remains in doubt.

John O'Toole draws our attention to a source of commitment in fiction-making that may sometimes override all other factors, in which the vested interest in the content of the drama by the participants is explicitly expressive of their 'real world'. O'Toole cites an example from my teaching in South Africa in 1980, made dramatic in both a fictitious and real sense by a black boy, towards the end of the improvised drama, taking my hand (he, in role as an old man living in the year 2050 and I in role as a 'white journalist'), and saying as he shook it, 'We are equal now'. Such a moment of 'identification' was 'true for us', 'spontaneous', and 'committed', but not necessarily dependent on dramatic skill, or, for my part, on extensive knowledge.

I have suggested that 'fiction' is the nucleus of all acting behaviour. It is possible now to see 'identification' as a further defining feature, so that a definition of acting behaviour would so far read as **fiction-making involving identification through action**. It is not meant to suggest, as Morgan and Saxton (with a different purpose in mind) do,[6] that the extent or depth of identification is paralleled by a matching complexity in level of action, but rather that maximum identification may be expressed in *any* kind of acting behaviour, whether it be the child described by Piaget who put her doll on an imaginary tractor because she is afraid of the tractor in the neighbouring field, or the ten year old boy in Heathcote's 'Making History' series who confronts the 'villeins' with 'You do not understand why this book is so important to us. It's part of our life. We need it so much. It's what our Lord said', or Finlay-Johnson's pupils who were 'so exceedingly good' as Rosalind and Celia. Just as the degree of identification does not determine its *quality*, so the intensity of identification does not determine the *kind* of acting behaviour, nor, conversely, can it be assumed that one kind of acting behaviour will guarantee a higher degree of intensity than another.

Degree or intensity of identification does, however, determine whether or not make-believe can occur. A major problem emerging from Marjorie Hourd's, Peter Slade's and Dorothy Heathcote's approaches, for example, has been the one of 'ownership' in the early stages of, respectively, Hourd's invitation to 'do the accompanying actions to a ballad', Slade's narration of a made-up story and Heathcote's use of teacher-in-role. Each of these exponents' methodologies, depends for its success on relinquishing the teacher's ownership of the fiction to their pupils while relying on considerable external input – a poem in (possibly) obscure language from Hourd; a series of teacher-timed instructions from Slade and a powerful acting display from Heathcote – and it is possible that none of these sufficiently capture the imagination of some children in their classes and that consequently their commitment remains too low for engagement with the fiction. On the other hand, in Hourd's classroom the poem may capture the child's imagination, but the techniques and personal exposure required to represent it in Mime may seem formidable. These are but examples from particular methodologies, but the problem of appropriate level of commitment is a feature of all acting behaviours.[7]

An aesthetic feature common to all acting behaviours: Fictitious time and space

If we search the publications of our pioneers and other leading figures for selected images of what they might have considered to be among the principal *aesthetic* features of classroom acting behaviour, we find in Harriet Finlay-Johnson (1910) a high tolerance for 'crude action' combined with a penchant for representational realism in costume, properties and scenery; Henry Caldwell Cook (1917) sought an intelligent use of the spatial proportions of an Elizabethan stage and the avoidance of realism; for Jacques-Dalcroze (1921) 'rhythm' created the basis for all the arts and he introduces the concept of 'musical gesture'; Irene Mawer (1932) emphasised mental and muscular control, physical fitness and imagination; Frances Mackenzie (1935) insisted on the importance of the use of the voice, facial expression, timing, holding pauses and effective exits; Robert Newton (1937) was concerned with 'form', by which he meant elements of surprise, contrast, mood and climax; Langdon (1948) saw the shape of the dramatic event, the plot, beginnings and endings and climax, as its key components; Marjorie Hourd[8] (1949) sought 'naturalism', by which she meant an untutored, unselfconscious, 'statuary' style of acting, as her pupils discovered the actions to accompany a ballad; Peter Stone (1949) introduced 'movement for movement's sake', in the Physical training space of the school hall; Peter Slade (1954) believed in a spatial/musical dimension that could reach heights of artistry; Brian Way (1967) favoured individual practice of actions to music, stimulating the pupil's image-making. Dorothy Heathcote (1995) pursues *signi*ficance in the use of the theatrical elements of sound/silence, movement/stillness/ and light/darkness; and Cecily O'Neill (1995) seeks dramatic irony. Such a collection of images may not entirely do justice to the individuals referred to, but they serve to give an overall picture of a range of aesthetic priorities pointing to considerable conceptual differences.

One aesthetic aspect they have in common, however, is a manipulation of time and space. The relationship of acting behaviour to time and space is of a different order from everyday actions to time and space, from what Schechner (1982) more poetically, if depressingly, calls 'the flux and decay of ongoing living'.[9] Acting behaviour is dependent upon, yet *outside* or *bracketed from* the time/space dimensions. Bateson's (1955)[10] analogy of 'picture frame' and 'wallpaper' which he used to demonstrate a different order of meanings within 'play' and 'not play' activities[11] may, I believe, be extended. Whereas his argument pertained to the 'denotation', and 'interpretation' of what was going on within the frame (as opposed to the wallpaper on which the frame is hung), I suggest the same metaphor could be applied to a 'player's' perception of 'time' and 'space' within the frame. The 'here and now' of acting is not the 'here and now' of existing. Schechner (1977) captures something of the difference when he says:

'Theater, to be effective, must maintain its double or incomplete presence, as *a here-and-now performance of there-and-then events*. The gap between the ' here and now' and 'there and then' allows an audience to contemplate the action, and to entertain alternatives.

Again, Schechner's focus, while seeing time and space as critical elements, is ultimately concerned with the meanings to be extracted and interpreted by an imaginative audience. I am interested here in establishing that this 'double and incomplete presence' requires the actor to be in the 'here and now', but, as it were, *outside* the bracket, *playing* with the 'here and now' inside the bracket. A vivid example of such 'playing with time and space' can be seen in Bertolt Brecht's instruction to his actors that in rehearsing a text they should render it[12]:

> not as an improvisation, but as a *quotation*. At the same time it is clear that he has to render, in this quotation, all the undertones, all the concrete, plastic detail of human utterance. His gestures, though they are frankly a *copy* (and not spontaneous), must have the full corporeality of human gestures.

In this example the actor is astride two time/space dimensions. He is located in space and existing 'in present time' and yet conveying implicitly, through 'quotation', a third person and a past time. In Chamber theatre, as we have seen, the *elasticity* of the time/space dimension is harnessed explicitly. Most 'living through' drama enjoys considerable freedom in time/space manipulation.

And yet in the first part of Peter Millward's experimental drama, action was avoided altogether. 'Why do you keep your village down here below this great volcano?', from teacher fumbling with his role as stranger, hardly seems to invite action of any kind. In fact, as we have already seen, he is addressing six children round a table in the staff-room – and that is where they stay for the whole of that first session. Does this qualify as drama? Where does this stand in relation to a theory that all acting behaviour is dependent on 'bracketed' time and space? In this episode action seems to have been reduced out of existence, but nevertheless a fictitious time and space are *implied*. That is not to suggest that incipient action is present: there is a huge gap between being round that table and the actions of living in that village; it would have required a very brave soul (and perhaps one insensitive to the medium) to have started doing 'volcanic village actions'. We have, therefore, a special kind of manipulation of time and space. Those dimensions grew and were 'played with' *in their minds* and did not become evident until the second session three months later. Thus the definition of acting behaviour as 'fiction-making involving identification through action' should be understood to embrace *implied* or *mental* action.

What is not brought out by Millward's thesis is the notion of double space/time dimensions. Part of being in the fiction is the chance to play with time and space, so that the most literal gesture, coinciding exactly with how it would be done in 'real life' in terms of time, space and energy, is done that way by *choice*; the participant is still outside the time/space bracket while deploying the dimensions within it. When Millward's pupils move into the school hall, space is immediately manipulated by giving status to the 'priest's place outside which 'shoes have to be removed', but time runs at a conversational pace until slowed down by the ceremony of 'meeting the priests' and we then, and only then, become aware of time and space being deftly handled to give meaning to their creation. When, out of choice, their timing and 'spacing' coincide with an everyday, 'conversational' usage, we are not aware of it as manipulation from 'outside the bracket'.

It is interesting that Dorothy Heathcote, the one writer who explicitly offers us an image of the manipulation of the three dimensions of 'space', 'time' and 'light' as central to her work should also present us with the greatest problem when it comes to trying to fit that image into her later practice, 'Mantle of the Expert'. Mostly her pupils are carrying out tasks in a way that suggests they are 'inside the bracket'. They are doing 'literal' tasks requiring 'everyday' timing – they are discussing, drawing, recording, cutting out, measuring, looking something up etc etc. Drawing a map demands the same spatial/ temporal dimensions whether or not one is in a role as 'expert'. Set against this, however, in 'Mantle of the Expert', we have another example of implied fictitious dimensions: just as a tilt of the head could suggest 'a volcano up there' in Millward's first session, so a glance at the the desk in the classroom corner indicates where you go to discuss a problem with the 'manager'; on the wall is the staff 'holiday' roster'; over the door shows the firm was established in 1907; and your 'Personal File' shows you have been an employee here for two years nine months. The whole activity is suffused with fictitious time while operating in the obstinate present of 'having in *actuality* to finish that map'. Nevertheless, traditional views of drama become challenged by the 'Mantle of the Expert' task-centred approach because it is traditionally assumed, by theatre theorists and child play theorists alike, that any 'character' drawing a map as part of 'a Play' or in 'Playing' will but *indicate* the action.

We can now add this time-space dimension to our definition of 'acting behaviour: **it is an act of fiction-making involving identification through action and the conscious manipulation of time and space**. I believe this definition applies across the range of classroom drama.

'Acting as generalisation' in all acting behaviours
That acting behaviour manipulates time/space from outside the bracket reinforces the notion, first introduced into education literature by Susan Isaacs (1930), that make believe play enables 'the emancipation of meanings from the here and now of a concrete situation.'[13] Drama as a medium for education is based on this capacity for generalisation from its particularity. The 'bracketing' of action invites that action to be attended to '*as*'action, of interest 'beyond itself', as Lars Kleberg (1993) has expressed it. Put succinctly: as well as being 'as if',[14] drama essentially is 'as'. This theoretical aspect is once again challenged by the 'Mantle of the Expert' role. Mantle of the Expert's reliance on *actual* behaviours seems, in this respect, to disqualify it as dramatic, although, of course, like geysers bursting out of a plateau, the most obviously dramatic structures of 'depicting', 'replaying the past' 'anticipating the future' and 'Chamber Theatre' etc are as integral to 'Mantle of the Expert' as the task work. But they belong to the *second* dimension of Mantle of the Expert. It is as though, although wearing the expert mantle, *drama* doesn't start for Heathcote's pupils until they are involved in drama-like contexts such as, say, 'setting up an interview with a customer'. To some extent this is paralleled by Caldwell Cook's pupils who see themselves as *players* but are not involved in drama until they actually start performing.

Thus our definition might now read: **Acting behaviour is an act of fiction-making involving identification through action, the conscious manipulation of time and space and a capacity for generalisation**.

The concept of 'audience' as a feature common to all acting behaviours

Interest in whether or not there should be an audience has been a major thread running through this history of drama teaching amounting, almost, to a plot-filled story of exponents' preferences. Finlay-Johnson wrote of 'doing away with an audience', by giving them responsibilities; Caldwell Cook's whole approach was with an audience in mind, developing what I have designated a 'platform' mentality; for Susan Isaacs' research of the play of her infants only observers were present; Langdon saw the presence or absence of spectators as a developmental issue – with no audience for infants, 'playing it out with an audience there' for lower Juniors' and beginning to understand 'the rights of an audience' for the older ones; Mackenzie (1935), Mawer (1932) and Newton (1937) saw their work as entirely audience orientated as did the Speech teachers of the 1920s and 30s; Hourd, like her colleague, Langdon, saw it as a developmental matter but interestingly perceived Junior school children (provided they were not turned into 'conscious artists') as stronger candidates for public performance than lower adolescents; Stone (1949), Slade (1954) and Way (1967) banished the idea of an audience, although Way does accept that small groups showing each other their work may be inevitable, if regrettable; Burton (1949) urged that the audience should 'know what we are experiencing' The Schools Council (1977),[15] while recognising the significant 'shift of emphasis' between 'acting-out' and 'performing', saw it as a matter of 'readiness'. Robinson (1980) makes a clear distinction between 'exploratory activities of classroom drama' and 'the activities of those who act a part to an audience.' Heathcote's (1979, 1984, 1995) teaching shows little interest in a traditional audience, but nevertheless generates a strong 'sense' of audience; in Millward's (1988) work an audience would have been irrelevant; O'Neill's (1995) 'Process Drama' includes, selectively, opportunities for rehearsal, with or without texts, and intense audience observation.

To argue as I have done above for 'manipulating time and space' as the common ground in spite of so may obvious differences in practice may seem to have challenged conventional wisdom. It may seem even more perverse to now argue in the light of the contradictory list in the preceding paragraph that *audience* is a common factor in classroom drama practice. However, I believe it to be important to do so.

It will be my purpose within the next few pages to replace the audience/no audience division with a tripartite classification based on the orientation of the players. In other words, in order to establish 'audience' as a *common* factor in all classroom drama, we shall be required to neutralise some of its related dichotomies[16] and at the same time introduce an alternative classification.

The concept of audience: 'Public/Private' dichotomies
This dichotomy is to be found in the writings of James Sully (1896) who draws a distinction between the 'contented privacy' of child play and the public face of art. In the history of drama education and professional theatre there have been two meanings applied to the notion of 'privacy'. One is linked with the need for protection from public scrutiny at times of vulnerability, such as many theatre directors guarantee their actors during rehearsals[17] and when Peter Stone insists that only selected guests may be brought in to observe the work. The other, relating to linguistics or semiotics, raises an important philosophical issue. Part of the progressive movement's ideology is the notion of an 'inner self' whose expression remains private, personal and inaccessible to others. Among the drama exponents, Slade and Way most notably, take this position, one which David Best[18] argues is untenable. He avers that not only is an individual's means of expression dependent on culturally determined media, it is the media (particularly language and the arts) that determine the kinds of thoughts and feelings he is capable of having in the first place.[19] In other words, all forms of expression are potentially 'public' because they are culturally derived.

If we take an example of classroom drama that clearly showed no interest in entertaining an outside audience, such as Millward's 'Volcano Drama', in the light of Best's theory, we can see that the young pupils' struggle to 'present experience dramatically' (to use Millward's phrase), has little to do with idiosyncratic, individual expression, but, rather, its opposite. They are seeking a *public* agreement about what is going on – and they are 'audience' to each others' endeavours.

The concept of audience: 'Process/Product' dichotomy

Caldwell Cook saw the value of his broad 'playway' in terms both of 'destination' and 'journey', the latter, he insisted, to have the greater claim. The first writer[20] to make a precise *distinction* between 'process' and 'product' in classroom drama[21] was E.M. Langdon (1948) who drew on a grammatical analogy of 'playing' and a 'play', which she used synonomously with 'pretending' and 'acting'. She saw the infant age group as the province of the former in preparation for a gradual change to the latter in the Junior school. The first was to be without an audience and the second was to go through a phase of 'playing it out with an audience there' and beginning to recognise 'the rights of an audience'. Exponents may have disagreed over the age groups, but Langdon's division into 'playing' and 'a play' is a thesis many have found acceptable. Just as the rehearsal process is seen as an opportunity for actors to explore and experiment without penalty, so 'playing' is seen as an essential element of improvised classroom drama. At its weakest it is intended to be regarded as exploratory, not 'public', and therefore not subject to critical appraisal; at its best it is intended to be regarded as a 'public', spontaneous, meaningful, dramatic presentation of experience, having, as in Millward's work, 'all the makings of a well-made play'.

It has made sense to a large number of drama teachers to emphasise the value of this kind of process for itself. The experimentation, risk-taking and discoveries involved have been seen as integral to personal development, whether the methodology be stage or child or content centred. It may be mistaken, however, to leave the impression, as some writers have done,[22] that 'process' is to be seen as an alternative to 'product', for they are *interdependent*, not polar, concepts. Fleming (1994) expresses it succinctly: 'For in an active discipline like drama every end product contains a process within it and every process is in some sense a product.' As he points out, we would hesitate to make a distinction between 'a football match' and 'playing football' and yet that is what Langdon did between 'a play' and 'playing' – to most practitioners' approval. However, the theoretical language applied to drama today tends to reduce the distinction. Millward's phrase, for example, 'presenting experience dramatically' implies both process[23] and product.

The concept of 'audience: a performing/experiencing dichotomy

To argue that there is in all classroom drama some sense of audience combined with some notion of performance is one thing, but to do this at the expense of ignoring key differences is another and here we begin to cry out for at least a sub category! One such will emerge in the following discussion.

An apparent dichotomy between what actors do and what children at play do was once more first mooted in England by the psychologist, James Sully (1896), who wrote 'A number of children playing at being Indians... do not 'perform' for one another. The words 'perform', 'act' and so forth all seem out of place here.' Harriet Finlay-Johnson rarely used the term 'performance', (although she did use 'acting') confining it to the rare occasion when her pupils gave a 'public performance'. Indeed she reiterates the point that she wants to 'do away with acting for display', which may seem at first sight to be an unconvincing protestation from someone whose pupils daily prepared (writing and rehearsing) plays for performing to the rest of the class. I believe, however, that **within Finlay-Johnson's expression 'acting for display' we have the seed of a major conceptual shift that will clear the way for a revised framework of classroom acting behaviour**.

I infer (and this is where I begin, necessarily, to reformulate *differences* in order to promote a truer understanding of audience as a common factor) that in banishing 'acting for display', Finlay-Johnson was attempting to remove from her pupils' acting behaviour that element that would normally have been seen as legitimate fodder for audience appraisal and appreciation – **the skill involved in the acting**. I noted above that she wanted to change the function of the audience, but she also wanted to change what they looked for: they were to give their attention to their fellow pupils' presentation as a medium for curriculum knowledge and avoid seeing it as an acting achievement to be applauded as such. Notice here that I have chosen the word 'presentation', not 'performance', for it did not seem appropriate to use the word 'performance' for an example of acting behaviour that sought to eliminate a proper attention given to **acting**. I want to suggest, therefore, **that the term 'performance',[24] in a drama context, is most meaningful when it refers to acting for which an actor would expect to be applauded**, and that it be replaced by the term **'presenta-**

tion'[25] **in respect of dramatic activity in which the acting is not highly relevant** *in itself.* In defining the terms in this way 'acting' and 'performing' are being used synonomously and *'performance'* may refer either to the acting retrospectively or to the occasion of the acting. Thus it follows that 'acting' or 'performing' is a *special sub-category* of that kind of acting behaviour one would expect of a 'presentation' [i.e. in which *showing* is the principal purpose].

It is this reordering of the basis for conceptual distinction that puts some of the activities of our pioneers in a different light. For instance, in respect of Finlay-Johnson, her intention to 'do away with display' places her work in the 'presentation' category – her pupils' endeavours at researching, script-writing and rehearsing are directed towards *presenting, not performing.* Caldwell Cook's work, on the other hand, unambiguously belongs to 'performing'. In other words, the principal purpose in *both* their classrooms is to *show*, but *additionally and significantly* in Caldwell Cook's classroom, the acting itself is up for approval as well as the content to be communicated. Thus 'performing', in this way of classifiying, is not separate from presenting, but a special version of it.

Finlay-Johnson's pupils, according to these terms, were engaged in 'acting behaviour as a vehicle for curriculum knowledge'; Caldwell Cook's were 'acting' in its traditional or pure sense, in what Slade designated 'Acting in the full sense' – with a Capital 'A'.[26] One fundamental effect of this change in rationale is that 'communication' can no longer be perceived as the prerogative of 'performing'. Other acting behaviours, involving some kind of 'presenting' (that is, depicting significant subject-matter[27] for an audience to examine) require clear communication to an audience, but not their applause. It is conceivable, therefore, that the *audience* in part determines how the acting behaviour is to be perceived – what was intended by the players as a presentation could be turned by the audience into a performance. Just as Lars Kleberg argued that for an event to qualify as 'theatre', there must be present a spectator willing to see it *'as theatre'*, so I am now suggesting that a spectator may also contribute to determining whether acting behaviour qualifies as 'performing' in its narrow or pure sense. The categories I am putting forward, 'performing' and 'presenting', are both concerned with conscious communication to an audience outside the drama. The extent to which skill of acting contributes to the meaning of that event, for actor or spectator, determines whether it belongs to 'presenting' or to its sub-category.

A further practical implication of this separation of 'performing', in a specific sense of being important in itself as an artistic skill, from other acting behaviours is that work by pupils on a script does not necessarily qualify the pupils' behaviour as *'performing'*. It is conceivable that while the performance of a play to another class or in school assembly or as a public performance is 'performing', the pupils' behaviour in the presentation of an excerpt from that same play as part of a classroom project on some social issue is not necessarily to be regarded as *performing* – unless, of course, the ethos of the school be such that pupils and teacher alike are conditioned to seeing enactment of any kind as demonstration of a skill awaiting applause. That is not to deny that there will be occasions within, for example, Process Drama when the artistry of the actors invites the expressed adulation of the spectators. This especially occurs in the final stage of the work when the students plan and rehearse a resolution of the story or issue, when the format being used is clearly of performance dimensions, *needing* the audience's approval of the performance as a performance for a sense of completion. Thus although I am making a conceptual distinction between 'performing' or 'acting in a pure sense' and other acting behaviours, this way of defining 'performing' by no means excludes it from the classroom. Indeed, training in stage acting might well be part of a course for upper adolescents in a secondary school specialising in the performing arts, in which case those students would necessarily concentrate their time within the 'performing' sub-division.

In the heading above, however, I have placed 'performing' and *'experiencing'* in polar opposition. There are, as we have seen, radical differences, to a point of mutual exclusion, between the performance behaviours, say, of Caldwell Cook's players and Millward's volcano-dwelling pupils, but 'experiencing' no longer seems the right choice of word for the culture-building at which the latter are working so hard. 'Experiencing' has a passive ring to it, but Millward's pupils are more than 'experiencing'; they are, as dramatists, forging a set of tacit laws within a cultural context; they are *composing* or constructing or, to give this kind of orientation a label, they are **'making'**.[28] Such a category of acting behaviour [which in the past I have called 'dramatic playing', a term that nevertheless lacks the *active, composing* connotation of 'making'] applies also to children's make-believe playing, to the kind of 'free' improvisations recommended in the 1960 textbooks such as 'be at the sea-side', to the sophisticated kind of tightly structured, small group exercises to be found in 'Process' Drama and to 'Mantle of the Expert' and all forms of 'living through'.

Thus I am suggesting the '**presenting**' classification, with its sub category, '**performing**' be set against a second category, '**making**'. It has sometimes been possible in the past to argue for 'performing' and 'experiencing' as alternative ends of a continuum, each with the potential for merging into the other, but the acting behaviour in 'making' taps everyday means of expression in order to signal the building, in 'now time', of a social or cultural entity and it could not logically 'merge into' either 'performing' or 'presenting' When Millward drew a distinction between 'presenting experience dramatically' and '*doing* Drama', he was alluding to a conceptual shift, not merely to a change of degree. 'Presenting'/'Performing and 'Making' are indeed in a dichotomous relationship.

A further practical implication of this distinction is that an invitation in the classroom to '*do* drama' will commonly feed *performance* expectations, in which pupils, functioning as 'pupils', under a teacher's supervision, enact an improvised or scripted play. 'Go into your corners and make a up a play for us to see, will invariably invite 'performing', unless there is already in place an overriding interest in the topic. In 'living through drama' (or, 'making', as I am now labelling the acting behaviour) the children's function is not primarily mediated by their normal 'pupil/teacher' school role. They are 'makers' (dramatists) of 'life under a volcano'. Similarly the child playing at 'tractors'is not *primarily* functioning in a child/adult relationship, even if the mother is joining in the playing. The child's primary role is that of a dramatist, 'making' a 'tractor context'.

A Sense of Audience and Self-Spectator

If it can be agreed that all kinds of drama are potentially communicable to others outside the drama and that there is always at least an implicit product, then it is but a short step to further argue that a 'sense of audience'[29] is properly present, whatever the methodology: if the pupil is 'performing', then s/he is subjecting herself/himself to an audience's appraisal, even if that audience is made up of just other members of the class or the teacher. If the child is 'making', whether in the sense of 'living through' under the guidance of a teacher-in-role or independent of an adult, then the pupil will be treating fellow pupils as audience in order jointly to present experience dramatically. If the drama is in the form of 'depiction' or 'tableau', or many of the other conventions now so popular in the classroom, then the demonstration is dependent on effective, accurate and economic signalling to a real or hypothetical audience. If the work is 'Mantle of the Expert', that special version of 'living through' drama, then the 'sense of audience', that is, a sense of who will need to understand what is being done to meet a contract, is paramount. This final example of 'audience', of course, resides in the participant himself, the 'self-spectator'. Emile Jacques-Dalcroze, writing in 1919 drew attention to the dual function of actor/spectator as follows: 'In the laboratory of his organism a transmutation is effected, turning the creator into both actor and spectator of his own composition.

Hourd sees the adolescent's phase of development as one of uncomfortable, but temporary, self-awareness, she sees the pervasive purpose of enactment as a means of 'losing oneself to gain oneself' Taking this expression further, it seems that through the fiction one can, to use Bruce Wilshire's phrase 'come across oneself'. The fiction-making exposes the self reflected in it. It is as if the fiction is a mirror in which one might glimpse oneself. It is this view of 'self-spectatorship' Heathcote has absorbed into her work, while avoiding the therapeutic connotation that Hourd's expression 'losing oneself to gain oneself' could have. Heathcote's insistence on self-spectatorship is a deliberate harnessing of our capacity through Mimesis to examine our own values. She feels it is not something that can be left to chance.

Thus 'self-spectatorship', at its best, can be said to promote a double valence of being an audience to one's own creation and being an audience to *oneself.* Mike Fleming uses the term 'percipient' to combine the participant/spectator function in drama. Such a concept takes us beyond *individual* spectating to the *collective* feelings shared by all the players as 'an audience' to what they are creating or presenting. It further extends the theory of self-spectatorship to take on board the notion of the 'percipient's' emotional engagement with what is going on. The dimensions of 'playwright' and 'director' could also be added. The four functions, 'dramatist', 'spectator', 'participant' and 'director' are occurring simultaneously. This is so in *all* kinds of improvised drama, including children's informal play. Most of the past research into children's play has focused on the expressive components of a child's make believe behaviour. Viewed from the perspective of a dramatist's or directorial functions, however, 'child-play' may be open to a new range of meanings, as evidenced by the research of Nelson and Seidman (1984), who see young children at play as making their own *scripts*.

The definition of acting behaviour may now be extended: **Acting behaviour is an act of fiction-making involving identification through action, the conscious manipulation of time and space and a capacity for generalisation. It relies on some sense of audience, including self-spectatorship.**

Acting as a 'focus of responsibllity'
Another dimension to a definition of drama resides in what could be described as the actor's 'burden of responsibility'. Even within broadly similar dramatic activities the focus of responsibility may be at variance. If we take, for example, Brian Way's methodology: in establishing that classroom drama was to be sans text, sans audience and sans acting, he was removing the traditional responsibilities of an actor. Furthermore little importance was to be attached to *content*, so that his pupils were not to feel responsible even in that direction. He wanted them, however, to see what they were doing in terms of personal development and their prime attention was to be given to skills of concentration, sensitivity, intuition, speech and movement. I wish to argue here, therefore, that that particular orientation, the monitoring, largely to the exclusion of other elements, of how one is using one's personal skills, may be said to constitute, the acting behaviour of the participants. It could be said that, in this instance, the participant's make-believe behaviour is, at least in part, determined by his *intention*[31] to privilege one kind of responsibility over another, to give attention to personal skills over content.

The idea of a 'defining orientation' in acting behaviour is perhaps more readily perceived in stage acting. Bert States,[32] for example, classifies acting into three modes, (self-expressive, collaborative and representational) as a way of describing the intention[33] of an actor respectively to (1) display his skill to an audience, (2) relate to an audience or (3) demonstrate a play to an audience. States seems to be making the point that actors tend to favour [not exclusively, it should be said] one of these modal categories, involving an identifiable orientation, as part of an 'actor's presence'. States had a stage performance in mind, of course, but it is conceivable that such orientations could to some degree affect how, say, a small group of pupils show their prepared work to the rest of the class.

If we look at the process in a rehearsal room rather than on a stage, it is again possible to define the acting in terms of a different kind of intention or disposition. Two such contrasted imperatives are to be found in accounts of Stanislavski's rehearsals, for example. In the earlier stage of his well-documented experimentation, he insisted on his actors being clear about a character's 'objectives' in order to justify each action; in his later career, however, he encouraged his actors to plunge into action, letting the justification emerge from the physical. In these contrasted examples from Stanislavski, the kind of acting behaviour, during rehearsal, is dictated by the actors' choice, either to be disciplined by an intellectual impulse, or to be freed by a state of kinaesthetic receptivity. (Neither of these would apply, of course, if the actors or pupils were at the stage in rehearsal when lines should have been learned – their focal consciousness would be 'burdened' accordingly!)

Thus we have, from the above classroom, stage and rehearsal room, examples of three different kinds of factors determining the acting behaviour, which might be labelled as: *educational priorities, the actor's presence* and *the actor's way into a part*. The latter of course includes how the actor comes to *own* the 'givens' he is required to absorb.

Let us look further at how the *classroom* dictates the factors affecting the acting behaviour. Perhaps the clearest example may be drawn from Harriet Finlay-Johnson's 'shopping practice'. The overriding intention, as in all forms of acting, including stage and rehearsal room, is an agreement to 'play the drama game'; the defining feature of the Sompting pupils' acting behaviour is a simulation of what one does when one shops, including getting the arithmetic right. There may be something too, for some of the pupils, of States' 'self-expressive' mode: 'Look at me! I'm good at this!'. In Caldwell Cook's 'Mummery', how to translate Shakespeare's lines into a Elizabethan Playhouse design could be said to define the acting behaviour. For many teachers of English the acting of pupils engaged with Shakespearean texts would, by contrast, be described as 'making the meaning clear'.

It seems possible, then, to classify acting behaviour, according to the actor's focus of responsibility. We have already introduced this notion of 'responsibility ' as the defining characteristic of acting in discussing Langdon's distinction between *'playing'* and *'a play'* when the added intention to communicate or entertain or please an audience *determines* the nature of the acting required of a 'play'. I suggest that to the extent that a participant consciously embraces one set of objectives over any alternatives, that commitment could be said to constitute his/her acting behaviour.

We may now put forward a conception of acting behaviour as a list of determining responsibilities.

1. distinguishing intention relating to content, character, dramatic form, self-spectator, performance skills and

2. where there is a formal or informal audience an expressive, communicative or demonstrative mode predominates and

3. extrinsic 'burdens', such as trying to remember lines, or a teacher-expectation, may further qualify or even dominate the acting behaviour.

Further determining responsibilities could be added relating specifically to Slade and Way's approach. We have already noted the 'temporal imperative' in their work where they use the fast action narration to accompanying actions by all the pupils together, and Way, we have earlier observed, created a new genre for the drama classroom: improvised drama as 'exercise', with all that entails of task-focused, short-term, practising or trying something out, or getting ready. Thus a fifth item of the above list of determinants would relate at times to a temporal imperative and/or to a limited expectation of the structure *per se*. At its worst, the latter 'exercise' form would invite an 'it's only an exercise' disposition. At its best, it could be seen as a tightly structured vehicle for honing in on some aspect of living in which the actor has committed interest. A dimension of responsibility thus can embrace the participant's attitude to the medium itself and to the understood purpose of doing the drama.

The actor's 'responsibilities' need to be seen as many-layered, variously relating to content, skill, style, audience, attitude and context. At times it would be appropriate to speak of 'intention' or 'disposition' or 'colour' or even, 'burden' as the defining metaphor, but I hope that my choice of 'focus of responsibilities' covers all these. This dimension should now be inserted into our definition above to read: **Acting behaviour is an act of fiction-making involving identification through action, a prioritising of determining responsibilities, the conscious manipulation of time and space and a capacity for generalisation. It relies on some sense of audience, including self-spectatorship.**

Summary

In this first section of the final chapter an attempt has been made gradually to build a definition of acting behaviours, a process of identifying the common ground or centre of its many forms. This involved a clarifying or even a reinterpreting of long-held concepts associated with classroom acting. The classification of the three major orientations of 'presenting', 'performing' [a subdivision of 'presenting'] and 'making' made way for challenging past dichotomies bound up with the previously divisive notion of 'audience'. Acknowledging 'audience' as a common feature of acting behaviour, along with 'identification', 'manipulation of time and space', 'capacity for generalisation', and 'focus of responsibilities' amounts to a reformulation of theoretical positions. The most radical departure from traditional perception however may be ascribed to the notion underlying the classification into 'performing', and 'presenting', that 'acting' in its narrowest sense may be determined, not so much by identifiable behaviours, as by the combined intentions of the actors and audience.

Significantly, 'performing' has no place in 'making'. They represent two contrasted modes of acting behaviours. **On this premise is my reconceptualisation founded**. I am aware, however, that contemporary writers either fail to see a difference between them or do not regard such a difference as of importance in practice. In Ray Mather's excellent array of conventions, 'teacher-in-role', which I have claimed lures pupils into a particular form of 'making', is listed as but one of many conventions. This is fine for Mather's purpose which is to find images for helping his students acquire a language of theatre, but *teachers* I believe will work best if they are aware of the difference in power within each contrasted mode. To choose 'making' over 'presenting' or 'performing' or vice versa is to recognise the kind of experience each offers. It is with this in mind that I now want to clarify and summarise those features of 'making' that mark it as a unique form of acting behaviour. To achieve this it will be necessary **to rethink the very basis of 'living through' drama and child make-believe play**.

Characteristics of 'Making'

It seems from the above arguments that we can no longer characterise drama that is not specifically prepared for an audience as a 'self-expressive', 'personal', 'private', 'individual', and 'subjective' process – all the characteristics that used also to be thought to belong to child make-believe. Certainly both child play and 'living through' drama are examples of 'making', but I am proposing that the principal determinants are not to be found in the egocentric list in the above sentence but in directions that have not previously been considered. I will now list below the alternative criteria on which our classification of 'making', embracing 'living through' and child play, has been based.

Characteristics of 'Making', in respect of child play, some dramatic exercises, and 'living through' drama'

1. Although there is an emphasis on 'process', a 'product' is being made to be reflected upon during or after the drama.

2. Each individual's contribution is part of a collective enterprise, culturally determined in language and action.

3. The activity is cultural in a second sense: the participants, are creating their own make-believe identify with the underlying

'laws' of the social context being created. I believe this to be true of all child make-believe play. A child playing with dolls is examining the rules that belong to a mother/baby context. It remains egocentric to the extent that s/he is also seeking him/ herself within those rules – to see where s/he stands, as it were. S/he may be constructing the make-believe out of fear or power-seeking or wishful thinking, but it is the 'rules' of contextual behaviours s/he is exposing to herself. Likewise, in 'living through' drama, tacitly identifying the inner laws of whatever culture is being created is pre-eminent. This common link between make-believe play and 'living through' drama is, I believe, the key feature of both, but, of course many differences remain, including 'living through's dependence on 'teacher-in-role'.

4. A third cultural feature is the kind of acting behaviours that 'making' requires. They are initially akin to the kind of common negotiating and affirming skills in language and non verbal communication required of people involved in establishing any social event in 'real life'. They reinforce a strong sense of 'it is happening now; we are making it happen; we are watching it happen'. But because of this existential sense of it *occurring* now, it is not repeatable and because of the initial dependence on a *collective* effort, the normal entry into dramatic fiction of pursuing an individual *character* is not so readily available. It may not be *repeatable* but in 'living through' drama it is *interruptible* and *episodical* – a good teacher will recognise when a plateau, dead end or crossroads has been reached and know that it is necessary temporarily to come out of the fiction in order to go back in again at an enhanced level.

5. A fourth sense in which the activity is cultural relates to *who* the participants see themselves as before they start their drama-making. If they are friends in a garden their identity, including past history as friends, determines how they enter the make-believe. If they are pupils in a school invited to 'make up a play', *who* they are is unequivocally determined by that teacher/pupil context. If, however, they are led into 'living through' drama by a teacher in role, the parameters of their role as pupils and their teacher's role as 'teacher' *slacken*. There is a sub-cultural shift, unique to 'living through' drama, easing them into the fictitious context.

6. There is a related *aesthetic* dimension. In the normal *'doing drama'*, there are a number of 'givens' – ideas, information, a plan, characters, their own or someone else's script or even a teacher's instructions. These givens exist in a medium of their own – pictures, memories, ideas, images, words on paper or words spoken etc., and the task is to translate them into dramatic form, what Schechner calls the raw food waiting to be cooked by art. In 'living through' drama the givens, provided by the teacher in role are already expressed in the medium of dramatic art (partially cooked) so that no bridging is required of the pupils from one medium to another.

7. The teacher in role provides a challenging model of belief, style and dramatist's skills, so that in every aspect of the art the participant [*inside* the dramatic event] is invited to reach beyond his/her present competence and to acquire an understanding of how theatre works at a deeper level than if s/he were *outside* 'doing drama'.

8. The scope for manipulating time and space is limitless and fluid providing it is meaningful to the other players.

9. The *responsibility* of each participant is that of a dramatist/actor/director/spectator. It is a multi artistic function. When a child enters make-believe s/he is remaking her known world (in so far as she is looking at 'what the rules are' of that known world] by trying out a dialogue, trying out a plot, trying out actions etc. that reflect those rules – and observing herself in all that. The *pretending* or *impersonating* is but *one* aspect of these multi-responsibilities. Much observation of child play I believe suffered from focusing merely on the pretending. The actor on stage, of course, does not have these extended responsibilities.

10. A quality that 'making' shares with 'stage acting' is what Frost and Yarrow[34] name disponibilité: 'It's a kind of total awareness, a sense of being at one with the context: script, if such there be, actors, audience, audience, theatre space, oneself and one's body.'

It is the combination of the above ten features that leads us to insist on seeing 'making' as a special category of acting behaviour, especially when a 'living through', that is, a 'teacher-in-role-led approach to drama is adopted. Our category table could now look like this:

classroom acting behaviours

presenting   making   performing

'Presenting' includes acting behaviours in a wide range of activities, such as tableau, depiction, sculpting, acting from a script, forum theatre, chamber theatre etc., – any of the forms of acting where the responsibility to 'show' has priority. It is rehearsable and repeatable. 'Making' includes the acting behaviours of children's make-believe playing, 'living through' drama, 'hot-seating' and the kind of acting in any dramatic exercise in which the participants are free to explore without any sense of preparing for showing to someone else. It is not rehearsable nor directly repeatable. **I should perhaps reiterate the warning that this classification of acting behaviour as 'making' should not be confused with Hornbrook's categorisation of 'making' and 'performing' as but two stages in a dramatic process.**

Is *theatre* a feature common to 'making' and 'presenting'?
Perhaps the crudest definition of theatre is Eric Bentley's[36] 'A impersonates B for C'. Bruce Wilshire[37] elaborates on this, pointing out that the Greek word for theatre [*theotron*, a place for seeing] is linked with *theoria* which can both mean spectacle and speculation or theory. 'Thus', concludes Wilshire, 'it is suggested that theatre, at its origins, was its own mode of speculating and theorising about human nature and action.' Such a definition, Wilshire admits, takes the wonder out of theatre until one appreciates that *theoria* can also mean 'to look god in the face' It is towards the mystery of theatre that Peter Brook turns. He defines theatre in the following terms: 'The essence of theatre is within a mystery called 'the present moment.'[38] He later extends it into a mysticism that would have appealed to Peter Slade[39]:

> It [theatre] is the truth of the present moment that counts, the absolute sense of conviction that can only appear when a unity binds performer and audience. This appears when the temporary forms have served their purpose and have brought us into this single, unrepeatable instant when a door opens and our vision is transformed.

Thus theorists of theatre appear to swing between the functional and the poetic. Ken Robinson (1980), for instance, sees theatre as a kind of social encounter between actors and audience; '...it is partly their presence [the audience] and their activity which identifies what is going on as theatre.' By comparison, for Peter Slade, theatre is 'a golden moment' He writes: 'I felt the light dying. If not of the real sun, it was the light of 'real theatre' when a great scene comes to a close.' It seems that the place where an encounter can occur between audience and actors may be called 'a theatre' and that, more importantly, the encounter itself is to be called 'theatre'. Sometimes, however, 'theatre' is used as a criterion of effectiveness – Fleming (1994) refers to Heathcote's 'Three Looms Waiting' as qualifying for the description of 'an effective piece of theatre'. From Brook and Slade we see that special moments of ecstasy are to be called 'theatre'. In describing 'Process Drama' Cecily O'Neill (1995) uses the contemporary language of theatre; her conclusion about a completed Process Drama experience is that: 'The experience was its own destination and the group an audience to its own acts.' In my 1979 publication I wrote, misleadingly I now believe, of theatre as being one of three broad kinds of dramatic activity to be promoted in schools: 'theatre' (meaning 'performing to an audience'), 'dramatic playing' (meaning improvisational and without an audience), and 'exercise' (meaning 'practising something'). Then, perhaps more usefully, in the same book, I introduced the idea of 'theatre form', referring to such elements as 'tension', 'focus', 'surprise', 'contrast' and 'symbolisation'. For Heathcote, as we have seen, theatre '...has many 'communicating faces' that surround and give variety of shapings to a few operant laws'. Its dimensions are movement/stillness', 'sound/silence, and 'light/darkness'.

I am reluctant to deny any of the above usages. It may be that in discussing formal elements it is more useful, as Hornbrook[40] does, to employ the term 'dramatic art', in which case the most common usage of 'theatre' could be left to a combination of place and occasion when actors perform to an audience. And yet to see Process Drama, a sequence dependent on a mixture of 'making' and 'presenting' as a new genre of *theatre* has its attractions. Perhaps it is the *overall* experience that qualifies for the name, leaving particular components of the sequence to be rated as *dramatic art*. I suspect that common usage will continue to use these terms loosely. I certainly have no conclusive feelings on the matter.

Conclusion

Let us now reconsider some of the positions briefly outlined in the Introduction to this book in the light of the historical account attempted in these eleven chapters and of some of the conclusions I have come to in this chapter. I began by quoting John Allen who argued that 'drama in schools is basically and essentially no different from drama anywhere else.' Out of the context of his 1979 publication this seems to be no more than a platitude. One cannot disagree with it, but does it mean anything useful? The answer, of course, is that it *did* at the time of his writing when the very language of drama teachers became exclusive, divisive and sectarian. Allen was responding to a philosophical schism that separated drama into public/private, audience-centred/child-centred, product/process, performing/experiencing, and theatre/play dichotomies. The model I have presented here serves, I hope, to break up these dualities. Of particular importance is my conclusion that all kinds of acting behaviours rely on a sense of audience.

If we turn, however, to the quotation cited in the Introduction from David Hornbrook, who claimed 'that conceptually there is nothing which differentiates the child acting in the classroom from the actor on the stage in the theatre', we will see that my model puts forward an alternative position without seeking to defend the kind of thinking about performing that led Hornbrook to make his rather extreme statement. I am suggesting that performing *per se* is defined by the interest of the actors and/or spectators. This is acting [I am using 'acting' and 'performing' synonymously] in its purest or most traditional sense, applying equally to what the actor does on stage and to what the child *may do* in the classroom. Differences in such features as quality, style, or spontaneity will vary from classroom to classroom and from stage to stage, but essentially it qualifies as 'performing' because it commands attention to itself as an achievement.

'Presenting' may or may not focus on 'performing'. The players and audience may be emotionally engaged by the material illustrated; it may qualify as 'dramatic art', but if for both the audience and the players *what* is being said excludes for a particular audience *how* it is being said, making applause for 'the performance' redundant, then it fulfils solely a presentational function. Of course, the spectators may spontaneously applaud their approval of the 'message', as one would applaud a speaker at a meeting, without giving undue attention to it as a performance. Clearly in practice the two forms of 'performance' and 'presentation' may be so fluid that which applies in relation to any particular piece of work could remain academic. In the educational context of a classroom it is not so important in itself always to be able to draw a clear distinction between the two as it is to recognise that in an educational setting there may be times when an inappropriate degree of attention is directed towards performing skills. Of course the School's sub-cultural context will often control how a piece of work may be seen. In responding to the *same* stimulus, a Theatre Studies class may automatically rely on a 'performance' frame of mind whereas a 'presentation' of the same piece would more likely satisfy a Social Studies class.

'Making' as a category of acting behaviour (not to be confused with Hornbrook's usage of the term) is unlikely to be treated as other than what it is, a form of behaviour distinctly different from 'presenting' and 'performing' Its ten characteristics listed above are an indication of how complex it can be, especially in its 'living through' version. It represents a hugely important educational and dramatic tool. To ignore 'living through' drama, as some recent publications appear to do,[41] is to deprive our pupils of a firm basis for understanding dramatic art. It is not enough to recommend 'improvisation', for much improvisation is mostly performance oriented.[42] The ideal teacher uses the strengths of 'presenting' (including 'performing') *and* 'making'. In Mike Fleming's latest publication[43] he shows teachers how approaches to texts can embrace a wide range of tableaux, depiction, games, script work, 'living through' drama, dramatic exercises, and 'hot-seating'.

I hope that the framework I am recommending allows for an eclectic approach. It may perhaps be most vividly illustrated by reference to the many versions of the ever popular 'blindfold' exercise recorded earlier. At one extreme we have Clive Barker's acting exercise from Peking Opera in which acting technique alone is required to convey being blindfolded [other examples include Brian Way's and Constantin Stanislavski's sense deprivation exercises 'to find out what it is like to be blind' and Cecily O'Neill's 'hunter and hunted' game as a means of reviving, after a break, the atmosphere of the 'Frank Miller' drama] and, at the opposite extreme we have Peter Millward's nine year olds' play-making in which they subtly create blindness in a character by the way they treat him: 'Ah, here he is now... Come on... careful... over here... come on... mind the steps... Right... he made it.' This latter may be seen as a perfect example of 'making' in that it illustrates the *dramatist* function, even in relatively young children; Clive Barker's may be seen as a 'pure' example of acting technique. I hope the framework caters for both these extremes and for the other examples too.

That fiction-making is at the centre of all the activities appears to support the educational advocacy that drama provides a creative way of looking at the world. In this respect I believe Edmond Holmes, writing in 1911, was wise to see drama as having a rather different function from the other arts, but that is a matter for others to look into. Holmes wrote of dramatisation as '...teaching them to identify themselves, if only for a moment, with other human beings' He claimed this demonstrated the 'sympathetic' function of drama as an educational tool. This may be to err in the direction of a degree of 'compassion' which I do not believe drama necessarily feeds. Nevertheless, Holmes seems to be feeling towards the recognition that drama promotes some kind of relationship between the 'self' and 'the world'. Of growing importance in the vocabulary of writers in recent years is the notion of 'self-spectator', a conception that enactment leads to seeing oneself reflected in the fiction one is making. I have argued for 'fiction-making' as the defining nucleus for all acting behaviours. Perhaps 'self-spectatorship' should be regarded as the definitive outcome.

Notes

1   This qualification is a reminder that some activities that became part of a drama teacher's repertoire were not always contributory to a fiction. For instance, the formal speech practice of W.S.Tomkinson; the 'efforts' exercises of Rudolf Laban; the 'Natural Dance' of Peter Slade when his pupils simply responded to music; Brian Way's notorious 'blind' exercise; the 'relaxation', 'warm-ups' and 'games' so popular from the 1960s onwards; and the game played in Cecily O'Neill's 'Frank Miller' Drama. This is not to decry the use of 'direct' experiencing. Often it was central to the sequence of work, as for instance, in' Frank Miller' in which the 'game' recaptures the theme of the fiction.

2   My assertion that the child 'abstracts a truth....as s/he sees it...' is taken from Charles McGaw, who writes: 'The actor's imagination allows him to abstract the essence of truth from the familiar and the everyday...'

3   Norah Morgan and Juliana Saxton include 'interpretation' as the fifth in their taxonomy of personal engagement. They subdivide interpretation into 'communicating'; 'experimenting'; 'adapting'; 'analysing'; and 'reflection'. [Morgan, N. Saxton, J. (1987)...*op cit* p.26]

4   Callow, Simon (1984) *Being an Actor* Penguin Books Harmondsworth, p.200

5   O'Toole, John (1992) *op cit* pp.86-8.

6   Morgan and Saxton (1987) classify 'identification' by reference to a hierarchy of dramatic structures, 'delineating the increasing complexity of becoming someone else', so that, for instance, 'dramatic playing' where the children are 'themselves' is seen as the lowest step and 'acting' as the highest. [See Morgan, N. and Saxton, J. (1987) *op cit* pp.30-36

7   The opposite kind of problem can exist, if rarely, of the fictitious context being too close to the participant's life to sustain the drama. I can recall setting up a drama about a psychiatric hospital to discover that one of the participants' daughter had just gone into such an institution. Robert Witkin, too, records a drama he observed about 'schooling' in which the 'real context' spilled over into what was supposed to be fiction, or, as he put it, 'permeate(d) the barrier between the simulated network and the real network.' [Witkin, R. (1974) *op cit* p.80]. I always felt that it was a pity his one full account of a drama lesson should be one that demonstrated this kind of excess.

8   I suggested in the section on Hourd that 'naturalistic' was not altogether a suitable term for the style of acting of her pupils, controlled as it was by the poetry of a ballad, for instance, while appreciating that she was anxious to indicate a deficiency in what she called 'perfected technique'.

9   Schechner, Richard (1982) 'The End of Humanism', *Performing Arts Journal Publications*, New York p.111. Cecily O'Neill uses this quotation in O'Neill, C (1991) *op cit* p.154

10   Bateson, Gregory (1976) 'A theory of Play and Fantasy' in *Play* by J.S. Bruner et al p.128; originally published in *Psychiatric Research Reports* No 2, (1955) pp.39-51.

11   Bateson's theory has attracted the attention of a number of social theorists [indeed his exposition is acknowledged as a source of inspiration by Erving Goffman. See Goffman, E. (1974) *op cit* p.7] and a number of drama educationists find support for their conception of drama education as derived from play (See, for instance, Bolton G. (1984) *op cit* P, 80 and O'Toole, J. *op cit* 25-26). The writer who most fully gives attention to time is Cecily O'Neill [O'Neill, C.C. (1991) *op cit* pp158-160]. In a Chapter entitled 'Time in Theatre and Improvisation' [pp.154-178] she writes brilliantly on its many facets. Here is an example in which, interestingly, she uses the term 'bracketed': 'A significant example of the operation of 'bracketed' time is *Waiting for Godot*. Here, actions occur within the 'dawn-dusk' bracket, but are not causally related to each other and are not repeated exactly or in the same order. Vladimir and Estragon have no grip on time. Their 'present moment' indicates a complete discontinuity, and is disturbing to both the

characters precisely because of the absence of any true relationship to past and future. All they know of time is that it passes. Time has lost its meaning but paradoxically has acquired total significance. Beckett is squandering time, putting the play outside all temporal reality while apparently immersed in its categories.' (pp.165-166)

12   Brecht, B. (1949 trans. by Eric Bentley) 'A New Technique of Acting' in *Theatre Arts*, 33 No 1. Jan, p.39

13   Isaacs, S. (1930) *op cit* p.104. Earlier I also introduce Bruce Wilshire's contribution to theatrical theory that 'there can be no enactment without typification and generalisation...' [Wilshire, B. (1982) *op cit* p.105] Marjorie Hourd, in writing of the dramatist's responsibility in creating characters says he can '...pass through the particularities of his characters to a value which is beyond and yet is contained in them...' [Hourd, M. (1949) *op cit* p.84]

14   I make this point in 'DRAMA/Drama and Cultural Values' in *IDEA' 95* Papers Edited by Philip Taylor and Christine Hoepper, NADIE Publications, pp.29-34.

15   McGregor *et al* (1977) *op cit* p.19. The authors write: 'the crucial question for drama in practice is whether or not for this group, at this time and in this context, such a shift in emphasis [that is, between doing it for themselves and for an audience – (this author's insert)] can fulfil any additional or worthwhile function.'

16   These 'dichotomies' are related to communication to an audience. Jonothan Neelands, in an unpublished article dated May, 1995, devises a much longer list of what he calls 'oppositions' by broadening the area to 'Learning through drama' versus 'Learning in Theatre', p.5.

17   Peter Brook writes: '...as the years go by, I see more and more how important it is for actors, who are by nature fearful and oversensitive, to know that they are totally protected by silence, intimacy and secrecy.' [Brook, P .(1993) *There are no secrets* Methuen London, p.100 of 1995 edition]. By contrast, Robert Breen [(1986) *Chamber Theatre op cit* p.70] notes Kenneth Tynan's account of a visit to the Berliner Ensemble where the actors rehearsed in front of a large mirror in the footlights with 'photographers continuously shooting pictures ...to provide visual records for the actors to study later.

18   Best, D. (1992) *op cit* p.18. Best explains that the picture of self he offers is one of 'the common human way of acting and responding, set in the context of cultural practices, which is the foundation of the self, not some supposed 'inner' spirit or mentality.'

19   Best, D. (1992) *ibid* p.82/3. He puts it that '...if people succumb to popular pressures, and are thus limited to the circulating library of cliché forms of expression, then their capacity for their own individual thought and emotional experience is commensurably limited.

20   *The Hadow Report* (1931) had already made an 'official' distinction between 'formal' and informal' drama [Board of Education (1931) HMSO, p.76] which paved the way for a 'process/product' dichotomy. Ten years earlier in *The Teaching of English in England* the authors' classification [(a) the performance of

scenes or pieces in class and (b) the public performance of plays by pupils] appeared to focus on all drama as 'product'. [See Page 142 above and Board of Education (1921) *op cit* p.315 Para 289]

21 Although Mrs. Langdon appears to have been the first to make a distinction between product and process in drama, progressive educationists before her had drawn such a distinction in respect of education, including Caldwell Cook who saw the goal of education as '...not for the destination, but chiefly for the journey.' It was also pointed out that although Finlay-Johnson used the expression 'finished product', we should not assume that she was placing it in opposition to 'Process'.

22 Following Langdon's use of the verb 'playing' others have adopted the idea of using the present participle to convey an emphasis on a continuing 'process'. Pemberton-Billing and Clegg, for instance, [Pemberton-Billing, R. and Clegg, D. (1965) *op cit* p.28] coin the term 'playing-out', and, as we have seen, [McGregor *et al* (1977) *op cit* p.10] the *Schools Council Secondary Project* use 'acting-out'. I have used the expression 'dramatic playing.'.

23 It is a pity, in some ways that recent authors have, for reasons that are understandable, included 'Process' in their book titles, isolating it once more from 'Product': John O'Toole (1992) in The Process of Drama makes a startling appeal for the return to 'Process' as characterising the purpose of drama education. He quotes from a young South African teacher, by the name of Brendan Butler, who sees schooling in his country as a weapon for oppression, using all the theatrical paraphernalia at its disposal to do so. For the pupils school is removed from 'real life', for they sense they are required to act in the authority's play. O'Toole writes: 'Butler sees the processuality of drama in education as giving teachers the opportunity to 'subvert this theatricality...' [O'Toole, J. (1992) *op cit* pp57-59] O'Toole recognises that to take 'Process' out of our drama education vocabulary as a counter to 'product' is, for Butler, to deny a political weapon. Cecily O'Neill (1995) who published her book under the title *Drama Worlds: a framework for process drama* needed a term for what she describes as 'the kind of generative dramatic encounter' her methodology promotes. Published in America, the title had to make sense to both Theatre and Creative Dramatics people. When such people read it, of course, they will see that a great many of the activities are to do with creating 'a product' [O'Neill C.C. (1995) *op cit* p.5].

24 I am aware that my definition of 'performance' here considerably narrows both its common usage and its application by role and performance theorists. For instance Schechner [Schechner, R. (1977) *op cit* p.xiii of 1988 edition] defines 'performance' as follows:

> Performance is an inclusive term. Theatre is only one node on a continuum that reaches from ritualizations of animals (including humans) through performances in everyday life – greetings, displays of emotion, family scenes, professional roles, and so on – through play, sports, theatre, dance, ceremonies, rites, and performances of great magnitude.

However, my definition may be close to that intended by Goffman [Goffman, E. (1974) *op cit* p.124/5 of Penguin edition] who writes:

A performance, in the restricted sense.....is that arrangement which transforms an individual into a stage performer, the latter, in turn, being the object that can be looked at in the round and at length without offence, and looked to for engaging behaviour, by persons in an 'audience' role.

This 'can be looked at in the round and at length without offence' is reminiscent of Heathcote's 'permission to stare'. This comparison with Goffman, however, should not be taken too seriously as he is searching for a theatrical metaphor to help us understand the everyday world, and not theatre itself.

Marvin Carlson, who introduces his book, *Performance* [1996], with a range of definitions for what he calls this 'contested concept' (p.5) gives an example of an incident illustrative of a conception of 'performance' very close to the one I have chosen to adopt. Carlson writes:

> I recently came across a striking illustration of how important the idea of the public display of technical skill is to this traditional concept of 'performance'. At a number of locations in the United States and abroad, people in period costume act out improvised or scripted events at historical sites for tourists...a kind of activity often called 'living history'. One site of such activity is Fort Ross in Northern California, where a husband and wife, dressed in the costumes of the 1830s, greet visitors in roles of the last Russian Commander of the fort and his wife. The wife...decided at one time to play period music on the piano to give the visitors the impression of contemporary cultural life. But she later abandoned this, feeling, in her words, that it 'removed the role from living-history and placed it in a category of performance.'

This is a nice example of the skill of the performance being relevant in *itself*, inviting a show of appreciation from the audience. [Routledge, New York, p.3]

25   The choice of the term 'presentation' for this category should not be confused with Peter Millward's expression used elsewhere of 'presenting experience dramatically'. I will continue to employ both terms, relying on the context to make the difference clear. The alternative choice of term for the second category would have been 'demonstration' or 'illustration'.

26   Slade, P. (1954) *op cit* p.35. Slade of course did not see what he describes as 'Acting in the full sense' as part of classroom practice

27   It should be noted that whereas by 'subject-matter' or 'content' exponents such as Finlay-Johnson referred to traditonal school subjects and Heathcotian followers usually referred to some important issue or centre of interest, within today's broader curriculum, presentation could equally apply to a demonstration related to a dramatist's craft or to Theatre History. For instance, Andy Kempe [Kempe, Andy (1990) *op cit* p.106] having drawn from his pupils that David Hockney's 'Big Splash' conveys a startling moment of contrast, invites them to consider 'how we capture a contrast in drama in such a startling way?' Such an exercise, demonstrating a dramatist's or director's technique would qualify, (in the model I am offering here) as 'presentation'.

28 'Making', a term first used by Caldwell Cook, has been popularised in the last two decades particularly by those arts theorists keen to find a generic base for all the arts, so that they can be grouped under 'making', 'performing' or 'responding'. See for example, Hornbrook, D. (1991) *Education in Drama* Falmer p.13]. Robinson (1980 *op cit* p.168) gave a more active slant to the dramatic experience by his use of the term 'heuristic'.

29 Ken Robinson adapts James Britton's phrase 'a sense of audience' [Robinson, K. (1981) *op cit* p.242 quotes from Britton *et al* (1975) *The Development of Writing Abilities 11-18* Macmillan] to drama: 'In Dramatic activity the audience is vividly present. Even in the drama lesson, the child works with other members of the group as audience to his/her actions... Similarly, the actor will adapt his/her performance... as he/she interprets the audience's reactions and responses.'

30 In North American schools, I have experienced in my students a further 'sense of audience' – that of the teacher who will be grading the work at the end of the session.

31 I am aware that the use of the term 'intention' in relation to the arts can be problematical. [See, for instance, the discussion by Mike Fleming (1982, *op cit* pp.233-236) and G.E.M.Anscombe's (1979) *Intention* Basil Blackwell Oxford.] I am using 'intention' here in line with David Best's position when he argues that 'To refer to an action as being done with a certain intention is to say what kind of action it is.' [Best, D (1992) *The Rationality of Feeling* Falmer London p.137]

32 States, Bert O. (1985) *Great Reckonings in Little Rooms* University of California Press Los Angeles pp.124 and 160

33 It is interesting that States writes of 'the intention of the speaker' [he is referring to the actor here as a 'speaker' addressing an audience] in his book (1985 *ibid*, Chapter 5, p.160), but when he repeats that chapter as a contribution to a later publication [States, B. (1995) 'The Actor's Presence' in *Acting (Re)considered* by Phillip B. Zarrilli (Ed) Routledge London and New York], he changes the manuscript to 'the 'intention' of the speaker' [p.24] i.e. putting intention in inverted commas.

34 Frost , A and Yarrow, R. (1990) *op cit* Macmillan, p.152

35 Hornbrook, David, (1991) *Education in Drama op cit* p.58.

36 Bentley, Eric (1975) *The Life of Drama* Atheneum New York, p.150

37 Wilshire, Bruce (1982) *op cit* p.33.

38 Brook, P. (1993) *There are no secrets: Thoughts on Acting and Theatre* Methuen London p.81 [of 1995 paperback edition].

39 Brook, P. (1995 edition), *ibid* p.96.

40 Hornbrook, D. (1989) *Education and Dramatic Art op cit*

41 An admirable publication by the joint authorship of Jim Clarke, Warwick Dobson, Tony Goode and Jonothan Neelands is an example of what I mean. It offers the reader a wide range of issues around which drama programmes have been prepared, but fails to include any significant 'living through' experience, i.e. a

form of existential 'making' led by 'teacher-in-role'. I am not suggesting that 'living through' drama should claim a large section of such projects [in my example of 'The Crucible', in terms of time, the teacher-in-role episode played a relatively small part] but I suggest 'living through' offers an occasional rich medium for dramatic exploration that other forms may lack. [Clark, J. et al (1997) *Lessons for the Living: Drama and the Integrated Curriculum* Mayfair Cornerstone Ontario]

42 North America's 'Theatre Games' is a classic example.

43 Fleming, Michael (1997) *The Art of Drama Teaching* Fulton London

BIBLIOGRAPHY

BOOKS

Abbs, Peter (1987) *Living Powers: The Arts in Education,* Falmer, London

Adams, John (1918) *The New Teaching,* Hodder and Stoughton, London

Adams, John (1922) *Modern Developments in Educational Practice,* University of London

Aers, Lesley and Wheale, Nigel [Eds] (1991) *Shakespeare in the Changing Curriculum,* Routledge, London

Alington, A.F. (date?) *Drama and Education,* Basil Blackwell, Oxford

Allen, John (1979) *Drama in Schools: its theory and practice,* Heinemann, London

Axline, Virginia (1947) *Play Therapy,* Houghton-Mifflin, Boston

Ballard, P. B. (1925) *The Changing School,* University of London

Barker, Clive (1977) *Theatre Games,* Eyre Methuen, London

Barnfield, Gabriel (1968) *Creative Drama in Schools,* Macmillan, London

Bateson, Gregory (1973) *Steps to an Ecology of Mind,* Paladin Books, London

Bazely, E.T. (1928) *Homer Lane and the Little Commonwealth,* Allen and Unwin

Beacock, D.A. (1943) *The Play Way English for Today: The Methods and Influence of H. Caldwell Cook,* Nelson, London

Ben Chaim, Daphne (1981) *Distance in the Theatre: The Aesthetics of Audience Response* UMI Research Press, Ann Arbor, Michigan

Bentley, Eric [Ed] (1968) *The Theory of Modern Stage: An Introduction to Modern Theatre,* Pelican, New York

Bentley, Eric (1975) *The Life of Drama,* Atheneum, New York

Best, David (1992) *The Rationality of Feeling,* Falmer, London

Bloomer, Mabel (1911) *A Year in the Infant School,* Blackie, London

Boal, Augusto (1979) *Theatre of the Oppressed* trans. by Charles A. and Maria-Odilia Leal McBride, Pluto, London

Boal, Augusto (1995) *The Rainbow of Desire: the Boal method of theatre and therapy,* trans by Adrian Jackson, Routledge, London

Boas, Guy and Hayden, Howard (1938) *School Drama: It's Practice and Theory,* Methuen, London

Bolton, Gavin (1979) *Towards a Theory of Drama in Education,* Longman, London

Bolton, Gavin (1984) *Drama as Education,* Longman, Harlow

Bolton, Gavin (1986) *Gavin Bolton: Selected Writings* by Davis, David and Lawrence, Chris [Eds], Longman, London

Bolton, Gavin (1992) *New Perspectives on Classroom Drama,* Simon Shuster, Hemel Hempstead

Bolton, Gavin (1995) [with Dorothy Heathcote] *Drama for Learning: Dorothy Heathcote's Mantle of the Expert Approach to Education,* Heinemann, New Jersey

Brandes, Donna and Philips, Howard *Gamesters' Handbook: 140 Games for Teachers and Group Leaders* The Growth Centre, Newcastle

Breen, Robert S. (1986) *Chamber Theatre,* William Caxton, Evanston Illinois

Britton, James (1970) *Language and Learning,* Penguin, Harmondsworth

Britton, James (1975) *The Development of Writing Abilities 11-18,* Macmillan

Brook, Peter (1968) *The Empty Space,* Atheneum, New York

Brook, Peter (1993) *There are no secrets,* Methuen, London

Bruford, Rose (1958) *Teaching Mime,* Methuen, London

Bruner, Jerome (1990) *Acts of Meaning,* Harvard Uni Press, Cambridge, Mass

Bruner, Jerome *et al* (Eds 1976) *Play,* Penguin, New York

Buber, Martin (1947) *Between Man and Man,* Beacon Press, Boston

Burton, Bruce (1991) *Act of Learning,* Longman Cheshire, Sydney

Burton, E.J. (1949) *Teaching English through Self-Expression: A Course in Speech, Mime and Drama,* Evans, London

Burton, E.J. (1955) *Drama in Schools: Approaches, Methods and Activities,* Herbert Jenkins, London

Burton, E.J. (1959) *Theatre: alive or dead?* The Joint Council for Education through Art, London

Burton, E.J. (1993) *Drama in Schools (1930-1960): Some Footnotes,* St. Radigund Press

Byron, Ken (1986) *Drama in the English Classroom,* Methuen London

Callow, Simon (1984) *Being an Actor,* Penguin Books, Harmondsworth

Carlson, Marvin (1996) *Performance,* Routledge, New York

Carroll, John (1980) *The Treatment of Dr. Lister Mitchell,* College of Advanced Education, Bathurst Australia

Cassirer, Ernst (1953) *The Philosophy of Symbolic Forms* translated by R. Manhheim, Yale University Press, New Haven

Clark Jim, Dobson Warwick, Goode Tony and Neelands Jonothan (1997) *Lessons for the Living: Drama and the Integrated Curriculum* Mayfair Cornerstone, Ontario

Coggin, Philip (1956) *Drama and Education: An Historical survey from Ancient Greece to the present day,* Thames and Hudson, London

Cook, Caldwell Henry (1917) *The Play Way: An Essay in Educational Method,* Heinemann, London

Cook, Caldwell Henry (1912) *Perse Playbooks Nos. 1-6,* Heffer, Cambridge

Cook, Caldwell Henry (1921) *Homework and Hobbyhorses,* Batsford

Cook, Caldwell Henry (1921) *Two Plays from the Perse School,* Heffer, Cambridge

Cook, Caldwell Henry (undated) *Littleman's Book of Courtesy,* Dent, London

Courtney, Richard (1965) *Teaching Drama,* Cassell, London

Courtney, Richard (1968) *Play, Drama and Thought,* Cassell, London

Creber, Patrick (1965) *Sense and Sensibility,* ULP, London

Creber, Patrick (1990) *Thinking Through English,* Cambridge Univerity Press

Curtis, Eleanor Whitman (1914) *The Dramatic Instinct in Education,* Houghton Mifflin, New York

Davis, David (Ed. 1997] *Interactive Research in Drama in Education,* Trentham with University of Central England, Stoke on Trent

Davis, David and Lawrence, Chris [Eds.] (1986) *Gavin Bolton: Selected Writings,* Longman, London

Day, Christopher (1975) *Drama for Upper and Middle Schools,* Batsford, London

Day, Christopher and Norman, John [Eds] (1983) *Issues in Educational Drama,* The Falmer, London

Dewey, John (1906) *The Child and the Curriculum,* University of Chicago Press

Dewey, John (1916) *Democracy and Education,* The Macmillan Company, New York

Dewey, John and Dewey, Evelyn (1915) *Schools of Tomorrow,* Dent, London

Diderot, Denis (orig. c. 1773 trans by Walter Haries Pollock, 1883) *The Paradox of Acting,* Chatto and Windus, London

Doolittle, Joyce and Barnieh, Zina (1979) *A Mirror of our Dreams,* Talonbooks, Vancouver

Dodd, Nigel and Hickson, Winifred (Eds 1971) *Drama and Theatre in Education,* Heinemann, London

Driver, Ann (1936) *Music and Movement,* Oxford University Press

Findlay, J.J. (1911) *The School: An introduction to the study of Education,* Williams and Norgate, London

Findlay, J.J. (1930) *The Foundations of Education Vol 2,* University of London Press

Fines, John and Verrier, Ray (1974) *The Drama of History: an experiment in co-operative teaching,* New University Education, London

Finlay-Johnson, Harriet (1911) *The Dramatic Method of Teaching,* Nisbet Self-Help Series, James Nisbet, London

Fleming, Michael (1994) *Starting Drama Teaching,* Fulton London

Fleming, Michael (1997) *The Art of Drama Teaching,* Fulton, London

Fogerty, Elsie (1924) *The Speaking of English Verse,* J.M. Dent, London

Fogerty, Elsie (1977) *Rhythm,* Allen and Unwin, London

Fowler, J. H. (Ed.) (1904) *The Teaching of History and other Papers,* Manchester University Press

Francis, Hilton (1973) *The Vocabulary of Educational Drama,* Kemble Press, Banbury

Frost, Anthony and Yarrow Ralph (1990) *Improvisation in Drama,* Macmillan, Basingstoke

Gardner, D.E.M. (1969) *Susan Isaacs,* Methuen, London

Geertz, Clifford (1983) *Local Knowledge,* Basic Books, London

Gibson, Rex [Ed] (1986) *Shakespeare and Schools, The Newsletter of the 'Shakespeare and Schools Project',* Cambridge Institute of Education

Gibson, Rex (1990) *Secondary School Shakespeare, Classroom Practice, A Collection of Papers by Secondary Teachers,* Cambridge Institute of Education

Goffman, Erving (1974) *Frame Analysis,* Harper and Row

Gorchakov, Nikolai (1954, trans by Miriam Goldina) *Stansilavsky Directs,* New York

Granville-Barker, Harley (1922, 2nd edition) *The Exemplary Theatre,* Books for Libraries Press, New York

Granville-Barker, Harley (1944) *The Use of Drama,* Sidgewick and Jackson, London

Groos, Karl (1901; orig. 1989) *The Play of Man,* trans by Elizabeth L. Baldwin, Heinemann, London

Grotowski, Jerzy (1969) *Towards a Poor Theatre,* Eyre Methuen, London

Hall, Edward T. (1959) *The Silent Language,* Doubleday, Chicago

Hall, Stanley G. (1904) *Adolescence,* Appleton-Century-Crofts, New York

Hamilton, D. *et al* (1977) *Beyond the Numbers Game,* Macmillan, Basingstoke

Heathcote, Dorothy and Bolton, Gavin (1995) *Drama for Learning: Dorothy Heathcote's Mantle of the Expert Approach to Education,* Heinemann, New Hampshire

Herts, A.M. (1911) *The Children's Educational Theatre,* Harper, New York

Hilliard, McCormick Ogleby (1917) *Amateur and Educational Dramatics,* Macmillan, New York

Hirst, Paul and Peters R.S. (1970) *The Logic of Education,* Routledge, London

Hodgson, John and Richards, Ernest (1966) *Improvisation,* Eyre Methuen, London

Hodgson, John (Ed.) (1972) *The Uses of Drama,* Eyre Methuen, London

Hodgson, John and Banham, Martin (1972) *Drama in Education 1: The annual survey,* Pitman, London

Holmes, Edmond (1911) *What is and What Might Be,* Constable, London

Holmes, Edmond (1914) *In Defence of What Might Be,* Constable, London

Hornbrook, David (1989) *Education and Dramatic, Art* Blackwell, Oxford

Hourd, Marjorie L. (1949) *The Education of the Poetic Spirit: A Study in Children's Expression in the English Language*, Heinemann, London

Hourd, Marjorie L. (1951) *Some emotional aspects of learning,* Heinemann, London

Hourd, Marjorie L. (1959) *Coming into their own,* Heinemann, London

Hourd, Marjorie L. (1972) *Relationship in Learning,* Heinemann, London

Hudson, Liam (1966) *Contrary Imaginations*, Methuen, London

Hunt, Albert (1976) *Hopes for Great happenings: Alternatives in Education and Theatre*, Methuen, London

Isaacs, Susan (1930) *The intellectual growth in young children*, Routledge and Kegan Paul, London

Isaacs, Susan (1932) *The Children We Teach: Seven to Eleven Years*, University of London Press

Isaacs, Susan (1933) *Social Development of Young Children*, Routledge and Kegan Paul, London

Jackson, Tony [Ed] (1993) *Learning Through Theatre: New Perspectives on Theatre in Education*, Routledge, London

Jacques-Dalcroze, Emile (1921) *Rhythm and Music in Education* trans. by Harold F. Rubenstein, Chatto and Windus, London

Jennings, Sue (1973) *Remedial Drama*, Pitman, London

Jennings, Sue (1993) *Playtherapy with Children*, Blackwell, Oxford

Johnson, Liz and O'Neill, Cecily C. (1984) *Dorothy Heathcote: Collected writings on education and drama*, Hutchinson, London

Johnstone, Keith (1981) *Impro: Improvisation and the Theatre*, Methuen, London

Jordan, Diana (1938) *The Dance as Education*, Oxford University Press, London

Joseph, Stephen (1968) *New Theatre Forms*, Pitman, London

Keatinge M.W. (1916) *Studies in Education*, A and C Black, London

Kelly, Mary (1939) *Village Theatre*, Nelson, London

Kelly, Mary (1946) *Group Play-Making*, Harrap, London

Kempe, Andy (1990) *The GCSE DRAMA Coursebook*, Blackwell, Oxford

Kempe, Andy and Holroyd, Rick (1994) *Imaging: A Teacher's Guide*, Hodder and Stoughton, London

Kilpatrick, W.H. (1915) *Montessori Examined*, Constable, London

King, Colin (1972) *A Space on the Floor: a planned approach to teaching drama*, Ward Lock, London

Kleberg, Lars (1993, trans by Charles Rougle) *Theatre as Action*, Macmillan, London

Klein, Melanie (1932) *The Psychoanalysis of Childhood*, Hogarth, London

Laban, Rudolf (1941) *Effort*, Macdonald and Evans, London

Laban, Rudolf (1948) *Modern Educational Dance*, Macdonald and Evans, London

Landy, Robert (1986) *Drama Therapy*, Charles C. Thomas, Springfield, Illinois

Lane, Homer (1928) *Talks to Parents and Teachers*, Allen and Unwin, London

Langer, Suzanne (1953) *Feeling and Form: A theory of Art*, Routledge and Kegan Paul

Langdon E.M. (1949) *An Introduction to Dramatic Work with Children*, Dennis Dobson, London

Lee, Joseph (1915) *Play in Education*, Macmillan, New York

Lindqvist, Gunilla (1995) *The Aesthetics of Play*, University of Uppsala

Lobb, K.M. (1955) *The Drama in School and Church,* Harrap, London

Mackaness, George (1928) *Inspirational Teaching: A Record of Experimental Work in the Teaching of English,* Dent, London

Mackenzie, Frances (1935) *The Amateur Actor,* Nelson, London

MacNunn, N. (1914) *A Path to Freedom,* Bell, London

Mc Caslin, Nellie (1975) *Children and Drama,* McKay, New York

McGaw, Charles J., (1964) *Acting is Believing,* Holt, Rinehart and Winston, New York

Mc Gregor, Lyn, Tate Maggie and Robinson, Ken (1978) *The Schools Council Drama Teaching Project (10-16),* Heinemann, London

Maier, Norman R.F. *et al* (1956; revised 1975) *The Role-Play Technique: A Handbook for management and Leadership Practice,* University Associates, San Diego

Maslow, Abraham (1954) *Motivation and Personality,* Harper, New York

Mawer, Irene (1932) *The Art of Mime,* Methuen, London

Merrill, J and Fleming, M. (Eds. 1930) *Playmaking and Plays: The Dramatic Impulse and its Educative Use in the Elementary and Secondary Schools,* New York

Midgely, Mary (1980) *Beast and Man: The Roots of Human Nature,* Methuen, London

Morgan, Norah and Saxton, Juliana (1987) *Teaching Drama: a mind of many wonders,* Hutchinson, London

Morton, David (Ed: 1984) *Drama for Capability,* National Association of Drama Advisers, London

Motter, Vail (1929) *The School Drama in England,* Longmans

McCaslin, Nellie (1975) *Children and Drama,* McKay, New York

McGregor, Lynn, Tate, Maggie and Robinson, Ken (1977) *Learning Through Drama: Schools Council Drama Teaching Project,* Heinemann, London

van Ments, Morry (1983) *The Effective Use of Role-Play: A handbook for Teachers and Trainers,* Kogan Page, London

Mitter, Shomit (1992) *Systems of rehearsal,* Routledge, London

Montessori, Maria (1912 – translated 1919) *The Montessori Method,* Heinemann, London

Moreno, Jacob Levy (1946) *Psychodrama,* Beacon House, New York

Neelands, Jonothan (1990) *Drama Structures,* Cambridge Universitry Press

Neill, A.S. (1962) *A Radical Approach to Education,* Gollanz

Newton, Robert G (1937) *Acting Improvised,* Nelson, London

Newton, Robert G (1949) *Magic and Make-Believe,* Dennis Dobson, London

Nicol, Alan (1991) *Tilting at Windmills: a tribute to Catherine Hollingworth OBE,* Northern College, Dundee

Nunn, Percy (1920) *Education: Its Data and First Principles,* Edward Arnold, London

O'Brien, Veronica (1982) *Teaching Shakespeare,* Edward Arnold, London

O'Neill, Cecily C. and Lambert, Alan (1982) *Drama Structures: A Practical handbook for Teachers,* Stanley Thornes, London

O'Neill, Cecily, C. (1995) *Drama Worlds: a framework for process drama*, Heinemann, New Hampshire

Overton, Grace Sloan (1926) *Drama in Education: Theory and Technique*, Century, New York

Parry, Christopher (1972) *English Through Drama*, Cambridge University Press

Parry, Christopher (1967) *The Mummery*, Chatto and Windus, London

Pemberton-Billing, Robin N. and Clegg, J. David (1965) *Teaching Drama*, University of London Press

Piaget, Jean (1926) *The Language and Thought of the Child* trans. by Marjorie Warden, Kegan Paul, London.

Piaget, Jean (1951) *Play, Dreams and Imitation in Childhood*, trans. by C. Gattegno and F.M. Hodgson, Heinemann, London

Pinto, Vivian de Sola (1947) *The Teaching of English in Schools*, Macmillan, London

Polanyi, Michael (1958) *Personal Knowledge: Towards a Post-Critical Philosophy*, Routledge and Kegan Paul

Read, Herbert (1943) *Education Through Art*, Faber and Faber, London

Redington, Christine (1983) *Can Theatre Teach?* Pergamon, Oxford

Ridley, Frank (1924) *A Manual for Elocution for Teacher and Student*, Samuel French, London

Robertson, Seonaid M, (1963) *Rosegarden and Labrynth: A Study in Art Education*, Gryphon, Lewes

Robinson, Kenneth [Ed] (1980) *Exploring Theatre and Education*, Heinemann, London

Rogers, Carl (1954) *Becoming a Person*, Oberlin, Ohio

Ross, Malcolm (1978) *The Creative Arts*, Heinemann, London

Ross, Malcolm (1982 Ed.) *The Development of Aesthetic Experience*, Pergamon, London

Rusk, Robert, R. (1933) *A History of the Infant School*, University of London Press

Rutland, Harold (1972) *Trinity College of Music: The First Hundred Years*, Trinity College of Music, London

Sanson, Clive (Ed) (1946) *Speech in our Time*, Hinrichsen, London

Schechner, Richard (1977) *Performance Theory*, Routledge, London

Schechner, Richard (1982) *The End of Humanism Performing Arts*, Journal Publications, New York

Seely, John (1976) *In Context: Language and drama in the secondary classroom*, Oxford University Press

Selbourne, David (1982) *The making of Midsummer's Night's Dream*, Methuen, London

Self, David (1975) *A Practical Guide To Drama in the Secondary School*, Ward Lock, London

Selleck, R.J.W. (1972) *English Primary Education and the Progressives 1914-1939,* Routledge and Kegan Paul, London

Schiller, Friedrich (1967; orig. c.1794) *On the Aesthetic Education of Man* trans. and commentary by Elizabeth M. Wilkinson and L.A. Willoughby, Oxford University Press

Sherborne, Veronica (1990) *Developmental Movement for Children,* Cambridge University Press

Slade, Peter (1954) *Child Drama,* University of London Press

Slade, Peter (1958) *Introduction to Child Drama,* Oxford University Press

Slade, Peter (undated) *Freedom in Education,* EDA Publications, Birmingham

Slade, Peter (1968) *Experience of Spontaneity,* Longman, London

Slade, Peter (1977) *Natural Dance,* Hodder and Stoughton, London

Slade, Peter (1995) *Child Play: its importance for human development,* Jessica Kinsley, London

Sontag, Susan (Ed) (1976) *Selected Writings,* Farrar Strausss and Girouz, New York

Spolin, Viola (1963) *Improvisation for the Theatre,* Northwestern University Press

Somers, John (1994) *Drama in the Curriculum,* Cassell, London

Somers, John (Ed) (1996) *Research in Drama Education Vols 1 and 2*

Stabler, Tom (1978) *Drama in the Primary Schools: Schools Council Drama 5-11,* Macmillan, London

Stanislavski, Constantin (1937) *The Actor Prepares* trans. by Elizabeth Reynolds Hapgood, Geoffrey Blis, London

Stanislavski, Constantin (1949) *Building a Character* trans. by Elizabeth Reynolds Hapgood, Theatre Art Books, New York

States, Bert O. (1985) *Great Reckonings in Little Rooms,* Universiy of Californian Press, Los Angeles

Steiner, Rudolf (1924) *Human Values in Education* trans. by Vera Compton-Burnett for Rudolf Steiner Press, 1971.

Stewart, J.I.M. (1949) *Character and Motive in Shakespeare,* London

Stone, R.L. (1949) *The Story of a School,* HMSO

Sully, James (1896) *Studies of Childhood,* Longman Green, London

Tarlington, Carole and Verriour, Patrick (1991) *Role Drama,* Pembroke, Ontario

Taylor, Philip and Hoepper Christine (Eds) (1995) *IDEA '95 Papers,* NADIE Publications

Taylor, Philip (Ed) (1996) *Researching Drama and Arts Education,* Falmer, London

Thornton, S. (1971) *A Movement perspective of Rudolf Laban,* Macdonald and Evans, London

Tomkinson, W.S. (1921) *The Teaching of English,* Oxford University Press

Trench, Paul, K. (1935) *Principles of Gestalt Psychology,* Trubner, London

Turner, Victor (1972) *From Ritual to Theatre: The Human Seriousness of Play,* PAJ Publications, New York

Tynan, Kenneth (1957) *Declarations,* MacGibbon and Kee

Ullman, Lisa (1984) *A Vision of Dynamic Space,* Imago, Thame, Oxon

Viola, Wilhelm (1942) *Child Art and Frank Cizek,* University of London (orig. Vienna, 1936)

Vygotski, Lev (1938 orig; trans by Michael Cole *et al* 1978) *Mind in Society the development of the higher psychological processes,* Cambridge, Massachussetts University Press

Wagner, Betty Jane (1976) *Dorothy Heathcote: Drama as a Learning Medium,* Hutchinson, London [1979 edition]

Ward, Winifred (1930) *Creative Dramatics,* Appleton, New York

Watkins, Brian (1981) *Drama and Education,* Batsford, London

Way, Brian (1967) *Development Through Drama,* Longman, Harlow

Way, Brian (1981) *Audience Participation: Theatre for Children and Young People,* Baker's Plays, Boston

Welton, James (1906) Principles of Teaching, *University Tutorial Press, London*

Whitehead, Frank (1971) *The Disappearing Dais: A Study of the Principles and Practice of English Teaching,* Chatto and Windus, London

Wiles, John and Garrard, Alan (1968) *Leap to Life: An Experiment in Youth and School Drama,* Chatto and Windus, London

Wilkinson, Elizabeth M. and Willoughby, L. A. (1967) *Schiller: On the Aesthetic Education of Man,* Oxford University Press

Willett, John (1964) *Brecht on Theatre,* Hill and Wang, New York

Wilshire, Bruce (1982) *Role-Playing and Identity: The Limits of Theatre Metaphor,* Indiana University Press, Bloomington

Winnicott, D.W. (1971) *Playing and Reality,* Tavistock, London

Witkin, Robert (1974) *The Intelligence of Feeling,* Heinemann, London

Winnicott, D.W. (1971) *Playing and Reality,* Tavistock, London

Witkin, Robert (1974) *The Intelligence of Feeling,* Heinemann, London

ARTICLES IN JOURNALS and CHAPTERS IN OTHER BOOKS

Abbs, Peter (1992) 'Abbs Replies to Bolton' in *Drama* Vol 1 No 1 Summer

Allen, Bob (1991) 'A School Perspective' in *Shakespeare in the Changing Curriculum* by Lesley Aers and Nigel Wheale [Eds], Routlege, London

Bateson, Gregory (1976) 'A theory of Play and Fantasy' in *Play* by J.S. Bruner *et al* (eds)

Best, David (1982) 'Generic Arts: An Expedient Myth' in *Journal of Art and Design Education*

Burke, Margaret (1996) 'Learning from a Master: Bolton at Ohio, 1995' in *The Journal of Ohio Drama Education Exchange* Vol 1, No 1.

Bolton, Gavin (1990) 'Opinion – Education and Dramatic Art – A Review' in *Drama Broadsheet Spring* 7 (1)

Bolton, Gavin (1995) 'DRAMA/Drama and Cultural Values' in *Selected Readings in Drama and Theatre Education: IDEA Papers* by Philip Taylor (Ed), NADIE Publications, Brisbane

Bolton, Gavin (1996) 'Out of Character' in *Drama Matters* Vol 1 No 1 Spring, Ohio

Brecht, Bertolt (1949 orig. trans by John Willett 1968) 'Street Scene' in *The Theory of Modern Stage: An Introduction to Modern Drama* by Eric bentley (Ed), Pelican, New York

Brecht, Bertolt (1949 orig. trans. by Eric Bentley) 'A New Technique of Acting' in *Theatre Arts* 33 No 1

Bullough, Edward (11912) 'Psychical Distancing as a Factor in Art and as Aesthetic Principle' in *British Journal of Psychology* 5, June 1912

Byron, Ken (1986 and 7) 'Drama at the Crossroads, 1 and 2' in *2D* Vols 6 and 7, Autumn

Campbell, Guy M. (1918) 'Physical Education' in *The New Teaching* by John Adams (Ed), Hooder and Stoughton, London

Courtney, Richard (1977) 'Goals in Drama teaching' in *Drama Contact* (Council of Drama Education, Ontario) 1st May.

Davis, David (1976) 'What is Depth in Educational Drama?' in *Young Drama* Vol 4 No 3 October

Davis, David (1983) 'Drama for Deference or Drama for Defiance?' in *2D* Autumn Vol 3 No 1 and in *The NADIE Journal* Vol 15, No 1 Summer 1990.

Davis, David (1985) 'Dorothy Heathcote interviewed by David Davis' in *2D* Vol 4, No 2, Spring

Davis, David (1990) 'In Defence of Drama in Education' in *The NADIE Journal* Vol 15, No 1 Summer

Dunlop, F.N. (1977) 'Human Nature, Learning and Ideology' in *British Journal of Education Studies* Vol XXV No 3, October

Elliott, R.K. (1966-7) 'Aesthetic Theory and the Experience of Art' in *Proceedings of the Aristotelian Society* Vol LXVii

Faulkes, Margaret (1975) 'Creative Dramatic Leaders Face Objective Examination' in *Canadian Child and Youth Drama Association Bulletin*

Findlay, J.J. (1924) 'Eurhythmics' in *Educational Movements and Methods* by John Adams (Ed), Heath, London

Fleming, Michael (1995) 'Progress in Drama and Aestheitc Unity' in *Drama: The Journal for National Drama* Vol 4 N1 Autumn

Garvey, Catharine (1976) 'Some properties of Social Play' in *Play* by Bruner, J. *et al* (eds) Penguin, New York

Gillham, Geoff (1979) 'Experiencing drama: what's happening when children are doing drama in depth?' in *Schooling and Culture* Spring

Gillham, Geoff (1988) 'What Life is for: An analysis of Dorothy Heathcote's 'Levels' of Explanation' in *Theatre and Education Journal* Issue 1 September and in *2D* Vol 8 No 2 Summer

Gilpin, E.M. (1920) 'The Dramatic Sense as a factor in Education' in *Drama* BDL, July, 1920

Grotowski, Jerzy (1973) 'Holiday' in *Drama Review* No. 17

Gullan, Marjorie (1946) 'Choral Speech' in *Speech of our Time* by Clive Sanson (Ed), Hinrichsen, London

Harré, Rom (1983) 'An analysis of social activity: a dialogue with Rom Harre' conducted and edited by Jonathon Miller in *States of Mind: Conversations with Psychological Investigators*, BBC London

Hayden, Howard (1938) 'Drama in the Classroom' in *School Drama Its Practice and Theory* by Boas, G. and Hayden, H. (Eds), Methuen, London

Heathcote, Dorothy (1967) 'Improvisation' in *Dorothy Heathcote: Collected writings on drama and education* by Johnson, Liz and O'Neill, Cecily (Eds.), Hutchinson, London, 1984

Heathcote, Dorothy (1972) 'Drama as Challenge' in *The Uses of Drama* by John Hodgeson (Ed), Eyre Methuen, London

Heathcote, Dorothy (1971) 'Drama and Education: Subject or System?' in *Drama and Theatre in Education* by Nigel Dodd and Winifred Hickson (Eds), Heinemann, London

Heathcote, Dorothy (1975) 'Drama and Learning' in McCaslin, Nellie [Ed] *Children and Drama*, David McKay, New Hamshire, USA

Heathcote, Dorothy (1976) 'Material for Significance' in *Dorothy Heathcote: Collected writings on drama and education* by Johnson, L and O'Neill, C (Eds) (1984) Hutchinson, London

Heathcote, Dorothy (1980) 'Signs and portents' in *SCYPT journal* Spring

Heathcote, Dorothy (1980) 'From the Particular to the Universal' in *Exploring Theatre and Education* by Ken Robinson (Ed), Heinemann, London

Hourd, Marjorie (1948) 'Androcles' in an 'Arena' in *Theatre in Education* No 9, July-August

Hyndman, M.T. (1980) 'Utopia Reconsidered: Edmond Holmes, Harriet Johnson and the School at Sompting' in *Sussex Archaelogical Collection* 118

Keysall, Pat (1995) 'Mime in the Classroom' in *Scottish Drama Spring,* Issue No 3.

Lawrence, Chris (1996) 'Drama for Learning' in *National Drama* Vol 4 No 2

Mather, Ray (1996) 'Turning Drama Conventions into Images' in *Drama* Vol 4 No 3/Vol 5 No 1 *The Journal of National Drama*

Millward, Peter (1990) 'Drama as a Well-made Play' in *Language Arts* February, National Council of Teachers of English

Moore, Olive (1954) 'Rudolf Laban' in the Special 75th birthday number of *The Laban Art of Movement Guild Magazine,* December, 1954

Nelson, Katharine and Seidman, Susan (1984) in *Symbolic Play* by Inge Bretherton (Ed) Academic Press, Orlando and London

Newton, Robert G. (1948) 'Let's Enjoy Drama' in *Theatre in Education Journal* No 7-8, March-June.

O'Neill, Cecily C. (1985) 'Imagined Worlds in Theatre and Drama' in *Theory into Practice* Vol 24 No 3 Summer

O'Neill, Cecily C. (1995) 'Talk and Action: Elements of the drama curriculum' in *Canadian Tertiary Drama Education: perspectives on Practice* by Saxton, Juliana and Miller, Carole (Eds), University of Victoria.

Pennington, Eileen (1995) 'Drama has to be about something!' in *Scottish Drama* Issue No 3, Spring

Rouse, W.H.D. (1901) 'The Direct Method of Teaching Modern and Classical Languages' in *Journal of Education* December Issue.

Shlovski, Victor (1965) 'Art as Technique' in *Russian Formalist Criticism: Four Essays* trans. by Lemon L.T. and Reis M.J.

Slade, Peter (1948) 'Starting Improvisation' in *Theatre in Education* No 7-8, March-June

Slade, Peter (1993) 'Afterword' in *Playtherapy with Children* by Sue Jennings, Blackwell, Oxford.

Smith, Louis M. and Schumacher, Sally (1977) 'Extended Pilot Trials of the Aesthetic Education Program: A qualitative Description, Analysis and Evaluation' in *Beyond the Numbers Game* by Hamilton, D. *et al* [Eds], Macmillan, Basingstoke.

States, Bert (1995) 'The Actor's Presence' in *Acting (Re)considered* by Phillip B. Arilli (Ed), Routledge, London

Vygotski, Lev (1933 orig; trans 1976) 'Play and its role in the mental development of the child' in *Play* by Bruner, J. *et al,* Penguin Education, Harmondsworth

Wagner, Betty Jane (1974) 'Evoking Gut-level Drama' in *Learning: The Magazine for Creative Teaching* (US) March

Withers, H.L. (1904) 'The Distinction between Work and Play' in *The Teaching of History and Other Papers* by J.H. Fowler (Ed) Manchester University Press

Wright, Nicholas (1980) 'From the Universal to the Particular' in *Exploring Theatre and Education* by Ken Robinson (Ed) Heinemann, London

REPORTS (in order of date)

Board of Education (1905) *Suggestions for the consideration of Teachers and Others concerned in the Work of Public Elementary Schools*, HMSO

Conference of New Ideals in Education (C.N.I.): *Report of the Montessori Conference at East Runton* (1914)

Conference of New Ideals in Education 1915

Eighth Conference of the New Ideals in Education (1920)

British Drama League conference: *Drama* (1920)

Board of Education (1921) *The Teaching of English in England* HMSO

Memorandum on the Teaching of English by The Incorporated Association of Assistant Masters in Secondary Schools (1923) Cambridge UP

Board of Education (1926) *The Drama in Adult Education: A Report by the Adult Education Committee of the Board of Education, being Paper No. 6 of the Committee* HMSO

Board of Education (1931) *The Primary School Report: Report of the Consultative Committee on the Primary School* HMSO

Board of Education (1933) *Syllabus of Physical Education* HMSO

Ministry of Education working Party (c. 1948-1950 unpublished) Drama Report

The Teaching of English by the Incorporated Association of Assistant Masters in Secondary Schools (1952) Cambridge University Press

DES (1967) *Children and their Primary Schools: The Plowden Report* HMSO

DES (1967) *Drama Education Survey 2* HMSO

Calouste Gulbenkian Foundation (1982) *The Arts in Schools: Principles, practice and provision* London

DES (1989) Drama from 5 to 16 HMI *Curriculum Matters 17*, HMSO

DES (1990) *Aspects of Primary Education: The Teaching and Learning of Drama* HMSO

THESES (unpublished)

Bowgett, David Richard (1996) *'Teachers' Perceptions as to the nature and Practice of Primary Classroom Drama'* unpublished Ph.D thesis, University of Leeds.

Bowmaker, Mary (1986) *'Harriet Finlay-Johnson 1871-1956'* unpublished MA dissertation, University of Newcastle

Cabral, Beatriz (1994) *'Toward a Reader-oriented assessment in drama in education'* unpublished Ph.D thesis, University of Central England

Cox, Tim (1971) *'The Development of Drama in Education, 1902-1944'* M.Ed thesis, University of Durham

Crompton, N.J.R. (1977/8) *'A Critical Evaluation of the aims and purposes of drama in education'* unpublished M.Phil., University of Nottingham

Eriksson, Stig Audin (1979) *'Drama as Education: A Descriptive Study of it development in Education and Theatre with particular relevance to the U.S.A. and England'*

Fleming, Michael (1982) *'A Philosophical Investigation into Drama in Education'* unpublished Ph.D thesis, University of Durham

Griffiths, David (1970) *'The History and Role of the Drama Adviser'* unpublished Advanced Diploma dissertation for the University of Durham

Heston, Sandra (1995) *'The Construction of an Archive and the Presentation of Philosophical, Epistemlogical and Methodological Issues relating to Dorothy Heathcote's Drama in Education approach.'* unpublished Ph.D thesis, University of Lancaster

Malczewski, Carol (1988) *'Towards a theory of Ownership in the Dramatic Process'* unpublished MA dissertation, University of Victoria, BC

Millward, Peter (1988) *'The Language of Drama'* Vols 1 and 2, unpublished Ph.D thesis, University of Durham

O'Neill, Cecily C. (1978) *'Drama and the Web of Form'* unpublished MA Dissertation, University of Durham

O'Neill, Cecily C. (1991) *'Structure and Spontaneity: Improvisation in Theatre and Education'* unpublished Ph.D thesis, Exeter University

Robinson, Ken (1981) *'A Re-evaluation of the roles and functions of drama in secondary education with reference to a survey of curricular drama in 259 secondary schools'* unpublished Ph.D thesis, University of London

Wootton, Margaret (1984) *'An Investigation into the Determining Influences on Drama in Education, 1947-77'* MA Dissertation Institute of Education, London University.

INDEX